THE LIFE AND TIMES
OF YOUNG BOB SCALLION

THE LIFE AND TIMES OF
YOUNG BOB SCALLION

by Mick Martin

JOSEF WEINBERGER PLAYS

LONDON

THE LIFE AND TIMES OF YOUNG BOB SCALLION
First published in 2003
by Josef Weinberger Ltd
12-14 Mortimer Street, London, W1T 3JJ

ISBN 0 85676 267 9

Printed by Watkiss Studios, Biggleswade, Beds, England

To my mother

THE LIFE AND TIMES OF YOUNG BOB SCALLION was first presented at the Northcott Theatre, Exeter, on 20 March 2003. The cast was as follows:

BOB SCALLION	Adrian Edmondson
MOLLY/BERNADETTE	Catherine Bailey
EDGAR/MR FAIRWEATHER TED/MR MENDEZ	Michael N Harbour
TOMMY/FLEG	Colin Tarrant
MRS FAIRWEATHER/ AUNTIE VERA	Lindy Whiteford

Directed by Ben Crocker

Designed by Kit Surrey

Lighting Designed by Robin Carter

Sound Designed by Duncan Chave

Fight Director Renny Krupinski

Casting Director Derek Barnes

An earlier version of THE LIFE AND TIMES OF YOUNG BOB SCALLION was presented at the West Yorkshire Playhouse in 1997, with the following cast:

BOB SCALLION	Jim Weaver
MOLLY	Alison Lomas
TOMMY/MR FAIRWEATHER/ FLEG	John Michie
MRS FAIRWEATHER/ AUNTIE VERA	Tilly Tremayne

Directed by Natasha Beteridge

Designed by Bernie Roberts

AUTHOR'S NOTE

This play is best performed with a cast of five, three men and two women, the breakdown of roles being best illustrated in the cast list opposite. There are a number of other very minor roles which can either be ascribed to one of the other four actors besides Bob, or could just as easily work on recorded voice-over. The stage setting could be as simple or as ornate as any given director/designer team might choose to make it.

Bob Scallion is a survivor, no matter what life throws at him, no matter how entirely culpable or foolish he is in the many pitfalls that engulf him, he will always come through and begin again. This is because deep down he is an archetypal underclass hero, one who has nothing but his wits to keep him. Alas, it's those same wits that will always ensure he never escapes the fate that his actions lead him towards.

The central device of the play is that of Bob narrating his own story, as such he speaks of himself in both the first and third person, he is in the scene as it unfolds but reserves the right to step out of it and address the audience as and when he feels the need to. Every other character in the play exists as Bob sees them and describes them, yet within these confines there is a whole world of business going on that Bob is too stupid to pick up on, but which the other characters and the audience are fully aware of. In keeping with classic eighteenth century fiction he is a remarkably erudite jailbird and scoundrel, and a breathtakingly stupid one at the same time. His role is partly to satirize, starting with the 1970s in general and moving onto the 1980s 'look after number one' ethos, which he embraces whole-heartedly whilst professing his deep disdain at certain of Tommy Marchbank's business avenues, all the while living for free at a house of ill-fame. Bob is nothing if not a hypocrite. As he moves into the 1990s he encounters the modern phenomena known as New Labour – finding it in the form of one Tommy Marchbank . . . but most of all Bob Scallion is here to entertain.

Mick Martin
February 2003

ACT ONE

The Hallelujah chorus fills the air. BOB SCALLION *adopts the pose of a soldier on parade, or a borstal boy more like, he salutes very properly in the manner of one who has been drilled round a parade ground for hours on end. The chorus fades out as he does this.*

>   Hallelujah, Hallelujah, Hallelujah
>   Hallelujah . . . (*Repeated.*)

BOB   My name is Robert Arthur Scallion,
Though I have always been known as Bob Scallion,
Or Young Bob Scallion, as it was when I choose to start my story.
On the twenty third day of October 1976,
I was released from custody.
My crimes were of an unseemly nature and I will not dwell upon them.
Contrary to popular myth, my own time in penal reflection
Was neither brutal nor unduly violated.
I spent six friendly months in a pleasant country location,
Somewhere out near Boston Spa it was.
I recall with what joy my fellow fallen and I
Would lay the same twelve kerbstones each day,
In varying patterns according to the differing demands
A real work place situation may make of us.
On Tuesdays a nice man called Leonard would come in
And genially strip down an old motorcycle for us,
Then smoke his pipe, a bemused onlooker
To our efforts to put it back together again.
'Think about it', he used to say, withdrawing his pipe,
'When you look at a motorcycle, where are the wheels usually placed?'
Our technical skills were often exposed.

But clearest of all, I recall the bright winter
morning,
When I stepped beyond the prison gate, and into
freedom.
My home, well, my parent's home, did not seem a
place I could go to.
Their furrowed look of deep disappointment and
disdain,
Held no warmth before which I could unfurl.
What follows is the story of my calamitous youth.
I boarded a bus with my dorm warden's words
ringing in my ears.

WARD   See you next week, Scallion, heheheheh.

BOB   I vowed to remember that place, and never see its
like again.

WARD   I give it a fortnight.

BOB   Indeed you will not sir.
No man ever achieved the most of himself through
solvent abuse,
Car theft, burglary or benefit fraud,
No sir, no man e'er did it.

WARD   Bollocks.

BOB   I see.

Aged seventeen years and eight months.
Bob Scallion journeys, but not to any home, any
parent's home.
To a city . . . a big swinging city where the ugly
meets the pretty,
Bob Scallion went to Bradford!

These are good days ahead,
Work, work is the order of the day,
This way alone can a fellow of sufficient fibre
make the best of himself.
All here take note of my tale.
I have twenty three pence.

The Department of Health and Social Security,
Or Ill Health and Anti-Social Insecurity if you've
ever been to it,
Was closed by the time I got to its fine wooden
doors.

I shall have to amuse myself until it opens,
Some money would be useful at a time like this, for
a cup of tea,
Or a sandwich perhaps.
I shall walk awhile.

I walked awhile, sat on a bench a bit, and so on.
It was fast approaching 6.00 AM when . . .

My gaze came to rest, on a shop door,
A sign, nestling amid Durex and Brylcreem
adverts.

It simply said,
'Help required, no skills necessary'.

My heart leapt, help required, no skills necessary!
If help is required I for one will always help!
And I have no skills necessary.

The shop was hidden almost, a few feet off the
street,
But marked by a red and white spinning thing,
And a picture of Kevin Keegan with his new perm!

This is where he got it perhaps?

Edgar Broughton, Gentleman's Hairdresser.

On the door a little clock made from card pointed
to nine o'clock.
I resolved to return there at nine o'clock, sharp,
And continued on my early morning stroll.
My step all the lighter for the opium of hope
That tickled through my veins.

At nine o'clock Bob Scallion received a rude
awakening.

Today is Sunday, the shop will not be open until
tomorrow.

I confess this blow would have been too much for
my ill-steered star,
Had it not been for one . . . blessed intervention.
As despair swept me away and laughed me its
cruellest laugh,
I heard the voices . . . singing . . . in the distance.
Church service was about to begin at St
Bartholemew's,
To be followed, crucially, by coffee and biscuits in
the adjoining hall.
I did attend, in piety, hunger and trepidation.

MRS F   You need not hold back from the Lord's house,
come in, join us.

BOB   It was here that I first met Mrs Elizabeth
Fairweather,
And was nurtured by that fine and generous
woman.
Though I knew neither tunes nor words the hymn
singing
That morning was of a ripe and rumbustious
nature.
As she read the psalm that sunny autumn morn,
Halo'd in the stained glass, window spread, of
yellow light,
She seemed to me the highest strain of goodness
This world can offer.

MRS F   The poor thing is half-starved,
You must come with Mr Fairweather and I this
minute,
Why, he is not washed this many days either!
Mr Fairweather the moment I have fed this child
I will put him in the tub and wash his body clean!

MR F   As you wish, dear.

BOB   I had not the impudence to refuse.
Dear, dear Elizabeth.

(He falls into a moment's silent reverie as the next scene is set up.)

Scene Two

Bob Scallion's new job.

We are in the barber shop, EDGAR *is cutting someone's hair and talking and coughing all at once.*

BOB	The Fairweathers were attending a public function and no offer Of a bed for the night was made. Nevertheless my new found relationship with the Lord Had yielded pleasingly well to say it was the first day, And I have slept out before so it was no real hardship. It was with a light and hearty step that I entered the barber's shop.
EDGAR	Morning sir, haircut sir? Take a seat, won't be a moment, sir. By hell it's turned out fresh again, hasn't it?
BOB	Edgar Broughton was a very large man who talked a great deal, Always in the manner of one so extremely reasonable and decent That it was impossible for his customers to disagree.
EDGAR	What about my team then, Huddersfield Town? By hell they've got some right players there now, haven't they? Well you see I've said it all along, geared for success you see. Mind you I like to see all the local teams do well, you know, Bradford Park Avenue, Farsley Celtic, Halifax Town, oh aye . . .

Frank Worthington used to come in here for his
hair cutting,
Nowadays he goes to Mario's Unisex Style Salon,
aye . . .
Smashing lad Frank, always has been.

BOB   His shop was in a cellar, beneath a gentleman's
outfitters.
Time was it would be busy all day.

EDGAR   That Elton John . . . he wants strangling like,
doesn't he really?

BOB   Excuse me . . .
Ahem . . . I am not here for a haircut, sir.

EDGAR   Hmm? Why not you need one, and a wash, heh
heh heh,
Well we don't sell 'owt else lad, hmm,
What's it about then eh, speak up?

BOB   It is about the card in the door . . . help required,
no skills necessary.

EDGAR   Aye . . . aye there is a card.
Have you done it before?

BOB   Done what before, sir?

EDGAR   Worked!
Done what before, have you worked before?

BOB   Oh yes, I have worked before.

EDGAR   Aye well you've got to ask, plenty haven't,
And wouldn't if they had the chance some of 'em.
What doing?
Come on lad, speak up, what is it you've been
doing?

BOB   First major problem.
I have . . . been away . . . at sea sir, working on a
ship, sir.

EDGAR   A ship? On the sea?

BOB   That's where it was,
            Were you in the navy?

EDGAR   Surely was, twenty six years!
            Can't you tell?

BOB   I can now you mention it, sir.

EDGAR   Well, a sea dog same as myself, eh?

BOB   And he began to speak again.

EDGAR   Aye, I were twenty six years in the navy,
            I'd never o' left but the wife moaned and wittered
            on like, aye . . .
            We'd a grand wee cabin under the wheelhouse
            Don't know what were up with her really.
            Tin't for everyone is it mind, a life at sea . . .

BOB   As ship's barber, sir?

EDGAR   Barber, dentist, saw doctor . . . special days
            indeed . . .

BOB   What might the job involve, sir?
            I can make tea for anything up to fifty men at
            once,
            And I enjoy killing rats . . .

EDGAR   Mr Scallion, welcome aboard,
            You'll be sweeping up, making tea, dealing with
            counter enquiries,
            Generally keepin' the place tidy, that sort of thing,
            Work a week in hand, can you start now?

BOB   My heart leapt!
            Yes I can sir, right away sir, Bob Scallion's the
            name.

EDGAR   There matey!

BOB   As we used to say on the ship sir,

'Land ahoy!'

EDGAR   I remember it well!

BOB   And, 'you don't need to worry about me letting
you down Cap'n
Because there's nothing for miles but the deep
blue sea,
So I won't be going nowhere!'
Do you know that one?

(BOB *roars with laughter at this, so much so that*
EDGAR *is obliged to join him in the merriment.*)

EDGAR   Or this one,
One foot out of line and I'll skin you to the bone
And throw the carcass overboard, you scurvy
little toe-rag!
What about that old sea smacker?
Do you know that one, young Bob?

(BOB *is left in no doubt as to where he stands in*
his new position of general assistant.)

BOB   Yes sir the sea, ahoy ahoo sir,
(*Wiping away a tear.*)
Oh dear oh deary me!
Good times indeed, sir . . .

EDGAR   Fine, put this on and make a brew o' tea,
We'll have a mug o' steamin', what do you say?

BOB   Tea it is Mr Broughton, coming right up, sir!
Then I'll get swept up in here and give all these
surfaces a good wipe!

EDGAR   Good lad.

And so it was that Bob Scallion went to work in
the barber's shop.

Scene Three

Mrs Fairweather and Spiritual Regeneration.

MRS F   Robert, how lovely to see you again!
We have enjoyed your company greatly these past
evenings.

BOB   Not to disparage my close friendship with Edgar,
I disliked the man intensely.
Indeed as the first day wore on he took to calling
me a donkey's knob,
Repeatedly.
At least I knew religion was making a better
person of me.

I fear it is I whom fortune has kissed, Mrs
Fairweather.

MRS F   Male voices are so hard to come by,
Especially one so redolent with melody and
warmth as yours.
The vicar tells me you are helping him decorate
the altar this week,
How nice of you.

BOB   Mrs Fairweather was the leader of the spiritual
regeneration class . . .

MRS F   For those . . . not quite in step with the stride of
Christ.

BOB   . . . and like a lifeline to my anchorless, drifting
soul.

MRS F   I've brought along some of my husbands old
shirts and pullovers
For you to keep warm these dark, lonely nights.
There, I have clothed you.
Have you read the relevant chapters in Matthew
and Luke?

BOB   I have read and digested the chapters you
suggested,

And what is more, Mrs Fairweather,
I have thanked my employer for his kindness
And generosity toward me.
As you said was only proper and decent.
Mr Fairweather is indeed a well dressed fellow.
These slacks are particularly comfortable.

MRS F   Casual smart, Robert.

BOB   Mrs Fairweather was a lady in her . . . forties,
          Though it be impolite to conject in such areas.

MRS F   Come here and tell me all about your job.
          Mr Broughton is a fine and decent man,
          Whose flower of faith has yet to fully open, I pray
          some day it will.
          Mr Fairweather was so pleased to hear of your
          position!
          Sit beside me, here, I will read to you from the
          Psalms.
          Oh come closer child, hold my hand . . .

          (BOB *moves slightly closer to her and holds her
          hand as she begins to read from the book to him,
          his eyes move from the book to their hands and
          back again.*)

                        Scene Four

Meeting Tommy Marchbank.

BOB   As six o'clock on that first Friday came around
          I began calculating my income with a quite
          Caledonian zeal,
          Five days at . . .

EDGAR   Oi you, Scallion, donkey's knob!
          Get out here and sweep this floor up!
          And don't think there's any sub for you tonight,
          ships' rat!

BOB   Any?

EDGAR   Sub!
Sub you thick get, money, don't you know what a
sub is?
What ship is it you were on?
I know your sort . . . bloody council estates . . .

BOB   But my wages for the five days . . .
I was brought up in a detached bungalow if you
must know . . .
I've got an aunt who lives near Harrogate mark
you, Mr Broughton.

EDGAR   I don't give a monkey's where your aunt lives
near . . .

BOB   Oh no, I bet you don't . . .

EDGAR   You work a week in hand son, I told you that,
No money till next week.
And if you don't like it you know what you can
do.

BOB   A week in hand means no money the first week . . .
I had not understood this.
Inside I raged at this callous twist of employment
practice,
Outside I said,
That's fine, Mr Broughton.

EDGAR   It is fine . . . where near Harrogate?

BOB   . . . Leeds.

EDGAR   Argh Leeds, you . . . !
I should have known it!
Now get it tarted up in here, no more o' your
gutter rat lies,
Poncing little . . .

    (*A very swanky looking individual enters in the
middle of this tirade.*)

    Oh . . . aha, hello, sir, how are you, my you just
caught us in time,

About to lock up there Young Bob, were we not?
Put the kettle on lad, there's a good idea.
Going away anywhere this weekend, sir?
Trim 'n' sideboards?
Bloody government's killin' the small
businessman . . .

TOM   Give the lad a sub, you miserable old twat!
           Christ stuck in here all day listening to you Edgar,
           You ought to be glad anyone'll work here at all!

EDGAR   Relations between employees and myself
           Are strictly private and confidential in this
           business . . .

BOB   The new arrival wore an expensive suit,
           His watch and name bracelet glistened 'neath the
           strip lighting,
           Shoes that clipped, crisp and smart on the cold tile
           floor.

TOM   Go on strike son, everyone else does . . .

EDGAR   Now listen up Tommy Marchbank . . .

BOB   Tommy Marchbank . . . the Tommy Marchbank?!
           I was making tea for the most important man I'd
           ever met.
           I put an extra tea bag in the brew and left it longer
           than usual.

EDGAR   It's none o' your affair . . .

TOM   Who is the lad anyway?

EDGAR   Oh, he's only some kid come in lookin' half
           starved the other day.
           I'm doing him a favour Tommy, take no notice of
           him . . .

TOM   You're a saintly man, Edgar, come here son.
           Well, what's your name?

BOB   Bob Scallion, sir.

TOM   Drop the sir shit, what brings you down here?
          He can't be paying you much.

EDGAR   It's as good as he'll get anywhere else . . .

BOB   It is the only job I have seen which I could do,
          And Mr Broughton was decent enough to set me
          on.

EDGAR   Says he's been away at sea, Tommy.
          I know the sea he's been away at,

          Delinquen-sea! (*Laughs loudly.*)
          Bloody training ship, that's all he's been on, you
          mark me.

TOM   That right, son?

BOB   I answered as honestly as I could find it within my
          heart.
          No sir, it is not.

TOM   There you go, Edgar . . .

BOB   And what is more Mr Broughton,
          If you are not prepared to pay me for the days I
          have worked
          I shall withdraw my labour and take heed of Mr
          Scargill . . .

TOM   (*wails with laughter*) By jove, I do declare!

EDGAR   Mr Scarg . . . You'll nothing of the like you cheeky
          little tramp!
          Withdraw labour . . . I'll bloody murder you!
          And what's more I'll pay you nothing for your
          beggarly thievin' neck!
          You give someone a chance and what do you
          get!?!
          Shit all over you!
          That's a blasted Labour government for you!

BOB   What's it got to do with the government?

TOM   Here here, up the Socialists!

EDGAR   What!?
               Answering me back are you now, urchin?!
               Get out of here, go on!
               That's it, you're sacked, go tell that to Arthur
               Bloody Scargill!

BOB   I may be sacked but you stink of Brylcreem!

               (EDGAR *sets about* BOB SCALLION *with the brush as*
               TOMMY *laughs his socks off in the chair.*)

TOM   Outrageous fare!
               Give the silly old get a slap, Bob!
               Splendid!
               Better than the wrestling!

               (EDGAR *gets at least two or three good shots in as*
               BOB *departs.*)

EDGAR   Bloody Labour camps!
               That's where I'd send 'em!

BOB   I grabbed my coat and dashed up the stairs in fear
               of my life,
               Without my money . . . without hope of seeing it . . .
               back at square one.
               But smack bang in front of the barber's door sat
               A bright brand spanking Ford Capri!
               3 litre Ghia . . . nice one, Tommy . . .

EDGAR   I've never heard the like in all my life!
               Decent businessman daren't give a lad a chance
               these days,
               Outrageous, it is.

TOM   Now then Edgar, where's the money you owe me?
               Decent businessman has to keep track of his debts
               'n' all.

EDGAR   I've got it, and can you get any more of them Afro
               perm kits?

TOM   Certainly can, how you fixed for moustache and
beard powder?

EDGAR   Always use some of that these days, Tommy.

BOB   It was evening time and Christmas was kind of sat
in the air.
On a sleigh, smiling.

Down the street a choir is singing,
O Little Town Of Bethlehem.

From across the road three men are also looking at
the Capri.
They watch it, without love.
They move towards Tommy's nice car.

BOB   Unattended, unprotected it stood proud like, no
double yellow lines
Could ever deny it's chrome smooth cylindrical
surge . . .
Yes . . . half a ton of sheer pussy magnet.
I recall my back slowly arching . . .

Still no sign of its' dashingly groomed owner . . .

BOB   At this point a sense of something dreadful
flushed down through me,
I looked around quickly . . . and would have run
away,
Had I thought of it.

Two police amble on pretending not to see.

TOM   Smartly trimmed Tommy emerges from the barber's
entrance,
Looking very pleased with himself indeed.

The gruesome threesome strike in a flash.
Collar Tommy by the throat, in a growl and a
slash!

Marchbank, you fraudin' bastard!

TOM   Lads, lads I can explain!

BOB   I do not know what possessed me at that point,
           But seizing up a dod of righteous timber the Lord
           God placed at hand,
           The good teacher's best friend,

           (BOB *hurtles across the stage swinging the lump
           of wood about his head.*)

           And flailing it wildly thus and thus!
           Smote those bearded ne'er-do-wells' a series of
           sickening belts!
           There on the street I battered them fierce!

TOM   Filthy scum, let 'em have it son!

BOB   For England and Tommy Marchbank!
           Wallop!

           The bad guys bled!

           That's the main thing.
           Then they fled, in bruised limps of anguish!

           A crowd gathers, the two police feel it is now safe
           For them to come and have a look.

           At Tommy and me, side by side, on the street.
           People probably thought we were mates, me and
           Tommy.

           He took his car keys back from the flags,
           straightened his hair,
           Then his tie, then checked his fingernails.

BOB   And ignored the coppers completely.
           Then he saw me.

TOM   Young Bob, I'm grateful to you.

BOB   I stood on the busy footpath in front of him.
           I remember being strangely nervous

TOM   You did me a good turn, why?

BOB   I saw them looking at the car and figured they
were waiting for you,
I got the feeling they don't like you . . .
I didn't know what to do so I picked up the bit of
wood . . .

TOM   Did you now . . .

BOB   Yes I did, and . . .
Tommy Marchbank looked at me properly, for the
first time.
And got stuck into 'em.

TOM   Good lad . . . only way.
Well, I ought to buy you a drink, what do you
reckon?

BOB   Sir . . . Tommy. . . . I'm sorry, but I don't drink . . .

TOM   No?
Damn fine thing you don't, young Bob Scallion,
Never apologize for that, or anything else.
Where do you live?
I'll give you a lift home.

BOB   I er . . . I don't live anywhere . . . as such.
Tommy Marchbank laughed . . . he always seemed
to be laughing.

TOM   Well where is it you're staying then?
Got to sleep somewhere.

BOB   Well it's . . . a bit . . . rough at the moment
There's a single man's shelter I've been to for the
past couple of nights . . .

TOM   Jesus Christ.
Get in.

BOB   I knew better than to ask who these attackers
were,

Or what their quarrel might be.
A few seconds later as we drove down the road in
the swanky Capri,
Tommy cracked out laughing.

Scene Five

At the house of Auntie Vera.

VERA   Why Tommy Marchbank of all people,
            How nice to see you.

TOM   I'm just sorry it's been this long Auntie Vera, I
            truly am.

VERA   And who might this be?

TOM   This?
            This here is Bob Scallion,
            A good friend of mine in need of a place to sleep,
            Auntie Vera.

VERA   Well any friend of Tommy Marchbank is a friend
            of ours!
            Molly . . . Molly!
            Where the devil is that girl?

TOM   Go easy on him now, Auntie Vera.

VERA   My word Tommy, he's but a slip of a lad!
            Still as I always say, a slip's as good as a fall
            when the snow's out.
            Isn't that right, young Bob Scallion?

BOB   Yes indeed Madam, pleased to make your
            acquaintance.

VERA   Why manners . . . what a refreshing change in a
            young man nowadays!
            Mary Whitehouse would be pleased.

BOB   I had no idea what or even where this place was.
            But I sensed at once a warmth and charity

I had but the scantest recollection of,
Way back in the slide of memory.

VERA   And how is your wife, Tommy?

TOM   She's very well thank you, Auntie.

BOB   In the doorway stood a girl, beautifully.
            Her shape, carved in red, against a dark, deep,
            cavernous hallway,
            She tilted her neck and her hair rolled down it,
            Like water, down a waterfall.
            Slowly she leaned her fine head on the hardwood
            frame,
            And yawned, noisily.

MOL   What?

VERA   Oh, you're awake are you?
            Molly this is young Bob Scallion,

TOM   A good friend of mine . . .

BOB   Again!

VERA   He's going to be staying here for a while . . .

BOB   Is he?

TOM   Yes he is, I want you to take care of him,
            Show him where to get a bath and clean himself
            up.

MOL   Anything you say, Tommy.

TOM   Listen up, young Bob,
            This is comin' up 1977, things ain't what they
            was.
            Young feller wants to make a shape of himself
            Then he's got to take a bath, trim his sideboards
            now and then,
            Look at that Dave Lee Travis or Noel Edmonds,
            That's what a modern guy is all about these days.
            You understand?

BOB   I do Tommy, this new deodorant stuff is
           wonderful, isn't it?

TOM   Good lad, Bob, I've got to be off.
           Good day to you Auntie Vera, Molly.

MOL   Bye Tommy, when are you coming back?

TOM   God knows, when I get the time,
           I'm a married man for God's sake.
           Be good Bob Scallion, I'll be calling by.

BOB   Aye well see you around there, Tommy,
           Thank you for taking care of me like this, I
           appreciate it.

TOM   One favour deserves another, Bob Scallion,
           remember that.

BOB   Before he left, Tommy went into a room off the
           main hallway,
           Where sat two large men with beards, reading the
           paper,
           Like they had been there for hours.
           He spoke to the two men in a hushed tone.
           We were alone.
           Molly and me, alone.

MOL   You better come up here then.

BOB   Where?

MOL   The attic, where all the urchins and strays go.
           It's warm and its' dry and you should have it all to
           yourself most nights.

BOB   Oh . . . who might I be sharing it with?

MOL   Well if we're busy we might need it an odd
           evening,
           Weekends'd be't most likely time.
           Where's he found you then?

BOB Tommy?
    I helped him . . . out of a tight spot, in town earlier,
    He seems an awful good natured sort.

MOL Hmmm, he's right good natured is our Tommy.
    Dear old Tommy.
    Don't bring any food up here, Auntie Vera's
    paranoid about mice.
    And no loud music.

BOB This is a massive house, do you take in lodgers?

MOL Well, you could call it that.

BOB Well either you do or you don't.

MOL Don't get shirty, just because you're a friend of
    Tommy Marchbank's.
    Sort of . . . on short term lets . . . if you see what I
    mean.

BOB (*perplexed*) Yeah ? . . . How short?

MOL Well . . . depends really . . . I mean, it can be
    twenty minutes . . .
    Sometimes a few hours . . . depending how they're
    fixed . . .

BOB Twenty minutes . . . ? You've hardly got time . . .
    to . . .
    Molly, what . . . sort of a place is this?

MOL This?
    It's Auntie Vera's . . .

BOB Auntie Vera's what?

MOL . . . House . . . ?

BOB Molly . . . is this a . . . a . . . brothel?

MOL Don't let Auntie Vera hear you callin' it that, it's
    not a nice word at all.
    But yes, that's what it is, young Bob Scallion.

BOB   Oh my God . . . I've never been in a . . . before,
             I must confess this is not entirely how I imagined
             one might be.
             She's your Auntie Vera as well as Tommy's?

MOL   She isn't actually anyone's Auntie Vera, strictly
             speaking.
             It's just what they all call her, you know . . .

BOB   Who?

MOL   The men . . . who do you think, and all the girls as
             well.
             She's always been known as that as far as I know,
             Ever since she decided social work wasn't for her
             and set up this place.

BOB   I see . . .
             So this was the place to which Tommy Marchbank
             had brought me.
             A house of ill fame . . . Elizab . . . Mrs Fairweather,
             would have wept.

             (*A voice from offstage.*)

VOICE   Fall to thy knees and beg upon redemption child!
             Ahhaarrghh!
             And does thou repent thy wickedness now, child?

BOB   What's that?

MOL   God knows, they go in for different things, playing
             games you know.
             A lot seems to hinge on which church they went
             to as children.
             Odd that, don't you think?

BOB   Not really.
             Even at that early age I was aware that
             Cultural heritage should be wholeheartedly
             embraced, not denied.

MOL   Some like to play different games, if say they went
to public school . . .

BOB   . . . what, Monopoly and stuff?

MOL   Yeah . . . that's the sort of thing.

BOB   She looked at me a moment, I could feel the
chemistry.

MOL   This is it, not much I'm afraid.
Bed, table, got your own sink,
Don't light the fire it's supposed to be dodgy,
A bloke died in here last year, I felt awful.
I'll sort you some bedding out later.

BOB   This is fine, Molly . . .

MOL   Well, I'll leave you to it, all work I'm afraid.

BOB   Of course, well thank you . . . and thank Auntie
Vera again,
When you see her.

MOL   Is that all you have with you?

BOB   This, er . . . yes it is all I have with me, at the
moment.

MOL   Wow . . . who'd be you Bob Scallion?
I've got some books and things you can read, if
you want them,
I'll bring them up later as well.

BOB   That would be lovely, thank you, will that be
soon?

MOL   As soon as I can, why?

BOB   Well I can't go to bed without sheets, can I?

MOL   Well no, you can't do that,
Bye now.

BOB   In years to come Molly would often conjure the
                 sight of him,
                 Standing there that day,
                 Kind of like an angel in the attic.

                 But that is how Bob Scallion came to reside
                 At the house of illicit fare.

                            Scene Six

Mrs Fairweather's Unhappiness.

BOB   As the weeks turned into months
                 I grew ever closer to Mrs Fairweather.

MRS F   Here, I have some socks for you and a book of
                 poetry, too.
                 Our faith in you is going to be more than justified!
                 He that will work will inherit the Kingdom of God,
                 Robert,
                 But those that won't should have their dole
                 stopped
                 And be forced into the army.

BOB   I had not the heart, or never quite got round,
                 To informing Mrs Fairweather that my new job was
                 already my old job.
                 Or go into any details as to my new place of
                 residence.
                 Your kindness is like a midnight sun to a lost ship,
                 Mrs Fairweather.

MRS F   Oh, greater is the shepherd's joy on finding the
                 one sheep that was lost.
                 Than the other ninety nine who were not.

BOB   I said a lost ship, Mrs Fairweather . . . not a
                 sheep . . .
                 I think you misheard me slightly.

MRS F   No . . . I am referring . . . I realise you said a lost
                 ship, Robert . . .
                 I see . . . well . . . it is a happily Christian duty.

Ours is a childless marriage . . . God's will,
But your visits have breathed a zest and gaiety
into the house,
I am sure of it!

BOB   Oh Lord, I thank thee for this . . . opportunity of
personal improvement.
I resolve to cleanse these my polluted rivers,
I will flail at my flimsy, sea-shook ways . . .

MRS F   Come here, child. . . . oh, when I see your sweet
boy's face . . .

BOB   Things were looking seriously up.

MRS F   There is a look, I see it in your eyes, a sadness
that . . .
That matches my own.

BOB   And why are you sad, Mrs Fairweather?

MRS F   Oh why . . . why indeed . . .
I fear my heart is drowning in a swamp of tears,
At so many things, at what has been allowed to
happen to you . . .

(*She turns away from him a moment, overcome
with emotion. She stands with her back to him as
she says this next speech.*)

Mr Fairweather lacks . . . sensitivity and
compassion toward me . . .
I feel so wicked and disloyal even saying so.
Do you understand how I feel, Robert?

BOB   Yes, Mrs Fairweather . . .

MRS F   Please . . . Elizabeth.

BOB   Elizabeth, I do . . . for I feel it, too . . .
If only there was more compassion and
sensitivity . . .

MRS F   Oh, Robert.

(She falls into his arms. There is a pause.)

BOB   In the world . . .

MRS F   If I can succour you in your areas of profoundest
             need,
             Perhaps some greater joy will consume me, devour
             me whole I pray.

BOB   Yes.
             Perhaps I should put some hymn cards out, Mrs
             Fairweather.

MRS F   Elizabeth.

BOB   Elizabeth . . . maybe polish a tambourine . . . or
             two . . .

                        Scene Seven

A trip out with Tommy.

BOB   I was soon steeped in a happy routine.
             In the mornings I did the chores around Aunt
             Vera's house,
             Hoovering and the like,
             Then after that I would . . . counsel . . . Molly a
             while,
             Before popping off to Church in time for
             Evensong.
             Mrs Fairweather was determined to help me,
             Her attentions were a force too strong for my
             feeble protestations,
             May God have mercy on me.
             Nonetheless in those years I ate well, and every
             day.
             But it wasn't all housework, oh no,
             As Auntie Vera often said,

VERA   No amount of bribing could ever make a copper
             honest,
             So just check the street as evening draws on, love.

We don't want the gentlemen compromised.

BOB   One day as I was changing the sheets upstairs,
           It being the second Tuesday of the month,
           Tommy Marchbank strode into the hallway.
           It was mid-afternoon and all the girls were on
           prison visits.

TOM   Hello the house!
           Anybody home?

BOB   Just me at the minute, Tommy, how are you?
           What do you want, tea or coffee?
           Only I can't stop long, I haven't done the
           bedrooms
           Or even started to hoover downstairs yet.

TOM   Never mind hoovering, come on.
           I need hand, dead quick, I've just had a phone
           call.

BOB   I took my apron off and left my slippers at the
           door,
           What's coming down, Tommy?

TOM   Business.

BOB   We got in the Capri and set off.
           Yeah, me and Tommy, in the Capri, on business.
           Four hours later we pulled up, in Dunoon, which is
           in Scotland.

TOM   Scotland, wonderful country, funny crowd, but the
           scenery's nice.
           Can you see 'owt?

BOB   Can I see 'owt?
           No, can I frig,
           What have we come all the way up here for?

TOM   To meet a ship, what do you think we've come all
           the way up here for?
           Thought you'd feel at home anyway, round the
           docks . . . sailors,

Swap a few old shanties,
Yo ho ho and a bottle o' rum an' all that.

BOB   I've never been on a ship in my life.
        You know damn well the only water I get near is
        the rain!

TOM   What?
        All that you told Edgar was all shit?
        Well blow me away if Bob Scallion's not a fanny
        merchant.
        And there's me thinking you were like that Captain
        Onedin,
        Off the popular BBC series, 'The Onedin Line'!

BOB   Are you Jack Regan off the hard hitting crime
        drama, 'The Sweeney'?

TOM   No.

BOB   Well then.
        Now why are we here?

TOM   Told you, to meet a ship.
        Come on.

BOB   We walked down toward the shoreline,
        The Munster Queen car ferry floated, thankfully,
        in the dock.
        I could see the lights glistening in the
        firmament . . .

TOM   Come on, slow get!

BOB   Piss off,
        Round a whale fin funnel blowing steam white
        kisses to . . .

TOM   Cop for these two oars.

BOB   A nude reclining sky . . . cop for what?!
        Get you out of here, I am no more rowing that . . .
        That milk carton of a boat!
        Out there into that . . . look at it!

That's the sea is that, Tommy!
Do you hear me man it's the sea!
We'll be drowned out there the pair of us for sure!
For God's sake see sense Tommy, please!

TOM   Shut up or your walking home.

BOB   No, absolutely not!
Under no circumstances!
That's final!

        (*Moments later on the open sea.*)

TOM   Come on limp wrist, we'll miss the bleedin' thing!

BOB   Oh my arms are killing me man!
Shit the bed, there's a ship behind us!

TOM   Well course there's a bleedin' ship!
What do you think we've come here for?

BOB   Oh God no!
We'll drown Tommy, drown as God's an elderly
white bloke!

TOM   Shut up you wittering tit!

BOB   Ahahaharghh!
Oh God no, Elizabeth, Molly, Mother, Mr
Broughton even!
That's how bad it is!
Help me, somebody, please!

TOM   Hello up there, how are you doing?

VOICE   Ahoy there!

TOM   Yes, ahoy there yourselves!
Good to see you!

BOB   A man leaned off the side of the ship,
And threw us a rope.

TOM   Don't let go o' that, handy for parking out here, isn't it?

BOB   Isn't there anything we could tie it to?

TOM   Your neck if you don't shut up whinging!
Christ.
Now then sirs up there on deck, are we in business?

                On the deck two men, with beards, strangely enough,
Lowered some boxes down to the slip shaky row boat.

BOB   Why didn't you get 'em to post it?

TOM   Shush.
There'll be fifty quid in this for you.

BOB   Fifty, when?

TOM   Yes, thought that might alter your tune.
You ought to be grateful instead of moaning all the while.
Last one, thank you very much indeed.
Now then Johannes, what do I owe you?

BOB   I will never forget Tommy.
Stood up in the rickshaw rowing boat, counting out tens and twenties,
With a fag in his mouth, two hundred yards out in the sea.

TOM   You holding that rope?
Nice dealing with you, Johannes.

BOB   Who the hell is Johannes?

TOM   A Dutch seaman.

BOB   Oh I see, you can row back, I'm knackered.

TOM   Bog off, I only brought you up here to row the
bleedin' boat,
Get to, while I get a butcher's at this gear.

BOB   The journey back to dry land was the hardest
twenty minutes
I have ever known.

TOM   Come on!
What's up with you?
It's only a bit of water you know!

BOB   So what's in these boxes?

TOM   Contraband.

BOB   What's contraband?

TOM   Mucky books in this case . . .

BOB   What!?
Oh, that is disgusting!
What did you have to bring me into it for?
What would Elizabeth say?
If I'd known it was that I'd never have come man, I
wouldn't.

TOM   Shut up moaning, for shit's sake!
You ought to go get your old job back,
See how quick you'd make fifty quid in that!
Christ you're thick!
No wonder you were kipping in hostels, sweepin'
up floors,
What did you think we came all this way for?

BOB   I don't know . . . never thought . . .

TOM   You never thought?
Well lay that on a judge some day and see what he
reckons,
There ain't neither time nor space in this old world
for,
'I don't know' or 'I never thought'.

Everything has a reason, and if you don't know
what that reason is,
Do you know what that makes you, Bob Scallion?
A sheep, sheep don't know why they do knack all.
Don't ever be anywhere or doing anything,
That you don't know what it is for and why you're
there.
If this boat had sunk out there tonight or worse
still,
The coppers'd been waitin' here for us when we
got back,
And you'd finished up in Armley,
Do you know whose fault that would have been?
Yours, and nobody else's!
Nobody else has the job of looking after you, Bob
Scallion,
I look after me, you look after you, that's how it
ought to be.

BOB   That's how, eh Tommy?

TOM   Now get them boxes put in that car and shurrup
for once!
Oh and another thing, who's Elizabeth?

BOB   Hmmm?
Oh er . . . someone I used to know, that's all.

TOM   Well, she'd think well of you now, eh?

BOB   And Tommy laughed, to himself, loudly.

Tom   Bob Scallion . . . you baffle me sometimes.
Listen to your politicians, there's gonna be an
election soon.
That Mrs Thatcher know's what's what,
enterprise, initiative, trade,
We've got to roll back the frontiers of Socialism,
That's what the woman says and she's right,
The market is king, people want to buy these
books and look at 'em,
You and me are simply a function of that demand.

BOB   Is that right.

TOM   Yes it is bleeding right, who the hell are you, Mary
             Whitehouse?
             Modern age like this, we've got blokes on the
             moon, atom bombs,
             Shit knows what else but people still can't get
             hold of stuff like this
             And you know what I say to that?

BOB   Amen.

TOM   Amen is right.
             You've got to pick a pocket or two, Bob Scallion.
             Their job is to make rules, ours is to make money,
             'Cos we're the poor silly buggers who starve, you
             hear me?
             Expensive things, morals, I've never been able to
             afford 'em.
             Amen to money in our pockets Bob Scallion, damn
             right.

BOB   As we drove back from Scotland we both sat in
             silence.
             Deep down I knew he was right of course but even
             so.
             I resolved to have no more to do with Tommy
             Marchbank
             Since he spoke to me in that way.
             There are things a fellow cannot but draw the line
             at.

TOM   Fancy a pint when we get back?

BOB   . . . Aye okay then, Tommy, where?

             Well, no sense holding grudges I thought to
             myself . . . no, none at all.
             Somehow we seemed to get along better for that
             little fallout,
             I think of it now as my coming of age.
             Tommy started trusting me to look after things for
             him,
             And as Elizabeth often said as I was leaving her
             house of an afternoon,

Mrs Thatcher would have been very proud of me.
You know what, I think she'd have been proud of
Tommy, too,
And I would have voted for her,
Had such things been of any interest to me.

Scene Eight

Dinner with the Fairweathers.

'Hark the herald angels sing, (*Hearty singing!*)
Glory to the new born King,
Peace on Earth and mercy mild,
God and sinners reconcile'.

(*The singing continues.*)

BOB   One evening, after choir practice, the week after
          Corpus Christi, 1981,
          Elizabeth invited me home to a good Presbyterian
          supper,
          As Molly worked evenings I saw no reason to
          refuse her offer.
          Elizabeth and I had become close, especially on
          our trip to London,
          To see the royal wedding, Charles and Diana . . .
          I have always been a hopeless romantic at heart
          and detest cynicism,
          So something about those two struck a real chord
          with me.

MRS F   Robert, would you bring a bottle of simple grape
          juice from the pantry?

BOB   However I sensed all was not well between Mr
          Fairweather and myself.
          Though we were the best of choirmates.

MRS F   For alcohol is . . . ?

BOB   Satan's best friend.

MRS F   And not for the righteous and kind, as you know.

BOB   Which you undoubtedly are, Mrs Fairweather.
           I have no palate for the stuff, have you Mr
           Fairweather?

MR F   Hmm?
           Alcohol, no no none at all, fool's paradise, Bob,
           Consider the gooseberry bushes . . .

BOB   What?

MRS F   Oh darling please don't use that dreadful word
           'Bob',
           His name is Robert, that's the name his mother
           chose to give him.

MR F   Alright, alright then, Robert it is. (*Chuckling*.)
           You can see who the master is in this house, eh
           Robert, ha ha ha,
           It's all this women's lib I shouldn't be surprised . . .

BOB   Indeed not sir, ha ha ha.

MR F   The owl, Robert.
           A wise and wily bird.

MRS F   And a good thing too, I might add,
           You men have ruled the roost for far too long,
           Why it's high time a little woman sense came to
           the fore,
           You mark my words, Robert, Margaret Thatcher,
           She's the woman for Britain.

BOB   Absolutely Mrs Fairweather, couldn't agree more.

MRS F   Bisto, darling?

MR F   Please . . . you couldn't agree more could you,
           Robert?

BOB   Well . . . everything has drawbacks of course.

MR F   Hmm, such as?

BOB   Well . . . if women are as good as men,
Why don't any of them get into the England team,
That's what you've got to weigh up.
On the other hand, what man could hold a candle
to Esther Rantzen?
It's a very complex area I think you'll find.

MRS F   How astute and well informed you are!
Isn't he dear, for one so young?

MR F   Hmm, indeed.
This new vicar fellow, what do you make of him,
Robert?

BOB   Well he seems a very committed and wholesome
type of reverend,
Wouldn't you agree, Mrs Fairweather?

MRS F   Yes I do.
And please, Elizabeth.

MR F   But what about all this new trendy guitar
strumming,
Tambourine rattling, let's all be happy for Jesus,
Cliff Richard type of thing, surely you don't
approve of that?

BOB   Mr Fairweather, the Lord's word sounds good in
any key.

MRS F   How right that is, Robert . . .

MR F   But it isn't conducive to any sort of spiritual
contemplation,
Any true sense of communion with one's maker,
In the quietude of His House.
Now is it, Robert?

BOB   Some would say that it enriches God's House like
sunlight on . . .

MR F   Well I aren't among them, and neither is Mrs
Fairweather.

MRS F   Endacott, don't adopt that tone with dear
         Robert . . .

MR F   Oh bollocks, dear Robert!
         I'm sick to death of having this squirming little
         gutter rat in my house!
         And you hopping up and down over him,
         Like he's the second bastard coming!

BOB   That was it, the moment I sensed things were
         wrong between us.
         Mr Fairweather, if I have caused you offence I am
         truly sorry . . .

MR F   Are you screwing my wife, you bastard!?

BOB   Sir, the Almighty himself strike me down if I lie!
         I am not!

MR F   Get out, you crawling git!
         Get out, do you hear me!?
         I've tolerated you in my house for years, well no
         more!

MRS F   Endacott Fairweather, I defy you!
         If this . . . poor boy!
         If this innocent is to leave this house this night,
         Then I am to leave it with him!
         You have cast a stain upon my constancy,
         A slur with which I cannot live!
         And may the shame of it be all over this district by
         morning,
         I mean it, I cannot possibly allow you to cast this
         . . . this
         Lamb among the wolves and vipers of this . . .
         wretched Socialist age!
         So help me God and give me grace in this!

BOB   Elizabeth clung to me as she spoke this,

MRS F   In proud and glorious defiance!

BOB   Mr Fairweather swallowed very visibly,
         Then sat down again in his chair, heavily.

Adjusted his napkin, and said,

MR F   Would you . . . pass me another dumpling please
            . . . darling.
            And er . . . the Bisto as well.

Bob   He ate his dinner quietly thereafter.
            Dear Elizabeth . . . how like Mrs Thatcher she was.
            Though the evening was otherwise most
            convivial,
            I was aware of a certain distance on Mr
            Fairweather's part.
            Mrs Fairweather glared at him.

MR F   I . . . I'm sorry about that . . . little outburst,
            Robert,
            I don't know what came over me, quite
            inexcusable . . .
            You know . . . how fond of you I've become.

BOB   That's okay Endacott, we've all done it.

MRS F   That's good.
            Now tell me how your piano lessons are
            progressing, Robert?

BOB   Most energetically, thank you, Elizabeth.

MRS F   You must play something for us, I insist you do!
            Don't you want him to play for us, darling?

MR F   Hmmm.
            Absolutely, love to hear it, Robert.

BOB   Oh no, I could not possibly . . .

MRS F   Oh don't be silly, of course you can!
            Whichever piece is your favourite.

BOB   My piano playing was at that stage somewhat less
            than it is today.
            Elizabeth, saying no to you, is a feat way, way
            beyond me.

MR F   Say it to me then.

              (*He goes to a piano and in comes the sound of*
              'Get Down' by Gilbert O'Sullivan, with him
              singing it, appallingly. MRS FAIRWEATHER *smiles*
              on lovingly while MR FAIRWEATHER *puts his head*
              in his hands.)

MRS F   Thank you Robert that was wonderful, truly
              wonderful,
              Wasn't it darling?
              Such a melodious and dexterous boy!

MR F   Hmm.

MRS F   And yet dear Robert, I feel compelled to ask,
              Does your tutor not teach you any more . . . more
              substantial pieces.

BOB   Oh indeed he does, Mrs Fairweather,
              But in all conscience I do prefer the Gilbert
              O'Sullivan
              Style of composition.
              I feel it best reflects my own creative self.

MR F   Really?
              Now why might that be, Robert?

MRS F   Well . . . of course.

BOB   And I have recently acquired a Boney M
              songbook,
              So you shall soon hear me heartily render
              The Rivers of Babylon, Ra Ra Rasputin and many
              more.

MR F   Smashing.

BOB   Elizabeth didn't invite me round very much after
              that evening.
              But Mrs Thatcher threw a couple of million into
              poverty and suffering,
              So I thought she'd be happy.

Scene Nine

Tommy's visit and some controversy at the races.

TOM   Put the kettle on there, young Bob.
Well Friday night is party night at Auntie Vera's alright.
Eight beds a creakin', by jingo business is booming!

BOB   Oh absolutely it is, I still haven't actually seen
Two thirds of the regular clients who come here.

TOM   And that is the best way, believe you me.
The less you know in this old world, is often as not
The saving of you, as my father used to tell me.

BOB   That can't be right or how would you have got to be where you are?

TOM   How indeed, another good trick young Bob,
Is knowing when to mind one's own business.
Do I make myself clear?

BOB   Aye, aye, sure Tommy, I'm only saying like,
You must know a thing or two to be where you are today, that's all,
I'm not sticking my nose in your affairs Tommy, wouldn't think of it.

TOM   Course you weren't, you're a sound lad, Bob.
Now then, guess where we're off tomorrow . . .

BOB   Saturday . . . Old Trafford? Elland Rd?

TOM   No, try again.

BOB   Not Bradford City again Tom, you know we both get depressed!

TOM   God no, try Haydock races young man,
And what's more we're getting paid for going!

BOB   We always do.
Gambling is a quite boundless source of pleasure
and relaxation
Most especially so if you know the outcome prior
to laying the bet,
Tommy was always highly astute in such matters
And I had to agree with him, it made far more
sense.

(*Both don binoculars and white hats of the
cricket and race course type. In comes some race
commentary. Across stage a bookie is standing at
his board with the runners and prices for the next
race on it, etc.*)

VOICEOVER   All set for this Pertemps Handicap Chase, winner
for the last two years and favourite once again
today Mr Standing at 6/4 on, hard to see past him
on current form but if you fancy a risk then you
could do worse than Bolton Abbey at three's or
Flockton Boy 7/2 but drifting in, nice sort this one,
colt out of Flockton Banger trained at Middleham
by Mrs Dalwinney, she doesn't bring them out for
the ride. 5/1 is Harvest Ranger and at sixes Lupino,
winner twice last year but nothing to speak of this
time, 8/1 Flight Commander and then the rank
outsider, friendless in the market is Gadfly at 25/1
and drifting, not a prayer here, I'm afraid . . .

TOM   That guy there, Alfonso Mendez Ltd of Buenos
Aires, see him, take it, a grand there, on Gadfly,
25/1 . . .

BOB   Gad . . . fly . . . (TOM *winks at him.*) Why, we
should see it as war reparations!

TOM   You're no fool, Bob.

(BOB *takes the money, goes over to the bookie.*)

BOB   Now then Mr Mendez, business flourishing?

(ALFONSO MENDEZ *sounds rather more Pontefract than Buenos Aires.*)

MENDEZ   Business is bloody awful lad, can't make a
             shilling . . .

BOB   Well here's a gift for you, Gadfly, the lot, on the
             nose . . .

MENDEZ   Are you mad?

BOB   Yes.

MENDEZ   Tommy Marchbank's money?

BOB   He's a sporting man you know that, he backs his
             instincts . . . oh, and Mr Mendez, which bit of
             Buenos Aires is it you're from then?

MENDEZ   Pontefract. My old man moved there years ago,
             why?

BOB   Just wondered.

             (BOB *takes the ticket and walks back to* TOMMY.
             In comes the commentary.)

VOICEOVER   They're away and Flockton Boy first to show,
             closely followed by Harvest Ranger and Lupino as
             Mr Standing settles in nicely at the back alongside
             Gadfly as they rise to meet the first and Mr
             Standing is a faller there already . . .

             (TOM *and* BOB *exchange a look of extreme
             surprise. The commontary comes back in.*)

             Three fences left Gadfly is tailed off last might be
             pulled up as Harvest Ranger and Flight
             Commander make a terrible mess of that one and
             they're both down, jockey's unseated, that leaves
             Lupino . . . where's he going? Goodness me
             Lupino's gone the wrong way! Bolton Abbey
             takes it up second last out it's there for the taking
             . . . the jockey's saddle appears to be loose . . .

he's fallen off, unbelievable stuff here and
amazingly two fences back down the field the only
remaining competitor here is the rank outsider
Gadfly . . . Gadfly it is, he's virtually walking over
the line and the silence is deafening here at
Haydock . . .

(*Gadfly strolls over the line with the favourite
beaten and all the rest having fallen or pulled
up, etc.*)

BOB   Well lo and behold!

TOM   My eye young Bob, I do declare our luck is in!

BOB   How do we do it?

TOM   I don't know but there's lads out in the South
Atlantic'd shed a tear to think what we did here
today.

BOB   We played our part Tommy, that's the main thing.

(*He returns to* MR MENDEZ *who is distraught.*)

MENDEZ   You pair o' bent, frauding, twistin', lyin arseholes!

BOB   Ah, that's how we do it!
That's us Mr Mendez, twenty five grand if you
will, good sir.

(MENDEZ *hands over the stash, takes down his
board and exits brokenheartedly.*)

Now, all would have gone most splendidly
according to plan,
Had Mr Mendez not observed me but half an hour
later doling out twenty pound notes in glorious
fashion to the jockeys and stable lads
Of every other horse in the race . . .
So it was that at ten o'clock that same night,
Amid wild whoops of laughter, glee,
Sweet sherry and the like at Aunt Vera's, Tommy
came to me . . .

TOM   Problems son, in the kitchen, come on, nice and
               quiet . . .

BOB   No one saw us slink away from the jolly party
               room,
               What's up Tommy?

               (BOB *sees* MENDEZ *now*.)

MENDEZ   You bent bastards . . . you give us me money back
               Or I'll shop you in, Marchbank . . .

TOM   You any idea what he's on about, Bob?

BOB   None at all Tommy . . .

MENDEZ   I bloody saw you Bob Scallion, flea on a rat's
               back!

BOB   Oh now really!

TOM   Harsh. You calling me a rat?

BOB   Surely we can discuss this amicably?

MENDEZ   As soon as I get my money back you cheatin'
               bloody English!

TOM   Bob, what do you reckon?

BOB   I reckon he's calling our integrity into question.

TOM   Damn it that's what I feared, too.
               Well, having heard you out Mr Mendez, here's
               what I say,
               Swivel on it.

MENDEZ   What? Swivel on it? You telling me swivel on it?

BOB   There it is, swivel like your boys did at Goose
               Green.

MENDEZ   Is that so, Marchbank?

Well maybe they'll listen when I tell them
everything I know about you,
About this house, I can ruin you Tommy,
Like you have me . . .

TOM   See if I care . . . you lost this time my friend, so
suck on it,
And piss off home!

(*At that* MENDEZ *leaps on* TOMMY *and there is a*
most unseemly scuffle with MENDEZ *on top of*
TOMMY. BOB *looks round for something to hit him*
with and finally locates a piece of wood. He hits
him with it, MENDEZ *rolls back with* TOMMY *on top*
of him now, BOB *is appalled at the ferocity with*
which he hit the man and turns away his head in
his hands. TOMMY *observes* BOB *to be looking the*
other way and in a split second grabs the piece of
wood and gives MENDEZ *three or four more solid*
blows with it. MENDEZ *is clearly not dead or*
lifeless until this moment.)

BOB   I have always detested violence,
Not least since I've never won a fight in all my life,
fairly.
But the sound of his head hitting the floor . . .

TOM   Jesus, Bob . . .

BOB   What's up?

TOM   I think you went a bit hard on him, son . . .

(BOB *turns to look at the man, laying prone on*
the floor as he now is.)

BOB   Is he . . . okay?

TOM   No . . . he's not.

BOB   Well . . . does he need a doctor, an ambu . . .
lance?

(TOMMY's *face tells* BOB *the grim awful truth.*)

BOB   (*disbelief*) No?

TOM   'Fraid so . . . you didn't mean to do it, it was an
             accident . . .

BOB   Will . . . well . . . will the coppers believe that?
             Oh God, Tommy, I didn't mean to do it!
             I was protecting you, we'll say he had a knife . . .

TOM   Shut it! We'll say nothing of the sort!
             Coppers my rump, do you hear me?
             No coppers, or we'll both swing for it, do you hear
             me Bob Scallion?

BOB   But . . . Tommy?

TOM   In for a penny . . . in for a pound, lad . . .
             Coppers'll weave whatever lies they want, they'll
             shut the house down,
             Send you away for life, me for a spell, too . . . oh
             aye, is that what you want?

BOB   No . . . but . . .

TOM   Don't worry, I can get you out of it,
             But you need to do everything I say, everything!

BOB   Everything. What exactly?

TOM   Think about it, no one saw him come in here, no
             one'll see him leave.
             Come on, get hold of him, get him out the back
             door quick!

BOB   Tommy this is out of my league man, I've never
             done anything . . .

TOM   Shut it!
             What do you think, I do this every bleeding day of
             the week
             Is that it?
             Is that what you think?

Now you killed him and all I'm tryin' to do is keep
you out
From under lock and key, now shut up wittering
and get hold of him!

(BOB *gets hold of him and the two of them carry
the dead man from the stage. Moments later* BOB
returns alone.)

BOB We dropped him, and some concrete blocks,
Into Scammenden reservoir . . . it's very deep.
We were back at the house by three in the
morning.

I know Tommy sought only to help me,
But I wished at the time we'd handled things
differently,
And I still do now.
It's a very, very terrible thing . . . to kill a man . . .
even by accident.
Especially after you've insulted his national
pride . . .
Things . . . happen so quickly.

(TOMMY *enters on this, comes up to* BOB.)

TOM You okay?

BOB I'm . . . fine.

TOM Coppers are the same the world over, Bob . . .
They never know a thing till someone tells them.
You and me are the only two people who know
about this,
On my honour, son . . . I'll never breathe a word
about what you did.

(*Enter* AUNT VERA.)

VERA Ah you two there you are, where've you been,
rushing about all night,
Never know with you two do we . . .

TOM Pressures of business Aunt Vera,

Glad I bumped into you actually.

Vera   Are you now,
              Bob, run down to the cellar and fetch up another
              crate
              Of creme de menthe, good lad, these religious
              types, eh?
              Well Tommy, what makes you so glad to see me?

TOM   Oh you know me Auntie Vera.
              Love . . . and money.

VERA   Ah . . . I haven't got it, not just yet.
              Can't I wait and give it you double next month?

TOM   Oh Vera, come on, how can I run a business like
              that?
              If you don't pay me how can I pay the bank
              manager?
              I bought this house, set you and all the girls up in
              it,
              And I can land the lot of you back out on the
              street in a breath,
              Now where's the rent money, Auntie Vera?

VERA   Tommy please listen, there's nothing to worry
              about,
              Things have just been a little bit slow lately,
              It's all the bad weather we've been having,
              People don't feel like coming out as they would
              another time.
              And the run up to Christmas is always quiet, you
              know that.

TOM   Don't give me this shite.
              I'll be here at four o'clock tomorrow for it and
              don't piss me about.
              You don't misunderstand me, do you Aunt Vera?

BOB   I had heard every word but could scarce believe
              it . . .
              So . . . on top of everything else that had
              happened . . .
              Tommy owns this house . . . he lives off . . .

It's fair to say that I was only just getting to know the real
Tommy Marchbank.

I hurried out of the hallway and back into the party room,
As the pimp strode straight out of the place.
He unlocked the swanky Capri, got straight in it and drove off.

(*Blackout.*)

ACT TWO

Scene One

The brothel is raided.

Bob *strides back onto stage, this time decked out in a suit,
looking good.*

BOB   As a year became two, and then three or four more
           That I had been staying at Aunt Vera's,
           The unfortunate business with the bookmaker slid
           into history, almost.
           I grew very fond of sweet Molly,
           She and I would often go for walks of a Sunday
           afternoon.
           I wore a suit by then and knocked about town in a
           car.

MOL   I don't think I'd like to live this way forever,
           would you, Bob?

BOB   No, no, not me, no.

MOL   What way would you like to live?

BOB   Hmmm, me?
           Oh I don't know . . .
           I knew full well . . . I wanted to live like Tommy.

MOL   Do you not look at the way other people live and
           think, ever?

BOB   Yeah, God knows how they stand it, it's so boring
           isn't it?

MOL   I wasn't going to say that.
           Do you never see your mum and dad any more,
           Bob?

BOB   No no, not for a while now,
           I must think on and get in touch with 'em.

I think I spent twenty years thinking on to get in
touch with them.

MOL   There's a man comes here, an elderly man,
of Ukranian origins I believe.
Nicest man I've ever met.
All he ever wants me to do is take my dress off,
And sit curled up with him on the bed,
He puts his head on my chest, and we sit like that
a couple of hours.
After a while he goes to sleep.
He's not been round for a month or more now,
I hope nothing's happened to him but he's never
said where he lives,
Or I'd go check he's alright . . .
It'll be dark soon . . . then it'll be evening, again.

BOB   Aye flat out again, it's all go round here . . .

MOL   Did I ever tell you how I came to be here, Bob?

BOB   Yeah Tommy brought you here, you said,

MOL   I told you about my family . . . you know, you'd
like my sisters,
Sometimes when I'm out with 'em, I wish I lived
like 'em.

BOB   And why don't you?

MOL   'Cos I can't.

BOB   Well that's daft talk, you could if you had a mind to.
You can be whatever you want to be . . .

MOL   How the hell could I?
I've been in here five years, Bob!
Five years and I aren't ever gonna not be here.
I hate it sometimes . . . I really, really hate it, Bob.
But I can't go anywhere else 'cos I can't actually
do anything else!

BOB   As she spoke those words,

I had no idea of the thoughts that had them
brought,
Or the world she could see in them.
Aye well, we're all a bit in the stew if you think
about it, Mol.

MOL   Bog off, Bob!

BOB   Well . . . if that's how you feel . . . I better get a
move on . . .
I knew not what had come upon her.

MOL   Chop, chop, eh?
Time is money.

BOB   By the mid '80s I was Tommy's full time assistant.
We had retail outlets all over town and money was
no problem.
The night Tommy opened his first discotheque,
'McQueen's', well,
It was one we'll all remember a long, long time.

TOM   Look at this, young Bob,
Every dignitary in the metropolitan district is here,
Half of Leeds United's first team is here,
Half the boxer's worth a toss, and all the Wendy's
you could wish for.

BOB   It certainly was a star-spangled event,
That Richard Whiteley, he was there, oh aye, and
Jack Sugden,
Him from Emmerdale.
Champagne, vol au vents, champagne, sausages
on sticks,
I was so well and truly landed!

MOL   Bob, I don't know how to tell you this.

BOB   These are the best days of my entire life, Molly!
Bob Scallion has arrived!

MOL   I've got something to tell you . . .

BOB   Let's disco on, everybody!

TOM   You all know me . . . I'm Tommy Marchbank,
And when Tommy Marchbank says enjoy and
imbibe,
You know it's time to!
Everyone get as much booze as you can,
You're all my friends and Tommy . . . well, Tommy
is everyone's friend!

BOB   Wahoo, hoo, hoo!

VERA   Come here Tommy Marchbank, you old bank
robber you!

BOB   Auntie Vera looked like only Cleopatra before her
ever did!

TOM   Auntie Vera . . . I would be nowhere without you.

(TOMMY *and* VERA *embrace and there is much
whooping and joyful exuberance.*)

BOB   Wahhooo, waheeyyy!
Let's hear it for Tommy Marchbank everyone!

TOM   And then when we've got to turn off here,
Don't want the police raiding us, do we Chief
Inspector?
Nice to see you here, sir,
Still, if they do you won't have to come out
special to arrest us all!

BOB   How we all laughed.

TOM   No, it's back to Auntie Vera's for a select
reception!

BOB   Disco on, Tommy!
I was twenty four years old and money grew on
trees.
It seemed like nothing could stop the party.

TOM   See everyone gets back to the house okay, would
you, Bob?

I've got to shoot off for half an hour, be along later.

BOB   Tommy, anything.
         I should have known when the Chief Inspector declined an invite
         Back to Auntie Vera's for the select reception.

         At 3:00 AM no sign of Tommy, but the brothel is swinging.

MOL   Bob, I've got something to tell you.

BOB   (*singing*) 'I'm just a love machine!'

MOL   Bob, listen!

BOB   Molly, what could it be . . . why so fevered?

MOL   I'm pregnant . . .

BOB   Oh . . .

MOL   Well, Bob we need to talk, I don't know what to do . . .

BOB   Well now you knew how to get pregnant.
         (*Singing.*) 'And I won't work for nobody but you!'
         La lalalala lalalala lala . . .

MOL   You are the father, you know that, don't you?

BOB   (*singing*) Woo, hoo, hoo . . . What?!

MOL   You are the only one with whom . . . I haven't taken any precautions.

BOB   What?!
         Why the hell not?

MOL   Well . . . because you and me . . .

BOB   How can you prove it was me?

You've no more idea who it was than I have,
No chance, girl, not this hombre you don't.

MOL   But Bob I do know it was you, I'm sure of it,
        It was different with you . . . you weren't
        paying . . .

BOB   Not then I wasn't, eh?
        By Christ you'll have your pound of flesh, won't
        you!

MOL   What?
        What about all the time we've spent together?
        Don't be like this with me . . .

BOB   You weren't laying this on me then!

MOL   I wasn't pregnant then, don't be like this, Bob,
        You are the father . . .

BOB   Go to court and prove it,
        You're a prostitute for God's sake!

MOL   Well . . . (*She is somewhat dumbfounded at this.*)
        Well, if you don't want to help me, then don't!
        I might be a prostitute . . . but you're a liar, Bob
        Scallion,
        And that's far worse.

        (BOB *looks on mortified as she speaks.*)

MOL   Go on, go away . . . rotten bastard, don't worry,
        Auntie Vera'll help me.
        You learn who you can trust.

BOB   I have never forgotten those words . . . nor will I
        ever.
        I went, back into the hallway . . .
        A baby? Like little Wills . . . or Harry . . .
        I glanced around and she was still there, looking
        at me.
        Her face, so sad, so pretty, her shape, carved in
        red,
        In the kitchen light . . .

MOL   Bob . . . please?

(*He thinks another moment and then goes back to her.*)

BOB   Molly I'm sorry, please don't cry . . . forgive me . . . I hate to see you cry . . .

MOL   Well don't be such an arsehole then!

BOB   I'm sorry, sorry . . . it's a tough habit to break, I suppose . . .

MOL   I know . . . and . . . you don't know your own mum and dad, do you?

BOB   What's that got to do with it?

MOL   Well, you haven't got . . . no one's ever . . . oh never mind . . .
Well . . . a baby, Bob . . .

BOB   Baby Bob . . . or William.

MOL   What?

BOB   That's what we'll call him, William, or Harry . . .

MOL   And if he's a she?

BOB   Molly, dearest, you're in no condition to stress yourself with
Complications and things that, please God, just won't happen . . .

MOL   I suppose not . . . oh Bob, I knew you were a good one at heart!

BOB   I'm glad you do . . . and I'm sorry I called you a prostitute . . .

MOL   It's okay.

BOB   Even if you are . . .
             She looked so beautiful that night . . . happy
             even . . .
             And I would have held her in my arms except . . .

VOICE   OPEN UP! POLICE! OPEN UP! POLICE!

BOB   Blasted mayhem through the air!
             My blood ran cold, without thinking,
             Like a disturbed rat I bolted for the back door!

MOL   Bob!

BOB   Only to see them same rat-catchers,
             A coming through there as well!

MOL   Bob where are you going!?

BOB   Startled guests groped for their trousers!

             (*For a second he is face to face with* MOLLY, *he
             knows not what to say, but the look they
             exchange tells her all she needs to know.*)

             Don't worry sweet pea I'll . . . I'll . . . be . . . back
             for you . . .
             Some day . . .

MOL   But . . .

BOB   Mr Fairweather appeared in the hallway in his
             underpants,
             And I did bid him good morning sir, as I hurtled
             for the cellar!
             Police were everywhere!

VERA   Please please, gentleman please!
             I'm afraid we're by appointment only on Fridays,
             Try us on a Monday, we're less selective then.
             You could have rung the bell, you know!
             Mind the door frame, you great clumsy pillock!
             Cost more than you earn all year!

MOL   Bob Scallion, don't you leave me!

BOB   As all hell broke loose around me, the house now
           full of police,
           I darted down the stairs and to a boarded up
           window at the back,
           No police behind as I kicked at the boards,
           Out into a gully below the yard.
           No one had seen me.

VOICE   Nobody move, the house is under arrest!

BOB   And so I climbed from out of the sewer,
           But yards from the police, the bearded police,
           And snuck under the fence into next door's yard.
           As I climbed the wall to the next yard down
           I could hear the cries of the lost and compromised.

VOICE   Name?

MR F   Oh God . . . Endacott Fairweather . . .

BOB   I felt strangely sorry for him as he was led away in
           his underpants,
           Head bowed, crying quietly.
           Touchingly clutching his trousers in one hand.
           Auntie Vera, her sails, like poor Cleopatra's before
           her, in tatters.

VERA   I'm ruined . . . don't cry, Molly . . . come on lass.
           No sign of Tommy, no sign of Bob Scallion . . .
           Didn't we just know it, eh girl.

BOB   A hundred yards behind me the house of ill fame
           was sacked
           And ultimately sunk by the grim faced and
           righteous.
           The picture is etched, seemingly, into my eyelids.
           Molly, poor Molly, handcuffed and weeping . . .
           I myself had done it to her.
           Though I had the strongest urge to go back,
           I did not.

Scene Two

Tommy's goodbye.

BOB   A couple of days later I went round to Tommy's
house,
His wife opened the door, and looked at me.

TOM   Ah Bob, Bob, er good to see you son,
This is Bob, he used to work for me.
Let's go sit in the garden, Bob.

BOB   It's not hardly warm yet, Tommy, but if you want.

TOM   You didn't get collared with everybody else then?

BOB   No, not me Tommy, too clever eh, us two?

TOM   Yeah that's right, Bob,
Listen son, things are still a bit warm, lot of fall
out from this,
If you get my meaning.

BOB   Hardly surprising, Tommy,
Thank God you and the Chief Inspector weren't
there,
That's all I can say.

TOM   Yeah . . . yeah, absolutely Bob.
They're going to be watching me like hawks for
the foreseeable.
I think I'm due for the high jump big style, any day
now.

BOB   What, they can link it to you?

TOM   Not half, Bob, so I'm one feller you want to steer
well clear of.
Whatever happens Bob, I won't breathe a word
about you.
Get well clear of me and don't come back, Bob,
Do you understand me?

BOB   But Tommy, I left Molly in the lurch the other
           night and well . . .

TOM   Don't worry about Molly, Bob.
           I'm sure she'll come through alright.
           All the girl's got released this morning,
           It seems Molly's sister was at the police house
           and took her off,
           Big tearful family reunion trip by all accounts.
           She'll be okay, I'll tell her you asked though.

BOB   He bundled a few ten pound notes into my pocket,
           And said . . .

TOM   I won't see you for a while Bob, good luck.

BOB   I left Tommy's house almost in tears at my good
           friend's generosity.

           So ended my time at Auntie Vera's, the balmy days
           of ease
           And familial warmth that had become so much a
           home to me.

                          Scene Three

Armed robbery with Ted and Fleg.

BOB   So . . . a dead man in his watery grave . . . a maid
           with child, abandoned . . .
           God has no place for such as I . . . no place at all.

           I cannot account for the next chapter of my life.
           That I am ashamed seems so paltry and worthless
           a remark
           As to make matters worse.
           I removed myself from the district and fell to a
           terrible state.
           Tommy's money soon went and,
           After a period upon the charity of the Christian
           Brothers,
           In their charming 12th century abbey at
           Giggleswick,

I fell to drinking heavily and gambling, and acting
the goat generally.
I am only thankful that Elizabeth never laid eyes
on me in those times.
I ended up sharing a flat with a fellow named Ted,
and his mate,
A punk rocker, called Fleg, so he said.
The entire winter of 1986,
We didn't do much, apart from bongs and listen to
The Grateful Dead,
Or The Stranglers if Fleg was in charge.
We got utterly banjaxed, wazzed every giro day for
a full six months.

FLEG   Aw shit man, no bog roll again . . .

BOB   No?

FLEG   No, give us Ted's shirt over. (*Wheezy laughter.*)

BOB   I hate winter . . . this flat is freezing, Ted.
              I haven't took my coat off since August.

TED   No . . . mind if you did Fleg'd probably nick it . . .
              Worse still hahahaha, he'd take a dump in't pocket
              of it man, hahahaha . . .

              (*They are both laughing wheezily at this low
              humour.*)

BOB   We had neither food nor money, nor the foggiest
              idea,
              But the crack was fine.
              At first we just robbed telephone boxes, then fish
              and chip shops,
              Ted said they were the easiest prey.

TED   Going to California, that's me man.

BOB   Yeah?

TED   Eh Bob, Fleg, listen, I've got an idea, man.

BOB   You haven't, have you?

TED   Aye it's a stonker!

BOB   Go on.

TED   Let's do a sub-post office, like that Black Panther
           bloke did.
           Then we can get out of this shit tip and rent a new
           one.

BOB   Ted, that's a stroke of genius!

TED   Aye, well . . .

BOB   He's doing life, isn't he, the Black Panther?

FLEG   Is he?
           Sound one!

TED   Aye well . . . he didn't do it right, did he?
           No, we'll sort it out proper man, in and out in two
           seconds,
           Then I'll be able to get an Harley and go to
           California!
           Beautiful, man!

BOB   That we would never see California was fairly
           apparent,
           Even in the state we were in.
           I think we should stick to phone boxes, Ted, it's
           what we know best,
           In spite of everything, the next morning we took
           the bus to Halifax.

TED   See comin' over here means less chance of us
           gettin' recognized.
           Got to think about that sort of thing.

FLEG   You are a master criminal, Ted, I've always said
           you had it in you.
           I'm really pleased for you man.

TED   Aye, look at this.

BOB   What about it?
           It's a piece of lead piping, Ted.

TED   Aye, but they'll think it's a gun, man they'll shit
theirselves
And cough us up the lot!

FLEG   Wicked tactics, Ted.

BOB   There's no way anyone could mistake that for a
gun, Ted.

TED   No man, you haven't got it, I'll put it in a bag
right, and point it at 'em,
They'll think it's a gun barrel and kak 'emselves,
nice one, eh?
It's knack all is this type of thing if you've got a
bit o' bottle.
Born to be wild, eh?

FLEG   Bang on Ted!
Made a fool of yourself there, Bob.

BOB   Aye.
Not just there, Fleg.
The bus moseyed its' sweet way to Halifax,
And if you've never taken it you should,
For it is without doubt a most picturesque and
uplifting journey.
We stole a Ford Capri . . . not Tommy's,
From the Halifax Building Society car park.
Why didn't we steal a car in Bradford and drive
over here?

FLEG   I didn't think of that . . .

TED   'Cos you said the bus ride were nice.

FLEG   Yeah, you did.

BOB   Yeah . . . I did, fair point . . . just wondered that's
all, seems daft . . .
Either way we were in business.
Three post offices and two hamburgers stands
In just over an hour and a half.

TED   Fast action man or what?!

(*Sings.*) Headin' down the highway . . .

FLEG   Five minutes and you're almost there!

BOB   I am a cider drinker!
Anyone remember The Wurzels?

(*The three of them generally whoop it up, drink cider and laugh their socks off.*)

BOB   For a time Ted and me worked as a fine team inside,
While Fleg was the driver.
I bought a new suit and went for my dinner at the Victoria Hotel.
For a time we did okay, but like I said,
Fleg was the driver.
One day outside Morrison's in Dewsbury.

(BOB *and* TED *are in full armed robbery mode like they've just robbed the till and are in full flight.*)

TED   Where the hell's the car gone to?
Fleg where the hell are you, man!?

BOB   Fleg you stupid useless . . . can you believe that?

TED   Oh shag it, man!
I'm gonna nut that Fleg!

BOB   We were wrestled to the floor by two ladies from a shoppers club,
And beaten and kicked by a variety of passers by,
Until the police arrived and saved us.

TED   That's Dewsbury for you that is.
Every time I come here I get punched.

BOB   That evening we were joined in the cell by Fleg.
Nice one, Fleg.

TED   You're a true pro.

FLEG   I'm really sorry about that lads, I've got no excuses.

But I saw this bloke I used to know, and we got
talkin' like,
He said he had some demon weed so I offered him
a lift.
I was sat in his house when I remembered.

TED   Easy done, don't worry about it.

FLEG   What I can't work out is how they got me,
When I weren't there you know when you got
collared like.
How could they o' known?

(BOB *and* TED *glance somewhat guiltily at one
another, since both grassed* FLEG *up instantly.*)

TED   Weird, yeah . . .

BOB   No idea, Fleg . . . uncanny.

Bob Scallion and Ted Fernyhough were each
sentenced to four years,
Increased to six when Ted employed a certain
metaphor
When addressing his honour, the judge, without
permission.
Fleg got three years.

And there I was . . . ten years after I had left it,
Back in prison.
My heart sank lower than at any point.
As they took me away to that bleak prison cell,
I would gladly have swapped anything I ever have
owned,
For just one tender minute with Molly.

Scene Four

Molly's prison visit.

BOB   For me the late 1980s were characterised
By a series of O and A level classes and all night
origami sessions.

Early release was denied me after an unfortunate
incident when
A bloke from Middlesborough took it upon himself
To borrow my Charles and Diana mug . . . he broke
it . . . my . . .
Bob and Molly mug, you might say . . . and then
he laughed.
Everything . . . Everything I could list that had
gone awry,
Every moments desperate misfortune and ill luck I
had suffered
Came back upon me in that momentary froth of red
mist and . . .
I very nearly killed him by all accounts . . . but I
recall none of it.

My spirit was severely dented by those years
And I scarcely care to recall them but for one day.
In the spring of 1990, four years into my term, that
I received a visitor.
I could not disguise my curiosity or excitement
At the thought of who it might be.
I went into the large room with tables and chairs
Where I made such an unfamiliar sight, and
stopped dead in my tracks.
To begin with she did not see me, but there she
was.
Oh there she was, messing about with her hair.
I was overcome, with a potent mix of shame and
adoration,
Shame at where she had to come that our eyes
might meet,
Like before in the dim lit cavernous hallway, with
its glistening walls,
The never gone days of Auntie Vera's house.
Tommy's house, as it turned out.
My only, only Molly . . . how are you?

MOL   I'm fine, you?

BOB   Very well under the circumstances . . . but not very
           well when I see . . .
           What I have missed in you . . .

MOL   I've brought you some books to read.

BOB   You've always been bringing me books to read,
             haven't you?
             You brought some to me once at . . .

MOL   I remember it, Bob.
             Bob, I've come to visit you for a reason.

BOB   I've realized some things, Molly.
             I never meant to just leave you like that.

MOL   Didn't you?

BOB   No I did not, I was going to come back to you . . .
             But next thing everything broke down in hell and
             policemen.

MOL   I remember it well, and you ran . . . left me, like
             your sort always do.
             Never mind . . . it's not your fault, Bob Scallion.

BOB   Oh Molly . . . you don't know how I lie awake in
             here,
             Thinking about you, and the little one, Jeremy.
             Though I wish you'd called him Jim or Harry or . . .

MOL   Or Bob . . . no way is he going to be anything like
             you, Bob.

BOB   Molly listen . . . I've learned so many things . . .

MOL   So have I Bob, it's too late now, though.

BOB   Oh Molly, beautiful Molly, say not so sadly,
             It's never too late . . . there is always hope,
             Look at me in here, hope is all I have, hope and
             you . . .

             (*He pauses, looks fondly at her and smiles.*)

             I . . .

MOL   Don't say you love me, Bob . . .

BOB   But I do . . . I do, Molly . . . I do.

MOL   Oh, Bob . . . say anything you like, but don't say
             you love me . . .
             These . . . are not times to love someone in.

BOB   Molly, oh don't cry, I hate to see you cry . . .
             Sweetheart, if I have learned one thing in my life it
             is this,
             It's always time to love someone, always . . .

MOL   Well . . . I'm not that someone, Bob.

BOB   Oh darling, yes you are, for me, the only one . . .
             I've . . . seen things, in here, Molly . . .

MOL   I'm pregnant again.

BOB   Aye, I appreciate that but since I've been in here
             well . . .
             You're what?

MOL   That's right, Bob, you remember the last time I
             told you that?

BOB   Aye, I do . . . well, I won't ask who it is . . .
             It's the price I've to pay I suppose . . . these minor
             infidelities.

MOL   You can ask who it is, and it's not a minor
             infidelity, Bob,
             Because you're not my husband, boyfriend, lover
             or whatever,
             For it to be an infidelity.
             You've never been anything like that, Bob,
             Because you never wanted to be . . .

BOB   Oh but I do now, Molly . . .

MOL   Well it's too late now.
             That's what I've come to tell you.

BOB   Well, I don't want to ask who it is,

This is the worst news you could have brought
me . . .
Are you saying . . . you and me, we can't be
together
Like I've been imagining it?

MOL   We never could have been, Bob.
And if I were naming this one after anybody, his
name'd be Tommy.

BOB   Tommy?

MOL   He's been very kind to me, Bob.

BOB   Tommy . . . ?
I bet he has, the lyin' swine . . . supposed to be
my mate . . .

MOL   He gave me some money, you know, that useful
item?
It's Tommy's baby I'm having, Bob.

BOB   Molly, how could you?

MOL   Oh Bob, whether he sold us all down the canal at
Auntie Vera's or not,
What difference does it make now, eh?

BOB   (*baffled*) What?!

MOL   That's why him and the Chief Inspector didn't
show at the house . . .
Didn't you never twig to that?
We were all set up so Tommy could get rid of us
all,
And shut the house down,
We didn't figure in his plans no more.

BOB   No . . . I didn't know . . . I never thought . . . the
bastard!
I've never said anything to you about this Molly,
But it was Tommy who owned that house, not
Aunt Vera at all.

MOL   Wow, Bob Scallion . . . I know that.

BOB   What . . . you knew all along . . . ?

MOL   Tommy . . . and me, Bob . . .
                I told you it was him brought me to Auntie
                Vera's . . .
                We've had . . . a bit of a thing all along, you know.

BOB   Molly, that swine sold you out before!

MOL   Well he didn't sell me out any worse than you,
                Bob Scallion!

BOB   Possibly not, but . . .
                Even when . . . I lived at Aunt Vera's and you and
                me were . . . ?

MOL   I stopped it with him for a while . . . I told him I
                was in love with you,
                He wasn't right happy but he always liked you so
                he didn't do nothing.

BOB   You were in love with me?
                You never said.

MOL   Well . . . wasn't it obvious?

BOB   Not without you saying something, how am I
                gonna know?!

MOL   Wow Bob Scallion . . . who'd be you.

BOB   Who'd be me?
                Same silly bastard who's always had to be me,
                From one bag of shit to the next!
                That bastard, I'll kill him!

                (*At this point he loses his cool a moment and
                bangs his fist on the table and so on.*)

WARD   Calm yourself down there, Scallion.
                You'll be losin' sweet rations any more of that,
                heheheheh . . .

BOB   Molly . . . there . . . there was a young man . . . on
          my wing . . .
          His name was Andrew . . . he was seventeen.
          I used to hear him cry himself to sleep every night
          just like I did
          When I was first in jail, all that time ago . . .
          But I never helped him . . . he was . . . ill-used in
          here . . . badly . . .
          One morning they opened the cell . . . and he'd
          taken his own life, Molly.

MOL   I . . . I'm sorry to hear that, Bob . . . I've no idea
          what it must be like . . .

BOB   No you haven't!
          Any idea what it's like for me . . .
          Molly listen to me, you loved me then,
          Love me now . . .

MOL   I can't . . .

BOB   Yes you can, please!

MOL   I can't because I love Tommy Marchbank . . .
          Look, Bob, it's how it is, so you better cop for
          it . . .

BOB   You can't go away with Tommy Marchbank . . .
          What about his wife, does she know?
          I'll tell her, there . . . you wait and see.

MOL   Bob, you'd be advised to stay well away from
          Tommy's wife,
          And well away from Tommy,
          He's bought me a house, in a suburb, it's nice . . .

BOB   Has he?

MOL   He says he and Mrs Marchbank have a modern
          marriage.
          He moves with some very swish types these days,
          Bob,

He owns a lot of property and he isn't anyone to
mess with.
And look at you, Bob Scallion, what do you own?

BOB   Where are you going?
            Molly don't go, please don't go, you can't leave
            me and go to him . . .
            Molly . . . you've been my only hope in here . . .

MOL   I'm sorry Bob, I couldn't tell you in a letter,
            And you'd have found out sooner or later,
            I'd like you to stop writing the poems to me
            please.
            Though the one about the snake dying was
            beautiful, it really was.

BOB   She got up and left the large room, and me in
            tatters.
            I have never put eyes on her from that day to this.
            1990, I understand the country was booming,
            forgive me,
            I missed it.

                        Scene Five

Scallion's Head Opener.

BOB   When next I saw the light beyond my joyless cell,
            My thirtieth birthday had been and long gone.
            Of the sixteen years since leaving school,
            Eight had passed in a prison cell.
            Things seemed very different, somehow.
            More and more seemed to be sleeping out rough,
            Unwashed, unlovely, then ignored.
            Mrs Thatcher had passed into history, her Soviet
            enemies with her.
            Charles and Diana were . . . on the rocks . . . Molly
            gone . . .
            The 1990s by jingo!
            One question, who the hell is Tony Blair?

            I decided to re-enrol for Mrs Fairweather's

Spiritual Regeneration classes.
I waited outside church for the service to end,
But there was no sign of her.
When it seemed everyone had left I moved
towards the door.

An old man came out and closed the door behind
him.
He shuffled some keys and put one in the lock.

EDGAR   Argh ... what is it you want?
Nay, I'm only locking the door, I've nothing to
steal, I'm an old man ...

BOB   Calm yourself old man, I only want to ... Mr
Broughton,
Mr Broughton, how strange to find you here.

EDGAR   Who is it ... who are you?

BOB   You don't remember me.

EDGAR   ... Yes I do ... it's Bob Scallion.
Indeed I do ... I've thought of you many times.

BOB   Well ... I never thought of you as a church-going
man.

EDGAR   Well ... like many a man, in my younger days, I
never thought ...
Life is lonelier than you know ...

BOB   Tell me about it.

EDGAR   I had to shut the shop after the wife died ...
The people here were only ever the kindest to me
you know ...
I ... think I er, owe you some money if you
remember ...

BOB   I never imagined I would need it.

EDGAR   Here, son, take this ... I don't have much, I'm
afraid.

(BOB *looks at the money a moment then back at* EDGAR.)

BOB   Mr Broughton keep it, I've had money many times
           and lost it all,
           It matters not the little you owe me.
           And love . . . I could say the same.
           I'm sorry to hear of your wife.

EDGAR   Aye, aye well . . . she'd o' loved comin' here every
           Sunday   . .
           But I'd never hear of it . . . then she was gone . . .
           in no time at all, gone.
           I think she comes here with me now, though.

BOB   I think so, too . . .
           Mr Broughton, do you know of Mrs Fairweather's
           whereabouts?

EDGAR   Ooh she's long gone now, is that one . . . there
           was a bit o' scandal like.
           I think she lives at Beverley now, we don't see her
           no more.
           Take care young Bob, look after your soul.

BOB   I'll try to, Mr Broughton . . . goodbye old man.

           (EDGAR *ambles slowly away,* BOB *looks on after
           him.*)

BOB   Poor Elizabeth had retired to the country.
           I resolved to let my thoughts stray nowhere even
           near to Mol . . .
           There, not at all, or that bastard Marchbank.

           Incredibly prison had not dulled my
           entrepreneurial spirit,
           And after a short spell at the YMCA in
           Huddersfield,
           I cobbled together the rudiments of a still, and set
           to brewing
           A fearsome wash of a broth which had proved
           very popular

With my fellows during our period of correction.
I gave it the rather catchy title of Scallion's Head
Opener.
Which I could produce at a cost of four pence a
gallon,
And retail at a pound for a quart bottle,
Thereby undercutting both Thunderbird and
Buckfast Abbey wine,
Crucial factors in my new whereabouts.
I set up shop in the flat where the council housed
me,
And for a year or so things went great.
Each morning there were queues down the
stairways,
And I bought a couple of new suits and lived on
pizzas.

BERNADETTE   There's someone to see you, Bob, says he knows
you of old.
I didn't ask what it was he knew.

BOB   Yes, thank you, Bernadette, please show him in.
I had an assistant called Bernadette, that was her.

FLEG   Nice to see you, Bob.

BOB   Fleg . . . my dear, dear Fleg, come in, how good it
is to see you.

FLEG   Heard you were here like, man . . .
What's this brew you're cookin' up?
You couldn't let us have some till I get sorted,
could you?

BOB   Fleg . . . the state of you . . .
That you were ever an unkempt slovenly
individual
Is beyond argument, but this incessant tremble . . .

FLEG   Only the natural aches of a fellow in these times,
Bob Scallion,
Like you, I am at the sharp end of a long-winded
recession, hahaha.

In spite of everything I've still got the same
convictions, Bob.

BOB   Are they not wiped off yet?

FLEG   Does it get you mashed, this wallop?
               You couldn't just let us have a little drop till
               tomorrow,
               I wouldn't normally ask but . . . could you, Bob?
               I'll pay you tomorrow man, you know I'm sound,
               Bob.

BERNADETTE   If he's sick on that carpet, Bob, you're bleedin
               cleanin' it!

BOB   Yes, yes . . . she has a . . . fairly direct manner, my
               assistant.

BERNADETTE   You're what?

               (*With* BERNADETTE *looking on contemptuous,* FLEG
               stands almost pleading with his eyes, BOB *turns
               away from him.*)

BOB   When realization hit me as to the source of Fleg's
               shivers and shakes,
               I confess to being filled with sorrow, and
               somehow affection.
               Prison can be very hard on some, and Fleg had not
               coped well . . .
               I saw it happen to many on my own wing . . .
               heroin.
               Physical escape is denied them . . . so a mental,
               chemical substitute
               Is the only option available,
               And it is a most inhuman and vulgar thing to see.
               Take it dear Fleg . . . for old times' sake, eh?

FLEG   Oh, nice one, Bob Scallion, cool as ever . . . you
               were always class.
               I'll be round and sort you out in a day or so, no
               problem . . .
               Hahaha, you're lookin' good, as ever, eh?
               Sound man . . .

(FLEG *departs with a succession of assurances nods, etc.*)

BOB   They found Fleg under a railway bridge.
Post-mortem said it was heart failure, brought on by a violent
Concoction of powerful alcohol and hospital drugs.
Twenty eight years old.

Though the charge of poisoning was dropped,
It signalled the end of Scallion's Head Opener as a commercial entity.
For the first time in his life,
Bob Scallion became dependent on state benefits.

BERNADETTE Oi, you! If you aren't earning any money to keep yourself round here
Least you can do's shift off your rump and clean up!

BOB   Yes dear . . . shortly . . . I'm just pondering . . . things.

(*She comes up and gives him a serious dig in the guts, he doubles over in pain.*)

BERNADETTE You can't afford to ponder!
Get out and earn some money if you want to ponder!
Your assistant my arse!

Scene Six

A trip out to Beverley.

BOB   For the next two years I lived with the woman Bernadette,
Though not without goodness,
She had a brutal temper and treated me with appalling violence.

I would not have stood for it had I had anywhere
else to go.
Then one morning I got up and left the flat . . . it
just seemed time.
Why my whole being yearned for further spiritual
regeneration!

So it was, fresh in hope, that I travelled to
Beverley.
It is a pleasing town in the wolds,
The air is fresh and clean there, disease less
prevalent and the people,
Of a ripe and simple nature such as one finds in all
country places.
I stood on the street outside the house I was told
she lived in.
It was hardly . . . salubrious . . .

Mrs Fairweather . . . it is I . . . Bob . . .

(MRS F *appears, as to answer the door.*)

MRS F   Bob? Bob . . . Scallion?
Robert . . . dear, dear Robert!
Do come in, oh my what a delight to see you, will
you have tea?
Or would you prefer coffee, oh look at me . . . I
haven't a piece of cake
Or a biscuit to give you . . . look at you . . .
Robert . . .

BOB   Mrs . . . Elizabeth . . . I . . . thought to find you in . . .

(*She attempts to pour him a drink but spills it.
That she is a gin soak is glaringly apparent, her
hands are shaking.*)

MRS F   In . . . church perhaps?
I . . . well . . . I do . . . still attend . . . from time to
time . . . however . . .

BOB   It matters not how oft we go to the altar,
Elizabeth . . .
It's whether the altar is dressed and lit within us
. . . our hearts . . .

MRS F   Yes, yes, quite . . . my altar burns brightly,
           Robert . . .
           As I trust does your own?

BOB   Well . . . I am . . . not the chap I hoped to be . . . yet.

MRS F   And your piano lessons?

BOB   Long gone . . . long gone.

           (*There is a moment's quiet between them. Slowly,
           painfully she looks up, and meets his eye.*)

MRS F   You should not have come here . . . look at me.
           Fucking look at me!

BOB   I stayed an hour, then left her there, alone.
           Take care, good Elizabeth, I'll trouble you no
           more.
           May some greater joy devour you, I pray.

                        Scene Seven

Tommy reappears.

BOB   Back in Bradford, Bob Scallion sat on the wall
           outside that other house
           That had been his home, and Molly's, too.

           Auntie Vera's School of Excellence, as we used to
           call it.

           It seemed so very different to him now, like all
           before was a dream.

           Sadly not.
           Nothing I tried could wipe thoughts of Molly . . .
           and hatred of Tommy
           Infecting each of my minutes.
           How respectable it looks, now same as then.
           This whole area has changed.
           All us low-life driven out, same houses worth
           double the money . . .

1997 . . . so much time had come and gone.
The trappings of the election smiled out from a
window.
Bob Scallion smiled back, and carried on
musing . . .
Then he looked up again.

Blood and sand!
How the hell has he got . . .
I don't believe that!

'A local man with a global vision, one of your very
own,
Things can only get better so
Vote for Tommy Marchbank, the MP you deserve!'

Oh no! That's not right!
Wow, Tommy, wow . . . that is all I want to say . . .
wow Tommy,
The Right Honourable Tommy Marchbank . . .

Inside of Bob Scallion's head, something terrible
dropped into place.

Tommy . . . an MP . . . junior minister . . . senior
minister
Elizabeth is a gin soak, oh my God . . .
Lord save us . . . for anything is possible . . . there
is no law . . .
There is nothing which cannot be undone.
This means . . . save us . . . God could be anyone
. . . Tony Blair even.

Scene Eight

Tommy's big speech.

TOM   Who is Tommy Marchbank?
                 What does he believe in?
                 What is it that putting him in as our representative
                 at Westminster
                 Is going to do for us exactly?

Well all I'll say is this,
Just what I've been doing for the last fifteen
years! (*Applause/cheers.*)
Walk soft, carry a big long stick, as my dear old
Aunt used to say!

(*Much applause.*)

Those who know me know I might have a rough
edge or two,
But the Labour party's always been in my blood
And the same age old values of community,
compassion, generosity,
Hard work, honesty, and Christian decency
That have always marked us out from the Tories
Remain the same for New Labour just as before.
But it's a new time, a new way – a time for change.

(*There is a crescendo of applause as* TOMMY
stands back to take it all in.)

Years ago, when I first pushed a barrow
Round my father's old waste wool products yard,
I learned the value of thrift, and fortitude, aye by
God.
I used to see how hard money was to come by,
I remember that man, his back arched and aching,
Some nights we'd hardly enough for to feed us all,
I said to myself, I said Tommy Marchbank . . .

BOB   I couldn't bare to listen to any more of him,
If the image of Satan is indeed just a man,
Then silken, split tongued Tommy Homespun
Marchbank
Was it . . . the beast in person.

TOM   Tommy, I said . . .

BOB   Be a pimp and a fraud and stuff this working for a
game o' soldiers!

(*There is much unrest and cafuffle.*)

BOB   Tommy stood, frozen to the spot, mouth open.

He looked straight at me, once again.

The whole assembled gathering turned on its seat.

BOB   And in that one moment I felt sure of one thing,
       No matter how high a man flies,
       It just makes him easier to shoot back down.

TOM   Tommy I said,
       Don't ever lose your dignity.
       Look at that, ladies and gentleman,
       Is that not the saddest sight?
       A young man, prematurely old, raving like a
       lunatic.
       That's what we've come to with the Tories.
       Drugs that is.

BOB   He's a pimp!
       Tell 'em about when we used to run the porn
       shops, Tommy!

TOM   That is the living image of dole culture, ladies and
       gentlemen!
       The nature of his . . . slur on my good name stems,
       of course,
       From an unfortunate and rightly publicized
       incident some years ago,
       When a house in my ownership was, I regret to
       say,
       Used for . . . unsavoury purposes. (*Muffled
       laughter.*)
       Yes indeed, thankfully the police were able to clear
       the rot out,
       And the subsequent enquiry exonerated me of all
       responsibility . . .

BOB   That's cos the Chief Inspector used to come for a
       shag himself!

       (*There is much uproar and general outrage.*)

TOM   I think the fellow gives an accurate account of
       himself.

BOB   And the pleasant, friendly crowd turned . . . on me.
         I could hardly believe my eyes and ears.

         (*Cries of derision start to filter in on* BOB, *the
         crowd dismiss him.*)

VOICES   This has all come out before,
         Have you got proof?
         Throw the loser out!
         Scandal peddling trash!

BOB   He's a pimp I tell you!
         Just ask Fairweather!

TOM   That's right, son . . . have you got any proof?
         Hmm?
         Look at him, he hasn't got anything . . .
         A generation that's lost its self-respect . . . needs
         discipline,
         Needs to learn what it is to get motivated and take
         its place in society!
         Aye society, for let me tell you there is such a
         thing and
         I'll die fighting for it, and you, young man . . .
         But this, dependence mentality, for that's what it
         is . . .
         Strikes at the very heart of what it is to be human.

         (*Murmurs of agreement all round.*)

BOB   What it is to be human!
         You are a lying swine!

         (BOB *suddenly hurtles at* TOMMY, *but* TOMMY *is too
         quick for him and hits him to the floor.*)

TOM   Er, could we have some security out here please,
         An awful lot of decent people want to hear the
         truth I'm telling them,
         They don't care for scandal-peddling rats out of
         the sewer!

BOB   No, course they bleedin' don't!

TOM   Be gentle with him, see he gets a meal, looks half
            starved,
            See, the Tories'd never give you that, would they?
            Any man deserves a bite to eat, a chance, a place
            to sleep . . .

            (TOMMY *looks direct at* BOB *as he says this next
            bit*.)

            But there's some that just can't respond to that bit
            of encouragement,
            Why, they bite the very hand that fed them, year
            on year,
            And people like that deserve nothing, nothing do
            you hear me?
            Get him out.

BOB   The entire audience looked on with dispassionate
            contempt
            As I was bundled out and into a police van.

TOM   Now, after that rather amusing interlude,
            Let's get back to the important issues at hand
            here!
            Education, education, education!

BOB   The local party activists and supporters got back
            to the business
            Of cheering Tommy and smiling warmly.
            Inside the van, the young constable looked at me
            and said,

            Are you barmy or what?

BOB   I did not answer.

                          Scene Nine

The final showdown.

BOB   I was released without charge at 6.00 AM the
            following morning.

Any later and they would have been bound by law
to feed me.
I had nowhere to go and nothing to do,
Tommy had everything . . . whilst I had less than
nothing,
Tommy had a future, I only a past where Tommy
stood large
And to blame for my fall . . . there was it seemed,
no alternative.
The following night, as he left the local Labour
club,
I had him in my sights. (*He produces a gun from
his coat.*)
Marchbank!

TOM   That's me, what can I do for you?
           Good God . . . steady on there . . . is that . . . ?
           Bob . . . Bob Scallion?

BOB   It is.
           You stitched me up and lied to me, Tommy
           Marchbank.
           You told me to be like you, Tommy Marchbank,
           You told me to be a clever get ridin' round in cars
           tellin' lies
           To everyone I met, to mess around with Molly till I
           blew the whole thing
           And then who did she end up shacking with?
           Tommy Marchbank.

TOM   I never told you nothin' you didn't want to hear,
           And you knew how to lie before you met me, Bob
           Scallion.

BOB   You did me one bad turn on another,
           And now no one wants to believe you're just a
           pimpin' fraud!
           And as for the New Labour one!
           What happened to Maggie Thatcher and
           Rolling back the frontiers of Socialism?

TOM   Why don't you put the shooter down, Bob
           And we can have a chat about it.

BOB   You sold us all down the river at Aunt Vera's,
             Them Police weren't on your tail at all,
             'Cos you were right in there with 'em!
             And no, you didn't want me hanging round Molly
             did you?

TOM   I don't know what you're talking about, Bob,
             And bustin' in on my meeting is hardly a way to
             conduct business,
             What did you think I was going to say?
             Oh everyone meet my old mate, Bob,
             Me and him used to do mucky vid runs!
             I'm trying to get them people to vote for me, Bob!
             Course they don't want to hear I was up to no
             good,
             I'm talking what they want to hear, Bob,
             First rules of sales, make sure you're floggin' what
             they want to buy!

             Hence it's not that hard to convince them
             Of what they really want to believe,
             Tommy's a sound fish all round!
             Listen, put the gun down, I don't want bad
             feeling, Bob,
             You were my mate once . . .

BOB   I was your lackey more like,
             And you even took Molly, you bastard.

TOM   You never would have looked after her and the
             kid.
             And if you were my lackey, then whose fault was
             that?
             Problem with you, Bob, is that you think you're
             clever,
             But actually you're thick . . .

BOB   You can't say that!

TOM   Why not?

BOB   'Cos I've got the gun.

TOM   Aye, but you're not gonna use it, so it's useless
           to you.

BOB   You don't know that . . .
           You just sound like you know things and it all falls
           into place for you.

TOM   Don't do it, Bob, you'll regret it the rest of your
           days.
           What's happened to you?
           I thought you'd have sorted yourself out,
           Lookin' good and drivin' a big car by now.
           You were a good mate to me,
           I invested a lot of time and trouble in you,
           And it wasn't to see you amblin' about like
           somethin' lost,
           Doin' armed stick ups with idiots, shoutin' insults
           at me in public.
           Put it down son . . . think about it . . .
           What's happened to you, eh?

BOB   What's happened to me?
           I don't know what's happened to me, or how it's
           happened.
           But I know . . . I know I miss you Tommy . . .
           I know I was never happier in all my life
           Than when I lived at Auntie Vera's and we had the
           shops,
           Going to the races, the boxing, all of it . . .
           And I was your mate . . . and Molly was mine . . .

           And then you sold us all out . . . why did you do
           that?
           You took everything from me when you did that.
           Everything . . .

TOM   Bob, I never took anyone more to heart than you,
           There you were in Aunt Vera's house, livin' high
           on the whores,
           And then off to church to shag Mrs Fairweather,
           You had style then Bob, I really have to give it to
           you.
           I did laugh about that,

Old Fairweather wanted me to do you a damage
you know.

BOB   And Tommy laughed . . . the way only Tommy
         laughed.
         The way I always remember him laughing.

TOM   He was hoppin' mad I'll tell you.

BOB   Shut up laughing!
         Do you hear me, shut up laughing, you bastard!

         (*The two of them sit down side by side like on the
         kerb or something, maybe* TOMMY *sits down first,
         so that* BOB *is watching him from behind, still
         with the gun in hand.*)

TOM   Oh dear Bob Scallion, I've got to be honest,
         I've missed you these past years.
         Things have been good don't get me wrong,
         I met that Peter Mandelson, he's a weird one he is.
         I went for tea with Bob Geldof and that Bono
         turned up,
         He talks shit, doesn't he?
         But the crack's not the same, you know, it's not as
         funny.
         What did you come here to kill me for?

BOB   Because I always thought you and me . . . were . . .
         mates,
         And we'd be mates and sidekicks no matter what.
         But you went and did me up like everyone else,
         Tommy!
         Just like I were another drongo and not your mate
         at all.
         I thought it was you and me doing them up, not me
         with 'em . . .

TOM   Bob, Bob that's business . . . and anyone who
         can't stand the fire
         Better get out of the oven, that's what these days
         are all about, Bob.
         I didn't make it like this, and neither did you,
         But it's how it's turned out.

Smart cookie sees what way the water's runnin'
and goes with it son.
Why don't you go round and see Molly, she'd be
happy to see you.
I'm gonna be in London a lot more of the time now
and . . .
Well, public eye and all that, can't afford any . . .
embarrassments,
Tony's adamant we can't have that and I agree
with him.

BOB   Tommy didn't offer me a lift,
In the shiny black BMW.
He shook his head as he walked away.

TOM   God bless you, Bob Scallion,
Life is strange and longer than you think,
And it don't go where you don't send it.
Take care, Bob Scallion.

BOB   And you know . . . for the first time in years and
years,
I didn't hate him.
After all, how could anyone ever hate Tommy?
I was glad I hadn't killed him and, typical of
Tommy,
He didn't take me trying to the wrong way either.
Take care, Tommy . . . goodbye . . . good luck.
He really was something else . . .

I walked home by the canal, and through the gun
into it's filthy depths.
Back in my one room I made a cup of tea, sat on
the sofa.
Like a condemned man just reprieved, happy even.
I'll have to get a clean shirt or two, pair o' shoes
polished,
Smarten myself up and get started, won't make no
sort
Of a shape of myself sat about mithering.
Huh, good old Tommy.
I turned on the ancient portable TV.

'Police say they are still trying to form an accurate
picture of the events,
Tommy Marchbank was shot dead as he drove his
car away from
A local Labour Party function.
Witnesses say he was seen talking to a man in an
alleyway
Just a few yards from the club, and that the man
may have been armed.
Police are appealing for witnesses to come
forward.'

BOB   I sat dumbstruck before the television set.

VOICE   (*off*) OPEN UP, POLICE!

BOB   Oh Jesus . . .

The Conclusion

BOB   Well . . .
           I have written every note of this from my little dark
           cell.
           My trial lasted just three days, and on April 1st,
           1998,
           I was sentenced to life imprisonment.
           Judge, jury, newspapers, television, small children,
           old women,
           Everyone in the country seemed to know full well I
           was guilty,
           And barely nine months after Tommy was laid to
           rest,
           Even less than poor Diana . . .
           I arrived here, in my cell, in Wakefield Prison,
           Where I have spent the last five years, where I will
           grow old.
           The irony is, to say the least, amusing.
           The one crime I did not commit, got me a bed in
           here.
           My life of crime and wanton living and abuse has
           netted its reward.
           And Tommy?

Poor Tommy . . . he was a good lad at heart was
Tommy.
The trial, and my defence strategy, left his good
name in tatters.
As the whole history of our association came out
in the open.
Tommy would have understood, though.

To the young people of the nation I will say only
this,
There ain't neither time nor space in this old world
for
'I don't know', or, 'I never thought'.
And never back the favourite in a handicap race.

WARD   Scallion, get yourself together,
          You've got a visitor.

BOB   A visitor?
          Well, a visitor indeed.

WARD   Aye, here she is.

MOL   Hello, Bob.

BOB   Molly . . . how good of you to come and see me.

MOL   Are you well?

BOB   I'm . . .fine sweet one, you?

MOL   I've brought you some books to read.

BOB   I'll be glad of them.

MOL   I've come to say . . . I'm really sorry, Bob.

BOB   What about?

MOL   I did it.

BOB   Did what?

          (*Blackout.*)

'You look beautiful

Logan's voice was hus[...]
made her shiver. Lyin[...], revelling
in her newfound sense of freedom, Amber
kept her eyes closed.

'And you like what you see?' she asked
innocently.

'Oh, yeah.'

Amber smiled, feeling very womanly and in
control. 'So what are you going to do about
it?'

'Whatever you want me to.'

Amber liked the sound of that. 'I want you to
seduce me.'

She sat up to get into a more seduceable
position and opened her eyes. A naked Logan
stood before her—a naked, aroused Logan.
Amber swallowed. 'Good job.'

The moonlight sculpted his muscles and a
hint of uncertainty shadowed his eyes.
'Amber, I—I don't want to mess up here. I've
waited too long…'

An endearing touch of humility. Damn, he
was good. 'Seduction accomplished,' she said
as she got up and slowly walked into his open
arms.

Dear Reader,

Oh, those sweet-talkers. You know the type—
they're silver-tongued devils, but we love them
anyway. They get away with more than they
should because we want to believe them, and
when we remember them, it's always with a smile.

I am raising a sweet-talker. Watching him in
action from this side of the telephone has been a
revelation. This new breed of sweet-talkers
depends heavily on modern communications.
Between caller ID, three-way calling, pagers,
e-mail and mobile phones, a man can sweet-talk
his way into a lot of hearts.

I invite you to let Logan, the hero of
Moonlighting, talk his way into yours.

Best wishes,

Heather MacAllister

MOONLIGHTING

by

Heather MacAllister

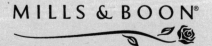

MILLS & BOON®

In memory of
Barbara Feurer Freise

*First published in Great Britain 2001
by Harlequin Mills & Boon Limited,
Eton House, 18-24 Paradise Road, Richmond, Surrey TW9 1SR*

© Heather W MacAllister 2000

ISBN 0 263 82802 6

21-0601

*Printed and bound in Spain
by Litografia Rosés S.A., Barcelona*

Prologue

"KISS ME."

"Logan! There'll be plenty of time for that later. We'll just have to make sure we sit in the back of the bus."

Logan Van Dell gazed into the excited brown eyes of Amber Madison, the love of his life.

He'd always known he and Amber couldn't last, not with their families despising each other the way they did. But he was afraid if he didn't kiss her right now, he wouldn't have the courage to do what had to be done tonight.

And then he was afraid that if he *did* kiss her, he wouldn't be able to let her go.

Either way, he was going to kiss her now and worry about the rest later.

Planting himself in front of her, he lowered his satchel to the grimy cement bus station floor, put hers on top, and adjusted her backpack, all the while smiling the half smile he knew she'd never been able to resist.

"Oh, Logan..."

And Amber Madison, the closest thing to a princess that Belle Rive, Mississippi had, was in his arms.

Just before he closed his eyes, Logan caught sight of the headlights of the approaching midnight bus. He and Amber had driven from Belle Rive north to Vicksburg to catch it, so nobody in the tiny town could alert

Amber's parents that their precious daughter was about to hop a bus with the disreputable Logan Van Dell.

Living up to his reputation, Logan slipped his hands under her sweater and allowed them to wander.

"Mmm, Logan, we shouldn't..."

He knew that. It didn't stop him, though.

He turned her slightly so that he shielded her from the approaching bus. "There's nobody here but the ticket clerk—and he's asleep."

Amber moved sensuously against him. "You always could talk me into anything."

He wondered if that would hold true in the next half hour. Breathing deeply next to the crook of her neck, Logan filled his lungs with the scent of her, then gave her soft skin one last caress before straightening her sweater.

Amber tightened her arms around his neck. "Just think how it'll be in New York," she whispered in his ear before giving it a nip. "We'll make love. We can spend the *whole* night together. We can wake up together. And we'll never have to get out of bed if we don't want to."

Logan squeezed his eyes shut as a spasm of pain shot through him. What a time for him to turn noble. He wanted her and, Lord knew, she was willing, but for reasons he hadn't figured out, he hadn't taken advantage. Yeah, he'd probably regret it. Or maybe he wouldn't. Nobility was new to him, so he didn't know.

What he *did* know was that he was tired of sneaking around to be with her, tired of not being able to call for her at the front door of her parents' home.

Reginald Madison, Mayor of Belle Rive, did not

open his door to the Van Dells, and right now, Logan didn't have the power or the resources to make him.

But that was going to change.

Belle Rive society had always considered the Van Dells vaguely scandalous and Logan had done his best to remove any vagueness at all until he was old enough to recognize the social snubs meted out to his mother— and his grandmother, as well, when she stuck by her daughter-in-law and grandson. For himself, he didn't care, but for them, well, that just wouldn't do.

He would *not* have people like Amber's family thinking they were better than the Van Dells. He intended to see to it that there were no Belle Rive doors closed to Gigi Van Dell, showgirl background or not, even if it meant turning respectable.

Even if it meant losing Amber. He was going to lose her eventually, anyway. She was destined for bigger things than Belle Rive. She just needed somebody to show her the way. It was the least Logan could do for her after the greatest spring and summer of his life. Once she got to New York, it was all going to be up to her, but whatever she ended up doing, he knew she'd make it. She was too stubborn not to.

"I can't believe that in two days I'll finally be in New York."

Logan couldn't, either.

Amber slid her arms down his neck as the bus rumbled into the station. It stopped with a squeak and a hiss and a cloud of diesel fumes.

"Do you know how many graduation teas I went to?"

Logan shook his head, content to listen to her babble about her favorite subject, the absurdities—to her—of

Belle Rive society, the same society he longed to have accept his mother and him.

"Thirteen! Thirteen, not including my own. Thirteen times I had to dress up and talk to the same people, drink the same sticky punch and not eat the food in case I should be considered unladylike. What a waste! I can't see why I can't eat at a party, do you? I mean, that's just silly."

Logan could tell that Amber was nervous. As for himself, he felt as though all the chewing gum he'd ever swallowed was sitting at the bottom of his stomach, just the way his grandmother had said it would. He'd known for a month that he was going to send Amber off by herself, so why was it bothering him so much now?

The fact was, even if he did go with Amber, her family had powerful friends—the kinds of friends who could make a person's life very difficult. The Van Dells had friends, too—friends who liked a good time. Going *mano a mano* against the Madisons was definitely not a good time.

Logan would miss Amber, miss meeting her at the tree house he'd built at the cold spring. He didn't want to miss her. He didn't want her to mean that much to him.

But she did.

"You know what they ought to do?" Amber continued, oblivious to Logan's inner turmoil. "They ought to make plastic sandwiches and just bring them out like decorations."

"If nobody ever eats them, then how do you know they aren't?" Logan managed a light tone.

Amber laughed—too much for his lame joke. "If I'd

stayed in Belle Rive, I would have had plenty of chances to find out. But you know the absolute best part about leaving?"

Logan swallowed and shook his head.

"I won't have to be Magnolia Queen for the pilgrimage."

"You could come back. Other girls have come back to be queen." *Please come back. It's the only way I'll ever see you again.*

"No." She shuddered. "I don't mind the homes tour, or even the plantation life reenactments, because that's part of our history. But I will *never* put on that stupid crown and prance around playing Scarlett O'Hara in an obscenely expensive dress just for a bunch of tourists. And I told everybody so."

"When?"

Amber watched the driver open the luggage compartments on the side of the bus. "At Sara Anne Jasper's tea."

"I'll bet your mama had a fit." It would have been something to see Lily Madison lose her cool.

"'Fit' doesn't begin to describe it. Her face got all red and you could see the veins in her neck pop out. That's why she wanted me to pay a call on practically everybody in Belle Rive. I was supposed to *apologize*." She looked up at him. "No way."

He studied her big brown eyes and shiny hair and felt his throat go tight. "You'd have made a beautiful queen."

"Oh, Logan," she groaned, then looked around and pointed. "Hey! People are getting on the bus. Let's go."

She reached for her satchel and quickly walked over

to the driver standing by the luggage bin. Handing him her ticket, she gestured to Logan. "Hurry up!"

Logan's own duffel bag was only filled with his dirty laundry. The driver hoisted Amber's satchel into the bin then looked questioningly at Logan.

Logan shook his head.

"Logan? Give him your ticket."

He shook his head again. Now that the moment was here, his tongue wouldn't form the words he had to say.

"Where is it? You couldn't have lost it."

"I didn't lose it."

"Anybody else?" the driver called, ready to shut the huge doors.

"Yes—wait!" Amber tugged on Logan's duffel.

Logan held on tight. "Amber," he croaked. "I'm not going."

Startled, she stared at him. The luggage doors slammed shut and the driver wrote something in the notebook in his front pocket.

"What do you mean, you're not going?"

"Look, Amber, New York is your dream—"

"It's *our* dream."

"Nah." Logan shook his head and took a deep breath. "You go on and make a big success of yourself. It's what you've always wanted. Me, I've got unfinished business back in Belle Rive."

She blinked rapidly. "You can't...you can't just..." Her lower lip trembled. "If you're not going, then I'm not going."

"Sure you are." Logan took her by the arm and half dragged, half pushed her toward the bus doors.

"Let me *go!*"

He stopped at the foot of the steps. "That's exactly what I'm doing."

"I don't want to go without you! I thought we were going to get...well, I'll wait, then. You can do whatever you have to do, and then we'll go."

Logan swallowed. Twice. "I want you to go now."

Her mouth worked and finally she wailed, "I thought you loved me!"

At her betrayed expression, he was ready to leap on the bus, dirty laundry and all. Instead, he raised a hand to her hair. "We sure did have some good times together."

She jerked away. "Good times? Is that all they were?"

"Weren't they?" She didn't answer, but he hadn't expected her to. She probably hated him right now. "Hey, Amber, it's time to move on." Reaching into his pocket, he withdrew an envelope. "This is the name of the youth hostel where we were going to stay. You still have a reservation." He took her unresponsive hand and curled her fingers around the envelope. "And here's some more money. New York is really expensive and you don't have nearly enough cash."

She flung it back at him. "I don't want your money!"

"Then don't spend it." With an outward calm that belied the knot in the pit of his stomach, Logan unzipped one of the compartments of her backpack and slipped the envelope inside. "Think how much satisfaction you'll get by mailing it back to me after you've got a job."

She lifted her chin. "I'll do that."

"Folks," the driver called down to them. "We've gotta be going."

Amber took two steps backward, then turned and climbed up into the doorway of the bus. Until that moment, Logan hadn't been sure that he could convince her to go to New York on her own.

The bus doors started to close, then jerked open again.

Amber looked down at him, her face regal and composed. "I loved you."

Logan gritted his teeth together and the doors closed, this time for good.

He backed away as the gears shifted and the bus pulled away from the station.

Logan watched until it turned the corner on its way north to New York.

"I loved you, too, Amber," he whispered.

1

Eight years later

"WHY DIDN'T YOU TELL ME that Lily Madison had invited you to tea?" A pretty, pink-suited, white-haired figure appeared in Logan's doorway.

"It's just tea."

"Nothing is ever 'just tea' with Lily Madison. And never say you're going to wear that tie!"

Logan frowned. "I like this tie. It sends the right message."

"If the message you want to send is that you have no sense of style, then yes, it sends a very clear message."

The thing was, the navy-and-white tie was the official tie of the Belle Rive Gentleman's Service Club and Logan wanted Lily Madison to know that he was a member. What was the point of spreading his money and time all over town, turning himself into a do-gooder so he could become a member if he couldn't wear the stupid tie so everyone would know it?

He glanced in the mirror at his grandmother before ripping off the tie. It made him look like a waiter in a yacht club, anyway. He reached for the expensive pearl-gray tie he generally wore with this suit.

His grandmother smiled her approval, tugged on

her white gloves and snapped her pocketbook shut. "Lily didn't extend the invitation to your mother and me, I noticed."

So had Logan. He always noticed. "Maybe she knows that you and Mama are at the garden club on Tuesdays."

"She could have chosen another day. One more day after several decades of snubbing the Van Dells wouldn't matter much."

"Maybe Miz Madison wants to discuss business."

"Lily Madison doesn't discuss business over tea."

Logan refrained from pointing out that as his grandmother had never taken tea with Lily Madison, she wasn't likely to know this for a fact.

"Camille?" Logan's mother called from the bottom of the staircase. "We'd best be going if we're to be back here to greet the Winchell family at three-thirty. Remember, they've booked the whole week this time."

"I told you not to book anyone over the weekend!" Logan's grandmother closed her eyes and pursed her lips in an expression he'd seen a thousand times since he and his mother had come to live here. Sometimes it was accompanied by a whispered, or occasionally shouted, "God give me strength!"

"Oh, pooh," Gigi said. "They're practically like family."

"Yes, I'm sure Mr. Winchell would love to be a kissing cousin," Camille said acidly.

Logan fixed her with a look.

"I know, she was only trying to help. But why couldn't your mother remember that the first meeting for the Azalea Pilgrimage is this weekend and we simply won't be able to give our guests the attention that they've come to expect at the Van Dell Bed and Breakfast? Unless, Logan, you...?"

Logan finished tying his tie. "I'll make sure I'm here for Sunday brunch to provide the appropriate local color." Thicken the drawl and smile at the ladies—he knew the drill.

"Oh, I knew I could count on you!" The tiny woman pulled his head to hers and gave him a resounding smack on the cheek, leaving a lip imprint of Revlon's most popular lipstick shade of 1955 on his cheek.

"Ca-miiii-lllle!"

"I'm admiring your handsome son, Gigi." Camille stood back and smiled. "You just remember that you are to hold your head up and don't let that Lily Madison lord anything over you. If she has her nose in the air, you just bring it right down by asking her how Stephanie enjoys married life. Though Lily's put a good face on it, her daughter eloping was a big disappointment to her, especially after Amber took off in the dead of night years ago and hasn't come back since."

"Thanks for the tip." Logan ignored the part about Amber. He'd never told anyone about his meetings with Amber—or his role in her departure.

And he'd never heard one word from her. But then, he hadn't expected to.

Camille gently nudged him away from the mirror and adjusted her hat. "It does make one wonder what kind of mother Lily is."

"Maybe she's the kind of mother who doesn't listen to her daughters."

She glanced up at him. "Well, those girls are obviously not the kind of daughters who listen to their mama. For some reason, it's harder to take that in a daughter than in a son." She turned to go. "Or a grand-son."

Logan chuckled, walked his grandmother to the top of the stairs and offered her his arm. She dimpled and swatted it away. "I'm not that old yet. How do you think I get up and down these stairs when you aren't here?"

Logan didn't like thinking about that, which was why he spent more and more nights here in the low-ceilinged attic bedroom instead of his town house. "I'll tell you all about tea."

"Yes, you will. And pay attention to the inside of the Madison house. I want to know how Lily has deco-rated. Now finish getting ready."

In spite of her protests, Logan stood at the top of the stairs until his grandmother had safely reached the bottom.

He was back in front of the mirror adjusting the knot on his tie when he heard a horrified gasp.

"Gigi! You can't wear a skirt that short to the garden club!"

"It's in style," Logan's mother protested. "You *said* to be stylish today."

"It's not ladylike."

"That's because the women who decide what's la-dylike and what's not are the ones with fat thighs."

"Gigi..."

"Oh, all *right!*"

His mother's heels clicked across the wooden floor and Logan grinned. Gigi would return with a longer skirt, but one still several inches above her knees, which would be the one she'd intended to wear all along. It was a ploy she'd used with his grandmother for years with her more outrageous clothes, and it always worked.

Sometimes he wished it wouldn't. If his mother would just try...

Logan's grin faded as he checked his appearance one last time in front of the mirror. He didn't want to care about this meeting with Lily, but he couldn't help hoping that it might lead to a social thaw between the Van Dells and the Madisons.

Proving he could be successful in Belle Rive without the social blessing of the Madisons was one thing. Wanting it was another.

LOGAN FELT STRANGE driving through the gates at the end of the long gravel drive in his BMW roadster instead of parking his ancient pickup around the back and scaling the iron fence so he could sneak over to Amber's bedroom to help her climb out.

Of course she'd gotten better and better at climbing down the huge old magnolia tree outside her room. As the summer had worn on, he'd only had to park outside the gates to wait for her.

After graduation, she'd been given her own car, and then he'd been able to wait for her down at the cold spring, which they'd both felt was better in case someone recognized his pickup and reported it to the Madisons.

He'd planned his arrival this afternoon with excruciating punctuality, pulling deep into the drive and parking in the shade of the interlocking branches of old trees.

It was early March and the house and drive were lined with hot-pink azaleas in full bloom. The Madisons lived in a smaller replica of their plantation home that had been destroyed during the Civil War. There were only three old plantation homes left in Belle Rive, which had had only five to begin with. The Van Dell Bed and Breakfast was one. Of the other two, one housed the Belle Rive city museum and library, and the other was now the Belle Rive Country Club.

The Madisons were members. The Van Dells were not.

The Madisons had fought and resisted the Yankee invaders. Their home had been burned to the ground, but they'd been rewarded by earning the lasting admiration and respect of Belle Rive society.

The Van Dells...well, the pretty Van Dell women pointed out that the officers would need somewhere to stay, and wouldn't they be much more comfortable with a roof over their heads and warm food in their bellies? Anybody could see that it was just silly to burn down a perfectly good house.

They'd earned the lasting scorn of Belle Rive society, kept alive by people such as Lily Madison.

In fairness, the Van Dells *had* produced more than their share of scandals and black sheep. The illegal liquor club during Prohibition hadn't helped their reputation, either.

Logan smiled wistfully. He missed his black sheep days.

He climbed the front steps of the white-columned house and rang the bell, savoring this small victory. A Van Dell was about to cross the Madison threshold— by invitation—and Logan expected thunder, or at least a minor earthquake.

To his surprise, Lily Madison herself, wearing a skirt

that fell well below her knees, opened the door. He'd thought there would have been a butler, or a footman, or at least a maid in one of those frilly starched outfits.

"Won't you come in, Mr. Van Dell?" Lily said in a lady-of-the-manor tone.

Logan hadn't ever heard her talk in any other way.

"His Honor sends his regrets that he won't be able to join us. Pressing business at city hall, you know." Lily gestured toward the front drawing room.

"I am relieved to know that the mayor of our fine city puts his responsibilities before pleasure." Logan doubted that Amber's father even knew he'd been invited.

Lily glanced at him, probably wondering if he was being sarcastic.

Logan smiled his sincerest fake smile and followed Lily into the room, remembering to discreetly look around so he could describe it to his grandmother.

Namby-pamby blue, antiques, and flowers, and not a big-screen TV in sight. That pretty much summed it up. He resisted the urge to say "Nice digs," sprawl in a chair and prop his feet on the coffee table, just to see her face. It was probably what she expected.

Lily sat on an uncomfortable-looking camel-back sofa in front of a silver tray containing two pitchers, a plate of cookies, glasses, and an ice bucket. She gestured for him to sit on an equally uncomfortable-looking side chair. "Would you care for iced tea? Or Bertha has made some of her famous lemonade in your honor."

"I'll have the lemonade then." Logan hoped whoever Bertha was, her lemonade was famous because she laced it with gin. Famous lemonade? Lemons, water and sugar—was he missing something?

He sipped cautiously and discovered that Bertha was thrifty with the sugar. Perhaps Lily was confusing "famous" with "infamous."

"Refreshing. Just right for a warm spring day." He knew they'd have to get through the weather before anything substantial transpired. Might as well get started.

"Yes, isn't it?"

Lily Madison poured herself a glass of iced tea, Logan noticed. "The azaleas are just brilliant this year. They're doing particularly well in the new garden over at the museum."

Well, well, well. His grandmother's rogue garden club was responsible for the new landscaping. For Lily to acknowledge it at all after she and *her* garden club had vigorously protested any changes at the city museum was astounding. And suspicious.

So. Logan knew all the signs—he had something Lily Madison wanted. It was as simple as that.

"Finding the old landscaping plans in the museum basement was a stroke of luck," he said. "We were especially fortunate that cuttings from the original azaleas were growing at Van Dell House so the garden could be restored with the same shade of pink." To Logan, pink was pink, but he remembered the huge fuss and his grandmother's triumph. She'd ordered two suits and a dress in exactly the same shade of pink and had insisted on wearing one of the outfits whenever she was likely to encounter Lily Madison.

"I do believe that tradition and authenticity are important," Lily allowed in what had to be a huge concession for her.

Logan waited, hoping that she'd reveal why she'd invited him to her home, but Lily launched into another innocuous subject, apparently prepared to overlook the fact that her family and his hadn't been on cordial terms for more than a century.

Logan easily followed suit, pouring on the charm. Making small talk was second nature to him, a skill he'd honed at dozens of pseudo-social business gatherings over the years.

He could sense her circling around the subject she wanted to broach, waiting for the right moment.

The right moment appeared to be when he'd choked down the last of the lemonade.

"Mr. Van Dell, I understand that you are a man of business."

"Depends on the business to which you're referring."

She set her glass on the tray. "I'll be brief."

Too late for that, Logan thought.

"Belle Rive traditions are very important to me."

So she'd said. Logan tensed. In his experience, "tradition" was synonymous with the Madison way.

"And one of the most important of those traditions is the Magnolia Pilgrimage which serves to remind us of the history of our city before the Late Unpleasantness."

She meant the Civil War.

"As does the Azalea Pilgrimage." Logan heard his drawl take on an edge as he referred to the rival pilgrimage started by his grandmother, mostly to annoy Lily.

"Yes," Lily allowed with obvious reluctance. "On a much smaller scale."

Logan let that pass unchallenged.

"It is fortunate that others who do not live in this region find the pilgrimages—both of them—informative enough to visit. As you may or may not know, the revenue from the home tours and the balls provides a substantial portion of the city's budget."

Logan knew. Everyone knew. Each year, Mayor Madison pointed out that the Magnolia Pilgrimage was officially sanctioned, and the Azalea Pilgrimage was not.

"During the last several years, revenue has fallen."

"And your husband raised taxes." Logan was beginning to get the gist of the conversation. Elections were in November and the city budget was due in September. Not a popular time to raise taxes again.

"I believe, and my committee agrees with me, that having two pilgrimages confuses tourists."

"Did you and your committee check with the chamber of commerce to see how they feel about it? Two pilgrimages means double bookings for the bed-and-breakfasts and restaurants." Logan's family was always fully booked during both times and he'd bet the others were likewise.

Lily's mouth pursed as though she'd been the one drinking the lemonade. "The fact is, Mr. Van Dell, that Belle Rive isn't big enough to support two pilgrimages. The tourists are heading to the ones in Vicksburg and Natchez and even attendance for theirs is down. We're dividing our efforts unnecessarily."

Logan cut to the chase. "Do I understand that you

wish me to convince my grandmother to cancel the Azalea Pilgrimage?''

"Do give me some credit, Mr. Van Dell. The pilgrimages obviously have to be combined. We would have no objection to the azalea group continuing with their traditions, if they wish. Naturally, always keeping within the overall scope and theme.''

Her dismissive tone grated. "Then what would be the point?''

Lily answered with a confidence that told Logan she'd anticipated his question. "Shared expenses for advertising and decorations, to name two advantages. Belle Rive resources are strained by having the pilgrimages within weeks of each other. We can get...'more bang for the buck'—'' She looked pleased with herself for coming up with the phrase ''—by having one larger pilgrimage than two smaller ones.''

She could call it "combining" or whatever she liked, but Logan knew the result would be the end of the azalea group. Sure they could have their own ball, but everyone would know it was for those who weren't on the list to attend the "real" ball—the pinnacle of the Belle Rive social season. Their queens would be girls who'd never be considered for the Magnolia Queen.

No way.

"Why are you telling me this, instead of speaking to my grandmother?'' he asked.

"I understand that you specialize in making deals, Mr. Van Dell. You have a reputation for bringing together people for whom it would be advantageous to work with one another, yet who would never consider doing so.''

"And I am usually well paid for this.''

Their gazes locked.

"*Always* with money?" she asked softly.

This was going to get interesting. Logan relaxed his posture, not quite slouching, but not the formally deferential seat he'd maintained in the uncomfortable chair, either. "No, ma'am. Not always with money."

"What do you want?" she asked bluntly.

"What are you offering?" he answered.

She looked away first. Taking a sip from her tea, she swallowed, then met his eyes again. "First, do you think you can convince your grandmother to combine the pilgrimages?"

"If I choose to."

"And what would make you choose to?"

"When I make a deal, both parties come away better off than they were before. If you agree to that, then we can talk terms."

She nodded once, tightly. "There's...one more stipulation."

There always was. "Lay it on the table."

"It is past time for a Madison to serve as Magnolia Queen. I was a queen. My mother was a queen. And this year, Stephanie, my younger daughter, was to have been queen. As you may know, Stephanie was recently married, and a married woman may not serve as queen."

"My congratulations and best wishes to the happy couple."

The way Lily took her breath told Logan she was still angry about her daughter's elopement. "Thank you. I'll convey your sentiments to her." Polite to the last.

Fixing Logan with a direct look, she said, "Since Stephanie cannot, Amber has to be queen."

Memories of Amber complaining long and loudly about the pilgrimage came to vivid life in his mind. Memories of Amber, period, came to vivid life. "Amber doesn't want to be queen."

She didn't ask how he knew this. "It is unthinkable that a Madison of this generation does not serve as Magnolia Queen. Royal blood runs in her veins."

Royal blood? Logan just managed to restrain himself from hooting. He got the picture now. The queen's family spent thousands of dollars entertaining. Mayor Reginald Madison, whose popularity was slipping, was going to use his daughter's coronation as a giant campaign party, hoping to erase the memory of those tax increases. Include the azalea group, and include their votes. As a bonus, insure that the pilgrimage made money this year. Clever.

Despicable, but clever.

Logan wished he'd thought of it.

However, he had no desire to help reelect Mayor Madison. He might want to run against him. Mayor Van Dell. That had a nice ring to it.

In fact, running for mayor might not be a bad idea. Snubbing the mayor's mother wouldn't be as easy. The more he thought about it, the more he liked the idea. He didn't need to go through the Madisons—he'd go around them. Why hadn't he ever considered politics before? With all the contacts he'd made over the years, people owed—

"Well?" Lily's voice rang with some of that imperialism she was bragging about.

"Not interested." He prepared to stand.

"Don't you want to see her again?"

Logan froze and wished like anything he could say no and keep walking. Knowing that he was going to be seeing Lily Madison had had him thinking about Amber a lot in the past two days. For the most part she'd been a memory he'd tucked away long ago in a darkened corner of his heart. He'd always assumed that with time and distance, she'd understand why he'd had to stay in Belle Rive. She hadn't, and he'd moved on. They were young, it had been spring, families warring in a Romeo and Juliet kind of way, et cetera, et cetera. Cliché city.

Now, looking into Lily Madison's knowing eyes, he settled back into his chair, curious to hear what she had to say.

Lily gave him a small smile. "Yes, I am aware that Amber had a youthful indiscretion with you."

Considering that they'd planned to move to New York together, it had been considerably more than an indiscretion, but Logan chose not to enlighten her.

"We made inquiries after she left home," Lily explained, though Logan hadn't asked.

"No one ever inquired anything of me."

"We had you watched."

Unease flickered through him at the thought of someone watching and reporting on his movements and he'd never had a clue. "For how long?"

"A few weeks. I hoped you'd follow her. Then I would have been able to find her and bring her back."

"She never wanted to come back."

"Maybe then." Lily smiled. "Now, I think it's a matter of being too busy. She's built a nice life for herself, but she works *much* too hard. She needs a break."

Logan felt as though he'd been sucker-punched. "You've *seen* her?"

"Of course I've seen her! I visited her in New York.

She has a gorgeous penthouse apartment and is the personal assistant to Peter Barclay of Barclay Jewelry."

"How personal?"

Except for a flash in her eyes, Lily ignored him. "We had a perfectly lovely time. But she has a lot of responsibility and I could tell that she was under a great deal of stress."

Logan thought he knew where the stress came from. "So ask her to be queen."

"I have."

"And?"

Exasperation crossed her face. "If she'd agreed, we wouldn't be having this discussion."

"And you expect me to convince her to change her mind?"

"I believe you're the only one who can."

"Why?" After all, Amber had contacted *them,* not him.

"Call it a mother's intuition," Lily said, leaving Logan with the impression that there was a lot left unsaid.

Enough to intrigue him. And he didn't want to be intrigued. He and Amber had parted ways. It had been clean-cut—at least for her.

He'd almost followed her a couple of times, but she'd left the youth hostel and he'd had no idea where she'd gone. And she'd never come back.

So she was a success, just the way she'd always wanted to be. It's what he'd wanted for her, wasn't it? "Amber and I haven't seen or spoken to each other since she left."

Lily gestured to the lemonade pitcher and Logan shook his head. She poured herself more tea. "When I

was in New York, she asked about everyone in town—
except you."

"There you are."

Lily smiled to herself. "You have a lot to learn about
women, Mr. Van Dell."

He raised his eyebrow. "I might take issue with you
on that."

"I'm well aware of your man-about-town reputation," she said coolly.

"So you aren't worried about me seeing Amber
again?"

"Not at all." She eyed him as she sipped her tea. "I
think you'll find Amber's years in New York have
given her a sophistication that the young women
who've spent their entire lives in Belle Rive have yet to
acquire."

Logan went very still. Lily Madison had issued a
challenge with her subtle insult, whether or not she'd
intended to.

Logan thrived on challenges.

"Now, I believe we have yet to discuss the particu-
lars of your fee."

Logan knew exactly what he wanted. "If Amber is to
be queen, then my mother will be in charge of the Magnolia Pilgrimage this year."

Lily's eyes widened. "Absolutely not! How could
you suggest that I allow a...a—"

"Careful," he warned.

"A *stripper* to run the pilgrimage!"

Logan stood, his jaw tight. "She was a dancer in Las
Vegas. She was never a stripper."

Lily had regained her composure. "She is an outsider."

"We've lived in Belle Rive for nearly twenty years and the Van Dells have been here as long as the Madisons."

"It's a tremendous amount of work and she doesn't have the experience."

"I didn't say she was to run it all by herself. I'm sure you have numerous committees in place. But she'll be the one in charge. And she'll open the coronation ball."

"What about your grandmother? I—I believe I could work with Camille."

Slowly, Logan shook his head. "My mother, or no deal."

Lily looked backed into a corner. Just how badly did she want Amber to return and be queen?

Pretty badly. She stood and offered him her hand. "All right. If Amber agrees to be queen, your mother will be head of the pilgrimage."

Her handshake was firm, he'd give her that.

"I hope you're as good as they say you are, Mr. Van Dell."

His lips curved. "I'm better."

2

WISHING SHE HADN'T SPENT her Christmas commissions on a new jewelry polishing motor with built-in extractor, Amber Madison dropped her bills into a metal mixing bowl and stirred them around with her hand.

Oh, the suspense. Would she pay off the phone company or the electric commission? Would she spend the week eating Ramen noodles or get to splurge on actual meat? Could she ransom her coat from the dry cleaner's or stun the landlord by paying the rent on time two months in a row?

Well, this was life in the big city, just the way she wanted it, right?

Amber cheated and felt around the bowl until she found the electricity bill and pulled it out. Her new polishing motor needed electricity and Amber had several pieces of jewelry she wanted to finish up. She couldn't sell unfinished jewelry, could she? She ignored the fact that she apparently couldn't sell finished pieces, either. Besides, computers needed electricity, too. And a phone line, which was why she next fished out the phone bill.

Oh, well. It was spring and she wouldn't need her coat for a while. She'd just walk a little faster to work. A brisk walk. There had to be countless untold health benefits to taking brisk walks.

And she liked Ramen noodles. Really liked them. Looked forward to them, in fact. She could eat them for days on end. And had. Once she added the past-their-prime limp veggies she bought for pennies from the Chinese restaurant she walked past on the way to and from her job at Barclay's, the meal wasn't too bad on the nutrition scale.

Besides, there was always the chance that she'd sell some of her jewelry pieces on the Internet for even more than the materials cost her. Maybe there'd be a bidding war. Maybe she should start one.

Just then Amber's fingers touched a familiar limp envelope. Sighing deeply, she pulled it out and stared at the yellowing edges. Originally, it had contained two hundred and sixty-seven dollars—the cost of the one-way bus ticket Logan Van Dell hadn't purchased on that long-ago night, the night she'd thought they were eloping. He'd scrawled "Green Street Youth Hostel" and a phone number in blue ballpoint pen across the top.

Penciled down the length of the envelope were the dates of her small failures, which now added up to one giant, huge mess-up of her life.

IOU $10—August 13
IOU $27—August 24
IOU $35—September 22

And so on, and so on. Over the years she'd put some money back—and had been forced to dip into the envelope again and again. Now it was empty and had been for some time.

The last of the money had been used to take her

mother to the Russian Tea Room before they'd closed it for remodeling. The entire time, Amber wondered what her mother would think if she knew she was having lunch on Logan Van Dell's money.

Logan had no doubt forgotten all about her by now, and Amber, herself, thought more of the debt than of the man.

He'd been a jerk. A big, drawling, handsome jerk who could kiss. She hadn't known just how good a kisser he was until she'd dated some of these New Yorkers. Or how much she'd taken for granted the little courtesies bred into the men back in Belle Rive.

Sighing, she set aside the envelope. Not this month. And the way things were going, maybe not ever.

Amber looked around her one-room efficiency apartment, crammed with her jewelry-making equipment and mailing supplies. She didn't even have a real bed. She slept on a sofa bed and had to move her worktable in front of the door to have enough room to pull out the bed at night. She told herself it made a great alarm system. Anyway, she didn't have time to waste on maintaining a fancy home. She could clean the whole place in forty-five minutes. She'd want a place like this even if she could afford better, she thought optimistically.

And then there were the dark moments, moments such as these when she had to decide what bills to pay...when she just wanted to give up and go home.

Even if going home meant living the kind of life that would make her numb inside. Sometimes she thought numbness might be better than feeling like a failure.

Then she remembered she couldn't even afford to go home, and the moments passed. Besides, she'd burned all her bridges more thoroughly than Sherman had burned Atlanta. Amber Madison was not going to stay in Belle Rive. Oh, no. Amber Madison was going out to make her mark on the world, and make sure everyone in three counties knew it. Only so far, her mark was more like a smudge.

There were people back in Belle Rive who would love to see her eat her words. They'd bake them up in a nice big humble pie and serve it to her on their best china with the sterling silver forks that had been handed down from their grandmothers—or before.

Her grandmother, she missed. Her sweet grandmother who mothered Amber and her sister, Stephanie, when their real mother was busy being a political wife. Her one regret was that it had been so long since she'd seen Memaw.

Maybe someday soon. Maybe she could talk Mr. Chan at the restaurant into letting her work Saturday nights for tips and leftovers. Amber took another look at her bank balance. She'd probably need Friday nights, too. And she should be getting the commissions for the Valentine's sales in her next paycheck. She'd sold three engagement rings—one while Monica, the blonde, had been batting her baby blues at the well-dressed man who'd ended up only buying a replacement watchband.

Amber decided to split the remaining money between her sky-high credit card balance and the rent, pay the phone and electricity bills and put Logan's empty envelope with the other unpaid bills, just the way she did every month. Before she could agonize over her decision, she ran downstairs and shoved the envelopes into the brass letter box engraved U.S. Mail.

She liked the letter box. It was the classiest thing about the whole decrepit building.

When she got back to her apartment, she turned on her computer and tied on her heavy canvas work apron. She didn't have to be at the jewelry store until noon, so she had a little more than two hours of prime work time ahead of her. Last year she'd finally talked Mr. McClelland, the manager, into letting her have a slice of one of the display cases to try to sell some of her designs—the slice where the lighting wasn't the best anyway. A couple pieces had actually sold and Amber counted those sales as the high points of her time in New York.

That and fooling her mother into thinking she was a huge success.

And fooling herself that her life was what she'd expected when she left Belle Rive so many years ago.

Amber logged on to the Internet and went to the jewelry auction site. She'd put up one of her elaborate pins twice and each time the auction had ended without a single bid. Frustrated, she'd impulsively relisted it for a two-dollar opening bid—even though the raw materials had cost her nearly fifteen dollars—thinking the low price would attract interest.

There had been two lousy bids and the price was now two dollars and fifty cents with only two hours left until the end of the auction.

"What's the matter with you people? Don't you know original, wearable art when you see it?" She rested her cheek on the gritty tabletop. Unless there was a flurry of bidding at the very end, somebody was about to get the bargain of the century.

There was a knock on the door, making Amber bolt upright.

The landlord? She wasn't even five days late with the rent yet.

Had she ordered something? Great. How was she supposed to pay for it?

It never occurred to Amber to answer the door. She just stared at it and listened for the sound of footsteps walking away.

There was a second knock. "Amber? Are you in there?"

Home was her first thought as the soft Southern drawl seeped into the room. That voice...like honey over sandpaper. Like— She brought her hand to her mouth.

"Amber? It's Logan Van Dell."

Logan. Amber's breath caught and guilt washed over her as she involuntarily glanced to the shelf with the empty envelope. Logan? Here?

Was her mother with him? No. Her mother would never arrive unannounced. And her mother would most definitely never travel with Logan Van Dell.

Logan. Was he really there, or had she imagined him?

"Amber?"

He was really there.

Think. Her first instinct was to ignore him, but if he'd tracked her down here, that meant he knew where she worked and would undoubtedly show up there. That wouldn't do. She could bluff her way through this. With a quick glance around, Amber shoved her laundry behind the screen in the corner that hid the rest of her clothes, then walked on shaky knees to the door. At the last minute, she fluffed her hair, then rolled her eyes for doing so, removed two security chains, threw the bolts on the upper and lower locks, turned an additional key lock and opened the door to an all-out Southern gentleman. A handsome Southern gentleman. A Southern gentleman with an ungentlemanly hint of the devil in his eyes.

"Logan?"

His lips crooked. "Hello, Amber."

Her mouth went dry. Her mouth wasn't supposed to go dry, dammit. Her heart wasn't supposed to thump, either, not just because Logan Van Dell, The Man Who Had Broken Her Heart, was standing at her door.

She'd imagined this moment a dozen times, maybe a hundred, but she'd never imagined being caught unaware. Where was her prep time? She was supposed to be dripping with sophistication, not sweating in panic.

Look at him smiling his crooked smile. He knew how he affected her. Or thought he knew. Well, she wasn't going to be affected by him. She *would not*. She wasn't an innocent little Southern miss anymore. She was a seasoned New Yorker.

"Why, Logan Van Dell! Whatever are you doing here?" She'd try for a little disarming Southern belle to put him off balance. She hoped she remembered how.

"I came to see you."

Amber just stopped herself from saying, "Little ole me?" This wasn't the Logan she remembered. He was wearing a suit and tie. She'd never seen him in a suit and tie before. And his clothes were expensively tailored, she noticed with the experience of sizing up customers. His hair was shorter and freshly styled.

And his smile was killer.

That she remembered.

There was just enough of the old Logan in that smile to reach through the miles and the years—and the hurt—to give a good hard yank to the old heartstrings.

Those heartstrings seemed to be attached to her knees in some way, she decided, because she had to hold on to the doorjamb to steady herself.

"You've got a smudge on your cheek." He reached out and lightly brushed a thumb about an inch from her mouth. "There."

Her skin tingled as he slowly removed his hand.

She remembered the tingling, too. No one else had ever made her tingle the way Logan could.

And he knew it.

They both stood in the doorway and stared at each other...until Amber remembered that this man, who was deliberately oozing sensual charm from every pore, had broken her heart. It had long since healed, but it was the principle that mattered here. Not smoldering looks trying to evoke memories of equally smoldering nights. Not the dark eyes, the intimate smile or the clean-shaven face that still allowed a rough shadow to show and keep things interesting.

She straightened and moved to one side. "Come in, won't you? How have you been?" She decided to drop the Southern belle for the busy New Yorker, after all.

"Just fine." He walked in and scanned the area, which took him about two seconds.

"I don't usually have visitors to my workshop." Amber held out her hands for his overcoat, self-consciously draping it over the bar stool because there wasn't any place else to hang it. She took a mental inventory of the pantry and the fridge. Not good.

"This was the only address Barclay's had for you."
Logan sat on her sofa and rested his ankle on his knee,
looking as though he had settled in for a long visit.

Amber didn't want him here for that long. "Barclay's gave out my address?"

He smiled that smile of his again. "Not officially."

"Monica." Amber sighed.

"Cute little blonde?"

"Yes." If he'd seen Monica, then he'd obviously been
to Barclay's in person. Amber swallowed in a throat
suddenly gone tight. What else had Monica told him?

"She figured out that we were old friends from back
home."

"And how did she figure that?"

"Something about the accent."

Amber had taken voice lessons to lose that accent.
Just being around Logan made her want to lengthen
her vowels and add an extra syllable here and there.

He was looking at her, in a way that no one else did.
She watched his gaze roam over her, making her glad
she was wearing the bulky bib apron over her black
skirt and funnel-neck sweater.

"What brings you to New York, Logan?"

"Business." His eyes returned to hers. "And pleasure."

Just the way he said the word...she shivered before
her early training kicked in. "Let me get you something to drink," she said with all the graciousness she
could muster to cover the silence before it got awk-
ward. "Though I don't really keep my workshop
stocked for entertaining..." She trailed off in front of
the open refrigerator. It was worse than she remem-

bered. "I can offer you milk or bottled water." She smiled brightly.

She couldn't read Logan's expression from across the room, small though it was. Never mind. As far as he was concerned, this was only her workshop. That was her story and she was sticking to it.

"Water is fine."

Amber got down two glasses from the cabinet and opened a bottle. "I've been trying to drink more water. People don't drink nearly enough, you know. It has so many health benefits. For instance, I don't get as many headaches as I used to."

She was babbling, she knew, but she was powerless to stop. As long as Amber kept talking, Logan couldn't ask difficult questions that would require difficult answers. "And the milk, well, you know women and osteoporosis."

When she looked up, it was to see that Logan had stood and was examining the bits and pieces littered across her worktable. He probably hadn't paid the slightest attention to her. *She* wouldn't have paid attention to her.

"You're making jewelry," he said when she approached him and handed him the one glass that didn't advertise Club Wen Kroy's half-price drinks.

"Yes. It's what I do."

He picked up a silver brooch that was waiting for a final polish, examined it, and set it carefully back on the table without comment.

Amber found herself wanting to hear his opinion. After laboring in obscurity, she was hungry for *anyone's* opinion, even Logan's.

"I thought you were the right arm of some high muckety-muck."

It took her a moment to absorb the implications of what he'd said. "You've been talking to Mother." How astonishing. And the sun was still coming up in the east and everything.

"Yes." He looked up at her. "Seems you've been talking to her, too."

"Of course. She's my mother." She had to go through her mother to get to her grandmother, but she didn't feel like telling Logan that.

"Mmm." Logan's dark gaze met hers.

Amber didn't know what "Mmm" meant and she wasn't going to ask.

He took a long swallow of his water. "Is this New York water?"

"Canadian," Amber mumbled, aware of being an inadequate hostess as only a one-time Southern belle could be. *Get over it! Logan just showed up at your door after eight years. He should be grateful that you're speaking to him at all.*

Inspection apparently finished, Logan sat again. Amber turned her work chair around and sat on it instead of joining Logan on the small sofa. He was taking up most of the room, anyway.

"You said you'd come to New York on business?" She'd ignore the pleasure part. "What sort of business are you in?" Just the sort of question one old friend would ask another. Amber relaxed a little. He seemed to have dropped the subject of her great job, which was a stroke of luck as far as she was concerned.

"My business."

"Logan, don't be that way. If you're trying to be

mysterious and intriguing, I'm not buying it." As if she could afford to buy anything.

"No intrigue intended, Amber. I'm a freelance consultant. Officially, I'm a facilitator on retainer with the Belle Rive First National Bank. I put deals together."

Sounded just like something a Van Dell would do. Amber remembered that no one ever knew precisely how the Van Dells made their money but everyone figured it was something shady. "What kinds of deals?"

He smiled. "Deals that need to be put together. For instance, you know the old battery plant outside of town?"

"That ugly old thing?"

"It's not so ugly anymore. The Peabodys wanted out. I found a buyer, but not just any buyer. I came across a computer power supply manufacturer that sells to several companies in Atlanta. Then I convinced the Belle Rive City Council to give them appropriate tax breaks in exchange for bringing new jobs to the area. As a bonus goodwill gesture, they spiffed up the place."

"And people *pay* you for that?"

"You don't think these things just happen, now, do you?"

Amber hadn't thought about it at all. "So what kind of a deal brings you to New York?"

He gazed directly at her. "You."

LOGAN WATCHED HER EYES widen and her face, already too pale, whiten even more. What had she done to herself? She was thinner than he remembered and her eyes had lost the sparkle that had made them the brightest brown eyes he'd ever seen.

And her mother called this sophistication?

Logan called it being beaten down by life.

"What about me?" she asked. He heard actual fear in her voice.

It saddened him. He'd expected...he'd expected to find a laughing Amber who would have flung herself into his arms. He would have spun her around and then he would have kissed her.

And then he would have awakened, because he surely would have been dreaming. A lot of time had passed. Too much time. Better to leave the past in the past. "I came to see how my old running buddy was doing," he said lightly.

"Fine. I'm doing fine." She gestured around her. "I have this cozy workshop and I adore designing and making jewelry."

Her "cozy workshop" looked like somebody's closet—in fact, it looked as if somebody was *still* using it for storage. There were cinderblock shelves holding boxes and tools. More boxes were stacked in the corner and under the worktable, and he was sitting on the world's most uncomfortable sofa. He thought it might have been green at one time. Now it had taken on the same brownish-green color bologna turned when it was time to throw it out.

"I don't remember you making jewelry in Belle Rive," he said.

"I've done a lot of things I didn't do in Belle Rive." Her face went hard for a moment, then relaxed. "I got into jewelry-making by accident. During the slow times at Barclay's, I'd hang out in the repair shop. They let me fix broken settings, restring pearls, tighten stones, that sort of thing, and it grew from there."

"So it's more than a hobby."

Her mouth twisted wryly. "I'd like for it to be."

"I guess your boss...is it Mr. I-own-the-store Barclay?"

"What?" She blinked. "Oh—yes." Looking down at the glass in her hands, she brought it to her mouth and took a sip.

"I hear he keeps you pretty busy."

"There's a lot going on. He's opening a store on the west coast. Rodeo Drive."

The way she said it, Logan knew he was supposed to be impressed. He guessed Rodeo Drive was about as far from Belle Rive as a person could get. "So why aren't you at work now?"

"I was. Now, I have a guest." She smiled.

"I meant at the store."

"I don't have to be in until noon today."

"Doesn't the boss man need any personal assisting before then?"

Her smile took on an edge. "I'll work late tonight."

He couldn't resist provoking her. "I just bet you will."

"And what are you implying by that?"

Some of the sparkle he remembered returned to her eyes. At least when she was mad, she looked more like her old self. "What exactly is going on between you and this guy?"

"*Nothing.* And even if there were, it would be none of your *business.*" She stood. "You made it quite clear that you'd moved on eight years ago."

Yeah, he'd been out of line to poke his nose into her relationship with her boss. Way out of line. But seeing

Amber so...so unlike the young woman he'd put on that bus had bothered him. "Sit down. Please."

When she didn't, Logan reached for her hand and tugged. Amber snatched it away, but she did sit down.

"Amber, you're the one who moved on," he said gently.

"We were supposed to move on *together*. I never would have planned to come here by myself."

Logan held her gaze. "I know."

"I was eighteen years old and all alone in *New York City*." Her lip trembled, stopping just short of a quiver. "Can you imagine what that was like?"

He had, plenty of times when he'd gone back to their special place by the cold spring and thought about her as he stared at the sky, wondering if Amber could see the stars, too, or if the bright city lights blotted them out. Or if she remembered to look.

"You never intended to come with me, did you?"

He shook his head, waiting for her to understand.

"Then *why* did you let me make all those plans about *us*?" He could hear the hurt in her voice, even though she was trying to cover it with anger. "Was there another girl?"

"No."

"Then what happened? Was I too clingy and putting me on a bus was a convenient way to get rid of me?"

"Amber..." He exhaled heavily. She didn't get it and wasn't going to. He supposed he couldn't blame her. "I never wanted to get rid of you. But you wanted out of Belle Rive so badly... I just helped you make it happen."

She stared at him. "So...I'm supposed to be grateful?"

"I imagined you might be once you'd had a chance to think it all through. All you had were dreams and no plans to back them up. You kept saying you wanted out, but you hadn't done anything about leaving."

She opened her mouth, then snapped it shut and looked off into the middle distance.

"I always knew you'd make it, Amber," he said quietly. "That's one thing I liked about you. You could have had an easy life in Belle Rive, what with your daddy being the mayor and all. But instead, you wanted to make your own way without trading on your family's name. That took guts. And now look at you."

"Yeah, look at me," she said hollowly.

"You've got a great job, and your mother says you live in a penthouse." He gestured to her worktable, not certain what to say about all the weird bits of metal. They didn't look like the kind of jewelry he was used to seeing on the women in Belle Rive. "And here you're starting another career. You've got it made."

"Made in the shade." Amber lifted her glass in a mock toast and drained it.

She wasn't reacting the way he'd expected and he didn't know why.

Maybe he *had* expected gratitude. At least a thawing by now. They should be laughing and sharing warm remembrances, but the warmest she'd been was when she'd opened the door. A definite cold front had moved through since then.

Logan had been working up to asking her to come back to Belle Rive and show off. As far as he knew, she'd never been back to prove to everybody that she'd made good.

But the vibes were all wrong. Amber didn't act as though she wanted to prove anything. He regarded her silently. There were several ways to go here. He could appeal to her better nature—since she and her mother were back on good terms, maybe Amber could be talked into returning to be queen because it would please her mother.

He'd even tell her that if she came back, then his mother could run the show, but he sensed that playing the sympathy card wouldn't work here, either. For one thing, Amber obviously still hadn't forgiven him for not coming to New York with her. For another, Logan didn't want her sympathy, her pity—or her scorn.

Now wasn't a good time, that much was plain. He probably should have called first, but he hadn't wanted to give her a chance to come up with reasons to not commit to the pilgrimage. Logan had learned that it was much easier for people to say no over the telephone than in person.

Although right now, Amber didn't look as if she'd have any trouble at all saying no.

Time for another tactic. Maybe a warm remembrance, or two. "Do you remember all those nights we'd lie in the tree house, looking at the stars, and you'd talk about having this kind of life?" He was gambling on her remembering the good and forgetting how she hated being forced to do the debutante drill.

She eyed him warily. "What's your point?"

Logan leaned forward and took one of her hands. "Hasn't enough time passed for us to remember the good and forget the bad?" He accompanied this with his most persuasive smile. It worked on every female except his mother. "That's your father's smile," she'd say. "And that's how I ended up with you."

But he knew Amber. And she loved his smile.

3

AMBER SNATCHED her hand back. "All right, what's going on?"

"Just talking about old times," he said, still with that sappy look on his face.

Old times, right. Logan Van Dell had gone soft in the head if he thought he could just waltz in and they'd take up where they'd left off.

The fact that he was probably more than half right bothered Amber. A lot. But she wasn't about to let him know it. "That bus has left the station, Logan. I was on it and you weren't." That sounded like a pretty good comeback to Amber. Very witty and I'm-so-over-you-ish.

His smile turned into one of amusement. He'd been caught, but wasn't too concerned. "Why haven't you ever come ho—been back to Belle Rive?"

Still in her that's-way-in-the-past mode, Amber lifted a shoulder. "Just never got around to it."

"Thinking of getting around to it anytime soon?"

"Not really." She glanced over to her worktable. "I keep myself pretty busy. Speaking of..." Pointedly, she looked at her watch, a big silver band holding a tiny watch face. One of her designs. "I'll have to leave for work soon."

Logan also looked at his watch, which Amber

couldn't help noticing retailed for four figures in the store. Had someone given it to him, or had he bought it for himself? Knowing Logan, he'd won it in a card game. It was probably engraved "To Guido, with love on our tenth anniversary" or something like that on the back.

"You've got well over an hour," he said. "Is traffic that bad?"

"I walk."

"Doesn't your boss send a car for his personal assistant?"

Good question. Amber would have to ask the woman some time. "Walking is good exercise."

"You're right. Walking is great exercise. So I'll walk with you." He settled back on the sofa. "Go ahead and get ready." Picking up the instruction booklet for the polishing motor from the crate serving as her lamp table, he started reading.

Amber's smile was tight. At this rate she'd never get rid of him, at least not without him knowing that she wanted to get rid of him, which was really her goal here.

She was feeling the strain of trying to remember everything she'd told her mother—who had obviously talked a blue streak if Logan knew about her supposed job and elegant penthouse—and keeping up the pretense for him.

And then there was the strain caused by Logan, himself. The strain of ignoring the fact that she wasn't totally indifferent to him. In fact, she didn't even hate him. She wanted to, but she couldn't.

His well-cut suit did everything to enhance his even better-cut body beneath it. But Logan had always had a good body. He worked out and was never shy about showing off the results of those workouts. Her mother had sniffed that it was vulgar for men to overdevelop their muscles, that they were only making up for shortcomings in other areas.

But Logan hadn't had any shortcomings. *Especially* in other areas.

Yes, he'd known exactly what he was doing by bringing up their nights at the cold spring tree house.

Originally, Logan had built the platform to dive off into the spring. She swallowed at the memory of Logan, cutoffs riding low on his hips, diving deep into the spring to retrieve the bottles of beer he'd weighted down to cool.

When Amber started spending time at the tree house, he'd added sides, but had left the top open to the night sky. Those late summer evenings when the moon was full and the stars were bright had been magical. Being with Logan had been magical.

Had been, she reminded herself as she gazed at him with cool detachment. Or a valiant attempt at cool detachment. Or at least lukewarm detachment.

Still reading the booklet, Logan grinned. "You want me to leave, don't you?"

"Yes."

"Why? You expecting company?"

"No."

"I thought I'd at least get a tour of the town while I was here."

"New York is a very big city."

"And I'd hate to see it all by my lonesome."

"That's why they have tour groups."

"I had something more personal in mind." He

tossed the booklet back onto the crate. "Could I take you to dinner tonight? I assume you get a break."

The thought of a free meal—one where she could order meat—nearly swayed her. But she was bound to slip up and reveal her true circumstances during dinner, especially when she got distracted by the dessert cart. "What do you want, Logan?"

"Would you believe me if I said you?"

Steady. "No."

"It's true." He smiled, adding the extra quirk that brought out his dimple.

Had she ever been so young and naive as to be charmed by this man?

She shouldn't be so hard on herself. He'd been a very youthful man then and his charm hadn't been nearly so practiced. Still, fresh and enthusiastic had a powerful allure all on its own. Now he was just another small-town man who thought he was God's gift to women. It was too bad he wasn't a customer in the store. How many times had such a man bought an expensive piece of jewelry thinking he was impressing *her?*

And how many times did you act impressed so he wouldn't change his mind and cost you the commission? Better not go there.

She ignored Logan and his dimple and stood to untie her apron, hanging it on the nail sticking out of one of the cinderblocks.

Mistake. When she turned back around she saw Logan, minus his dimple, looking at her in a way that was neither practiced nor charming.

"I'm thinking that I ought to meet your boss and

make sure he gives you time off for dinner. You look like you could use a meal."

"It's just because I'm wearing black. Black makes you look thinner."

"It's doing a helluva job."

Self-consciously, Amber ran her hands down the front of her thighs, then crossed her arms over her chest when she noticed Logan's gaze following her movements. The outfit had a jacket that went with it and she glanced around, then groaned inwardly. She must have gathered it up with her laundry and thrown it behind the screen when Logan knocked on the door.

Oh, great. It was a blustery March day and Amber didn't dare walk the twenty-two blocks without some kind of jacket, yet she couldn't dig around behind the screen with Logan watching her.

Stalling, she gestured toward the bathroom. "I'll be just a minute."

Once inside, Amber put on lipstick and tried to cram all her cosmetics into the one tiny drawer under the sink. They didn't fit. Okay. She balanced everything she could on the wire shelves in her shower and dumped the rest of the jars, bottles and towels into her dirty clothes hamper, trying to make the place look as though someone didn't live there. She'd offer Logan use of the facilities and while he was in here, she'd grab her jacket. Everything would work out and they'd be gone in minutes.

Emerging from the bathroom, she saw Logan studying her shelves. Fortunately, Amber kept nearly everything in the decorative storage boxes she'd scavenged. In fact, that wicker two-drawer one by his head held her underwear. "I'm almost ready to leave, if you want to make a pit stop."

Logan reached for his coat. "I'm fine."

He would be. "Did—did you see my briefcase some-where over there?" Amber waved vaguely toward her worktable as she edged toward the screen. "It's...black."

"What a surprise."

Amber exhaled as he obligingly turned to look. She quickly felt behind the screen, but couldn't find her jacket. Rather than folding up the screen, she pulled the edge out just enough to stick her head and shoulder behind it. There was her jacket—on the far side, natu-rally. She lunged for it.

Too late, she realized she would have been better off if she hadn't made such a big production of retrieving her jacket and had nonchalantly fished behind the screen as though the jacket had been hanging on a hook, or something.

As it was, the screen wobbled and fell, landing against the kitchenette bar, effectively trapping her in the corner.

Naturally, Logan noticed. If the crash hadn't been loud enough, Amber's un-Southern-belle-like excla-mation would have been.

Logan stared at her—or rather stared at what was behind her—a clothing rack with her shoes underneath and assorted belts, as well as purses and jewelry hang-ing from a Peg-Board on the wall. It looked like a makeshift closet. Which it was.

She reached for the screen. "This is what happens when you hurry!" She laughed. Okay, tittered. "Did you find my briefcase?" Anything to distract him.

He started toward her. "Let me help you with that."

"I've got it." She waved him away, but he ignored her and silently picked up the screen. Amber grabbed her stupid jacket and stepped out of the corner. "Don't worry about setting the screen back up. I can do that later."

"It'll only take a second."

Logan hadn't commented on what he'd seen, but Amber was ready when he did. She'd go into how she sometimes worked all hours in a creative haze and fell asleep in exhaustion. That would explain the clothes and everything. In fact, it sounded pretty good.

But Logan didn't mention the clothes. Carefully balancing the screen, he asked, "If I spring for a taxi, do you think you could let me have a few more minutes of your time?"

Amber found herself nodding, responding to the tone of his voice, which contained not a hint of innuendo or nostalgia. Even his dimple was gone.

"Actually, if I can leave within fifteen minutes, I've still got plenty of time to walk. I find walking...clears my head." If she avoided having him ride with her to work, then he couldn't possibly run into Peter Barclay, who'd be surprised to find himself with a new personal assistant.

"Sure." Logan draped his coat over the arm of the sofa and sat to one side, leaving plenty of room for her.

Though she'd rather keep her distance, it would be churlish to avoid sitting on the sofa with him. "What's up?"

He regarded her silently for a moment. "My latest project involves the Belle Rive pilgrimages."

Logan involved with the pilgrimages? That boggled her mind. "Do go on."

"Tourism has dropped, and with it, revenue for the city budget. It's been decided to combine the pilgrimages and have one great big blowout that can compete with Natchez and Vicksburg."

Amber searched his face, waiting for the punchline. He wasn't kidding. "And my mother agreed to this?" Her mother had been irate for years over the fact that Logan's grandmother had started a rival festival of sorts. Lily refused to call it a true "pilgrimage."

"Your mother was the one who approached me."

Amber was stunned. Her mother had actually sought out a Van Dell? To help her with the sacred pilgrimage? "And so now you're working out all the details?"

"Essentially."

"Oh, that's rich." Just thinking of Logan trying to deal with the pilgrimage women made Amber start laughing. They were so picky about flowers and themes and food and the order of the homes on the tour. Hair-pulling had been known to break out over shades of blue and whether it was tacky to put dark meat in the chicken salad at the luncheon for the queen and her court. "Oh, Logan, you've got yourself right in the middle of...of, well, I know how my mother felt when *your* grandmother started her own pilgrimage and I can't imagine... Oh, you poor thing." She laughed again, almost admiring her mother for coming up with a clever and brilliant way to torment a Van Dell. She was surprised Logan had fallen for it.

He wasn't laughing. Far from it. In fact...Amber sobered, belatedly noticing the tightness of his jaw and the polite mask he wore. "Well, good luck. You've got your work cut out for you," she said, wondering what all this had to do with her. Maybe he wanted hints for dealing with her mother. As if Amber could be any help.

"It hasn't been so bad. Each group has agreed to some basic ground rules, contingent on a couple of factors."

"If they agreed on anything, it would have to be basic—like holding the pilgrimage in Belle Rive."

He smiled faintly. "We've made more progress than that."

Amber imagined Logan being forced to sample punch recipes and mediate between color swatches. She shook her head. "I can't believe this. I'd almost like to see it."

Logan leaned forward. "You can."

Something in his eyes told Amber what he was going to say in the instant before he said it.

"I'm here to officially invite you to serve as this year's Magnolia Queen—"

"No!" Amber leaped to her feet. She should have seen this coming as soon as he'd started talking about the pilgrimage.

"Think about it—"

"Hell, no!"

"Amber—"

"Are you *crazy*? Are they crazy?" She backed away from the sofa. "How many times do I have to tell them that I will never be a queen, or princess, or empress, or goddess, or grand poobah, or whatever title they come up with? You, of all people, should know how I feel about it."

"I know how you *felt* about it," he said in that overly reasonable tone men use when dealing with hysterical women. "But it's been a while."

"And I still feel the same way." If he thought *this* was hysterical, just wait. She could show him a hair-pulling, shrieking hysteria that would send him back to Belle Rive pronto. She wouldn't even have to exaggerate a whole lot from what she was feeling right now.

"Your mother believes that if a Madison is queen, then it'll signify to the community that the combined pilgrimage has the official stamp of approval."

"If you need a Madison, ask Stephanie."

"Your sister is married and not eligible to serve as queen."

Amber could hear her mother saying the same thing. "That's right, she is. Smart girl." Even after three months, it was still hard to think of Stephanie as married.

"Heard you didn't make it back for the big reception your parents had for her," Logan commented.

"No." And she'd listened to enough complaining about *that*. "The holiday time is so hectic and our schedules didn't mesh." Amber avoided looking at the polishing motor. It had cost about what an airplane ticket home would have cost and she'd earned the money by not missing out on the Christmas sales which she would have done if she'd gone home for Christmas and her sister's reception.

She ought to be grateful to Stephanie for eloping, because Amber sure couldn't have afforded to be in the wedding. Missing a party her parents threw to stifle gossip was bad; missing a wedding would have been unthinkable.

And the cost of a wedding was nothing compared to what she'd have to spend on all the Magnolia Queen glop. "Logan, I appreciate that you came all this way, but it's not going to happen. You can go home and tell my mother anything you want, except that I have changed my mind."

Logan remained sitting on the sofa as Amber walked toward the door. "Would it kill you to make a bunch of old ladies happy?" he asked.

"It might. Competition for sequins gets pretty cut-throat during the pilgrimage."

That drew a reluctant smile from Logan. "Then do it for your hometown. Your daddy has had to raise taxes two years in a row to make up for the shortfall."

"So?"

"It's an election year."

"Again, so? He's been mayor for as long as I can remember. It's time for him to give somebody else a turn."

He looked at her and a little of the old Logan crept back into his expression. She missed the old Logan. "I don't suppose you'd consider doing it for me?" Slowly, one side of his mouth quirked upward.

Oh, no. Not the dimple. Amber gritted her teeth. "No."

"You sure?" he asked softly.

"You think you're worth it?"

"Ouch." He laughed softly. "I am, but you'd have to take my word for it." His eyelids lowered. "Unless you'd like a demonstration."

He had such a self-satisfied look on his face that Amber couldn't stand it. "I don't need your word or a demo. I've got the word of three-fourths of the women in Belle Rive."

"There're some I missed?"

Amber started laughing. She couldn't help it. "You're incorrigible, aren't you?"

"Come back and find out."

She sighed. "Logan..."

"Let's look at this situation another way," he said, his voice eminently reasonable.

Sighing again, Amber returned to the sofa. He was persistent, she'd give him that. But even if she *did* have money, she wasn't about to waste it on sequins.

Logan gestured with his hands. "Think of the irony—you left Belle Rive because you didn't want anything to do with that sort of life. I heard the talk after you'd gone and I can tell you, it was universally decided that you'd come to no good."

"I just figured they'd think I was pregnant." And she might have been if Logan hadn't been so much of a gentleman. She'd never been able to figure out why he'd been a gentleman with her and anything *but* a gentleman with anyone else.

"Yeah, well..."

From the look on his face, Amber could just imagine the gossip.

"Now they need your help and you're in a position to come back, help them...and prove you don't need them all over again. Think how it'll stick in their craw."

Laughing, Amber perched on the frayed arm of her sofa. "You're really good at this, Logan! I'm impressed. You've tried duty, guilt, love, pride, revenge—I'm waiting for the bribe."

"How much would it take?" he asked at once.

He smiled when he asked, but after looking into his dark eyes, Amber knew that if she named a price, and he could pay it, he would.

For a moment she was even tempted. Money might not be everything, but it was a far sight ahead of whatever was in second place. "I'm sorry, Logan. I'm not going back."

"It's been eight years, Amber," he said quietly. "Don't you want to go home?"

Amber opened her mouth to say no, but a vision of her home flashed in her mind. Home and her family. In all this time she hadn't seen her grandmother, or her father, or her little sister, who wasn't so little anymore. Logan probably didn't know that, probably thought they'd all visited her. Amber had discouraged visits until her mother just flat told her she was coming and did. "Not really," she said in a small voice, but the hesitation cost her. Logan had trumped her with the home card.

She checked her watch again, then stood. This time, she truly had to leave. "Have we gone through your bag of tricks?"

"No."

"Then what's left?"

His smile turned lethal. "Blackmail."

LOGAN THOUGHT he'd pretty much sized up Amber's situation. Apparently, she and Mr. High Muckety-Muck had had a falling out. In fact, he was guessing that it had been *his* penthouse she'd been living in when her mother had visited her. And though she was calling this her workshop—and it may have been at one time—she was obviously living here now.

Logan didn't like the thought of Amber living here on her own almost as much as he hated the thought of her living with anyone. A person didn't have to be familiar with New York to know that this wasn't the most exclusive area of town.

No, Amber Madison wasn't doing so hot. In fact, he'd even go so far as to say she was having money troubles. As someone who'd experienced money troubles himself, he knew all the signs.

Her boyfriend must have dumped her from her high-flying job, too.

Logan admired her for hanging in there, but now she was just being stubborn. She wanted to go home—the yearning on her face had been almost painful to see. The only thing keeping her in New York was her pride. All right, he'd make it easy on her.

"'Blackmail'?" she repeated, looking scared for just a minute. Then her face cleared and she rolled her eyes. "Why is it everybody thinks New Yorkers lead these wild lives? I hate to disappoint you and all those old sourpusses back in Belle Rive, but I haven't lived the type of life people get blackmailed for."

Okay, if she wanted to play it out..."Did you ever actually live in that penthouse, or just borrow it to impress your mama?"

She stared at him. "What are you talking about?"

"Your mother stayed with you in a penthouse."

"That's right."

This was almost too easy. "I'd like to see it."

"No."

"Because...?"

"Because your fifteen minutes are up." She stood and determinedly stuck out her hand. "It's been great seeing you, Logan. Have a nice life."

"I do, but I'll venture a guess that you don't."

"It's time for you to leave."

It was time for him to play hardball. Standing slowly, he reached for his coat. "If I leave now, I'll go back to Belle Rive and tell everybody that you've got a two-bit job as a salesclerk in a jewelry store and live in a shabby little one-room hole in a rundown building. I'll tell them that you're practically starving and you look twice as old as when you left." He hadn't meant to say the last part out loud, even though it was true.

Her hand crept to her whitened cheek. "They won't believe you."

"Your mother just has to make one phone call to the jewelry store to find out, doesn't she?"

Amber's face regained some of its color and she reached for her purse. "But she won't."

"Somebody else will."

"So what if they do? It won't prove anything. For all they know, I could be working as a clerk because it's routine training for executives. In fact, I might call Mama and tell her that's what I'm doing even before you get back to Belle Rive."

"Spiking my guns?"

She slung her purse bandolier-style across her shoulder. "Whatever I have to do."

He didn't doubt it. "You remember when I said I was guessing?"

Amber went still.

"You just confirmed my guess." He could see her mentally replaying their conversation and the moment she realized what she'd said. "How close was I on the other?"

"Go to hell."

"That close?"

She glared at him, then smiled. "It doesn't matter. No one in Belle Rive will believe you, anyway."

"Because I'm a Van Dell?"

"Because you're *Logan* Van Dell."

He was surprised that her words could hurt him. "Things have changed since you left. They'll believe me."

"Things haven't changed that much," Amber said. "And you have no idea what my life is like now."

"No, I don't. Unlike your mother, I haven't heard from you since you left."

"Did you expect to?"

"Kind of. If I recall, you were going to fling that money I gave you back in my face." Logan was still going for the "triumphant return" angle. Amber's reaction caught him by surprise.

Tight-lipped, she banged her purse on the kitchenette bar and peeled open the flap. Digging through it, she removed her checkbook and a pen. He could swear that her hands were shaking as she flipped through the pages.

"What are you doing?"

She scrawled something on one of the checks, then signed her name. "I'm paying you back."

"It was a gift."

When she ripped it out, the check tore and she had to hold the edge down with one hand while she separated the paper with the other. "It was a loan." She held out the check. "Here."

"Keep it."

"I don't want it."

When he didn't take the check, she flung it in his face, just as she'd threatened to do so long ago. He made no move to stop it as it drifted to the floor and lay there.

They stared at each other and what he saw made Logan determined to not leave New York without Amber.

"Shouldn't it have bounced?" he asked quietly.

Throat working, Amber blinked rapidly. "If you—" She stopped and swallowed. "I just paid bills, so if you would kindly wait to cash that for a few days while I transfer funds from another source, I would appreciate it."

Logan knew Amber had no other source. He stooped and plucked the check from the floor. It was made out for two hundred and sixty-seven dollars. He couldn't remember how much had been in the envelope, but it was telling that Amber had.

"Should I have added interest?" she snapped as he continued to stare at it.

"No." Watching her face as he did so, he slowly and deliberately tore up the check and dropped the pieces on the counter. Next, he took her checkbook and tucked it back into her purse, carefully closing the flap.

Then he opened his arms.

Amber's eyes were bright and her hands were fisted at her sides. Logan took a step toward her and her face crumpled. A second later, his arms closed around her shaking body.

She cried without making a sound, which Logan

found much worse than if she'd screamed or yelled or called him names.

"Come back to Belle Rive, be queen, and I'll see to it that everyone hears how you've hit it big in New York."

"And if I don't, you'll tell everyone I'm a big fat failure?"

"I'll tell everyone you're a big skinny failure."

"Logan, why do you hate me so much?" Her voice was muffled against his chest.

"I don't hate you."

"I hate you."

He closed his eyes. "I know."

4

AMBER HATED LOGAN Van Dell almost as much as she hated the idea of impersonating Scarlett O'Hara for two weeks.

He'd blackmailed her into a way of life she thought she'd escaped forever and subjected her to humiliation after humiliation, though to be fair, he hadn't set out to do so. It just seemed to work out that way.

The first utterly humiliating moment came when Amber had to admit that she didn't have enough money to buy an airplane ticket. It was even worse when Logan anticipated what she'd been about to confess and informed her that the pilgrimage organization committee always brought their queens home first-class.

Yeah, right. But she was in no position to argue. Especially when Barclay's agreed to give her an unpaid leave of absence. And so several weeks later, she found herself humiliated again when Logan returned to personally escort her.

Obviously, no one trusted her to keep her part of the bargain and return home. Amber liked to think she would have, even if Logan hadn't behaved like a bouncer in a nightclub and herded her from her workshop down the stairs and into a waiting cab.

Oh, well. At least they served meat on the airplane.

Amber ignored everything on her plate but the prime rib. Somehow—she suspected it had been Logan's doing—the flight attendant had brought her a second serving without Amber asking. It never occurred to Amber to refuse it. Really, who started that vicious rumor about airplane food? Her meal was excellent. They offered a choice of red or white wine with names other than "house" or "table" and everything. First-class was definitely the way to go.

They were met at the airport in Vicksburg by the mayor of Belle Rive and his wife—conveniently Amber's parents, though no one would ever know it—and an entourage, which included a tall and striking dark-haired woman, who lifted her cheek for Logan's kiss.

Amber was completely unprepared for the prick of jealousy, which, to be honest, was probably more like a stab and completely inappropriate for a couple reasons, one of which was that this was Logan's mother.

She held a bouquet of white roses, which she presented to Amber. "Hi, hon, I'm Gigi, Logan's mom," she told Amber with breezy informality.

So this was the infamous Gigi Fandana Van Dell, former Vegas showgirl who'd married the considerably older Auden Van Dell, Logan's father, though that fact was disputed in whispers accompanied by raised eyebrows until the adolescent Logan developed the unmistakable Van Dell jaw.

Amber glanced over to find him gritting the Van Dell jaw, his eyes boring into hers. What? Did he actually think she was ill-mannered enough to insult his mother? She threw him a withering look and thrust her hand from behind the flowers. "I don't believe we met when I was living in Belle Rive."

Gigi shook her hand with an enthusiastic clanking of bracelets. "I sure heard a lot about you, though. I just knew Logan would be able to talk you into coming back."

Amber looked toward Logan, curious to see if he was gloating. He wasn't. "He had a very persuasive argument."

Gigi patted her arm. "He always does, hon. Just like his father." She sighed.

Amber's parents reached her. Or, no, it was the mayor and his wife, judging by their campaign faces and stiff body language. Couldn't they just once act like her parents? she wondered wistfully. Amber eagerly looked around them for her grandmother, but didn't see her. She swallowed her disappointment. So it was to be an official event all the way.

"Amber, dear." Lily leaned close to air kiss her, while Amber's father, the same father she hadn't seen in eight years, patted her awkwardly on the shoulder. Amber tried not to notice that he glanced toward the hovering photographer as he did so. The photographer showed the good sense to pass on the photo op.

Lily whispered, "Darling, you look like you're in mourning."

In a way, she was. "Black is chic."

"Black is for funerals and cocktails with republican governors."

"And how did the last election go?"

Lily ignored her. "Put on some lipstick."

Amber licked her lips. "I'm wearing some."

Lily squinted down at her. "I can't tell."

Because she knew there'd be plenty of arguments later, Amber let this one go and obligingly dug in her purse, withdrawing a tube of lipstick that she swiped across her mouth. Putting on lipstick while holding an armful of roses—yes, she was back home.

Lily stayed her hand when she would have put away the lipstick. "What color is that?"

"Blushing Nude."

"Don't be vulgar, Amber."

"Wouldn't it be worse if the nude didn't blush?"

"Put on some Revlon." Her mother thrust a black tube at her.

Amber looked at the glowing cherry red and shook her head. Lily lowered her voice. "A reporter and photographer from the newspaper are here. We want everyone to be able to see your smile on the front page of the *Mirror*."

"They'll be able to see it in the next county," Amber mumbled, and gingerly touched the red stick to her mouth just as a breeze blew a piece of her hair into her face.

It stuck to her lips and her mother pulled it away. "Did you forget to spray your hair before you got off the plane? I wondered why it didn't have any oomph."

Amber remained silent rather than explain that nobody in New York appreciated "oomph."

Lily continued to fluff Amber's hair. "Can't you do anything with this?"

Amber tucked a few strands behind her ears.

"Oh, not that—wait." Lily brought one side forward. "Yes." She smiled for the first time since Amber stepped off the plane. "That'll do. Now remember, shoulders back and hold your flowers low."

Amber sincerely hoped Logan was taking all this in.

Maybe he'd realize just what he'd blackmailed her into.

Assuming he cared. She glanced toward him, surprised to find an intent look on his face that she couldn't read. Gigi's face, however, was a cinch. She wore the universal wary-mother look—narrowed eyes glancing from her son to Amber. *Don't worry. You're eight years too late, anyway,* Amber wanted to tell her.

"I'd planned to pose you next to the car," Lily was saying, "but since it's black you'll look like a disembodied head and a bunch of flowers in the pictures." Lily walked to the front of the limousine, frowned when she realized the airport parking lot would be in the background, shook her head slightly and gestured for Amber to follow her. "This angle, I think." After repositioning Amber's flowers and gently pulling Amber's father closer so that he'd be in any photograph, Lily raised her eyebrows at Gigi.

"What?"

Lily nodded toward Amber.

Gigi blinked, then rolled her eyes. "Oh, please. You're not going to make me—"

"Tradition, Mama," Logan interjected quietly, and urged her forward.

Since when had Logan been interested in tradition?

The photographer's camera flashed. Smile wide and practiced, Gigi struck a pose, jutting her hips forward and bending her knee slightly so her already short skirt rose another inch. After more flashing, Gigi tossed her hair.

"The mayor has a very tight schedule," Lily pointedly told the photographer.

Amber was having a hard time keeping from laughing until she caught the stoic look on Logan's face. He was embarrassed for his mother. Why? Wasn't Amber's own father the biggest picture hog in all of Mississippi?

Well, she'd better not laugh or he'd no doubt think she was laughing at his mother rather than at the whole situation.

He'd changed and she kind of missed the old Logan—the one who would have given the photographer two minutes to get his shots, and then swept her away.

The one who'd be wearing jeans with the suit jacket.

Amber bit her lip, then remembered the bright lipstick and wiped her front teeth with her finger just as the photographer appeased the mayor's wife by flashing the camera their way.

"Well, there's the front page," Amber muttered, and received a motherly nudge in the ribs.

Gigi approached her. Wrinkling her forehead, Logan's mother laced her fingers together and in a twangy sing-song began reciting the official Magnolia Queen pronouncement.

"'O daughter true of Belle Rive . . .'"

During Gigi's recitation, Amber glanced at her mother, whose eyes were closed as she silently mouthed the words along with Gigi. That's right—her mother usually pronounced the Magnolia Queen. Maybe she thought it would look funny this time since Amber was her daughter. But why Logan's mother?

"'The next fortnight you will be seen
To be our fair Magnolia Queen.'"

When she finished, Gigi beamed a smile at everyone. "I guess I should have waited until now to give you your flowers, huh? Oh, well." She dipped in an impromptu curtsy, which caused her tight skirt to ride up to reveal a great set of legs.

The photographer's flash went off. Several times.

Amber's father coughed. "Thank you, Mrs. Van Dell." He turned to Amber. "As Mayor of Belle Rive, I am here to present you, Amber Madison, with the key to the city."

He held out a tacky gold key with a white ribbon on it and turned toward the photographer in a seasoned pose.

"Oh, for heaven's sake! This is your daughter. Give her a hug!" Gigi urged.

Reginald Madison looked taken aback. Hugs weren't in the script, they were never in the script. Impulsively, Amber leaned toward him on tiptoe and kissed his cheek.

"Hold it for me!"

The photographer knelt and snapped half a dozen pictures before Amber pulled back, leaving a big, red lip print on her father's cheek.

Lily promptly wiped it off with a tissue. "We'd like some more traditional poses, if you please. For the archives," she added when the photographer seemed reluctant.

He must be new on the staff, Amber thought, or he'd know what her mother wanted from the photo sessions.

Prompted by her mother's elbow in her ribs, Amber smiled just as she'd been taught—cheeks down, mouth stretched. That way, her eyes wouldn't be squinty in photographs.

And so help her, she'd thrust her shoulders back.

How many times had the mayor and his family been photographed? The only thing missing was Stephanie's dark head fitting neatly to the left, just under Amber's chin. Amber wondered if Stephanie had grown any taller. She'd only been twelve when Amber had left home.

They held their smiles as the photographer worked.

Amber wanted to look at Logan, who'd been remarkably silent, but doing so would take her eyes off the camera.

Her mother had completely ignored him. What was up with that? According to Logan, her mother was the one who'd wanted him to retrieve Amber. Shouldn't she be showing a little gratitude?

In fact...just what exactly was Logan getting out of all this? Amber had assumed he'd been hired the way anybody hired him, but now she doubted that. There was something else going on here.

Blackmail.

Interesting thought. He'd blackmailed her, why not blackmail her mother?

Or her father. Amber dared to turn away from the camera to glance at the man next to her. Had her father done something, say, some shady business deal, and Logan had found out about it? Amber tried to imagine her father as shady and couldn't.

But her mother... Under the pretext of presenting her other side to the camera, Amber glanced at the woman standing next to her with the perfectly frosted helmet of hair that could withstand a hurricane and still look perfectly coiffed should the mayor and his wife happen to be photographed while surveying storm damage.

Then she looked at Logan.

He was angry and getting angrier. Gigi touched his arm and whispered something to him. Logan shook his head and started forward.

"Shouldn't the chairwoman of the pilgrimage be in the group photographs?" he asked in a low voice, looking straight at Amber's mother.

The breath hissed from between Lily's teeth, but she nodded stiffly. To Amber's astonishment, Logan turned and called to his mother. "They're ready for you now, Mama."

Logan's *mother* was the chairwoman of the pilgrimage? *The* Gigi Van Dell? Wow. How had that happened? "Mama?"

"Later." That one word brought back so many memories. Sometimes later came, but more often it didn't because Amber and her sister would forget all about whatever had triggered their curiosity. This time she'd remember to ask.

"Where shall I stand?" Gigi shined her smile at the photographer.

"How about next to Mrs. Madison? It will make a good frame."

Gigi stood next to Amber's mother, dwarfing the older woman. Logan's mother must be six feet tall, Amber thought, seeing that her father was practically on his toes trying to match her height.

The photographer gestured. "Move in closer, please."

"Well, let's all get cozy!" Gigi squeezed toward the middle and slung her arm around Lily's waist.

Amber felt her mother stiffen and knew she wouldn't relax until the photo session was over.

Come to think of it, neither would she.

LOGAN WAS COMPLETELY and utterly fascinated. Yeah, and irritated that Lily Madison was ignoring his mother, but what a show they were putting on. He had to admire the way they milked that key-to-the-city bit. Politics at its best.

And Amber...he'd never seen this side of her, this fake-smiling, dutiful political daughter. He didn't get it, either. Amber hadn't been back in eight years and her parents acted as though she'd only spent a week-end at the beach.

It was as though he was looking at a synthetic family, one manufactured by the media.

Guilt pricked the edges of his conscience at the grim set to Amber's mouth and the way she slipped into a plastic shell so she'd match her plastic parents.

In watching the interaction between Amber and her mother, and the complete lack of meaningful contact with her father—the man had nearly fainted when he was kissed by his own daughter—Logan began to understand what had driven her away from Belle Rive. So why had she wanted to come back? Logan would have sworn that Amber, in spite of the uncaring front she presented to the world, had desperately wanted to come back. If she hadn't, he wouldn't have been able to blackmail her. She wouldn't have cared. But she cared a lot, unless he missed his guess. Logan didn't miss many guesses.

His gaze slid to his mother. Sure, she had the posing bit down pat, too, but her smiles were real. He watched as she put her arm around Lily Madison's waist and urged everyone to get cozy. When they were all squeezed together, she winked at him.

Reluctantly he grinned back, knowing that his mother was aware that she was in Lily's personal space and that Lily didn't like it.

Gigi hammed it up for the camera, while the Madisons maintained the stilted pose they'd perfected years ago.

Logan's eyes sought Amber, as they'd done all afternoon.

She gazed back at him, expressionless. She was smiling, but there was nothing in it. With a wave of uneasiness, Logan realized that she'd stepped back into her old life much faster than he'd expected, and more completely than he wanted.

So THAT WAS THE DEAL. Gigi Van Dell was chairman of the pilgrimage and Amber Madison was Magnolia Queen. Logan had achieved the impossible.

Amber hoped he was satisfied. She wanted to have been angrier at him but knew that she had as much to do with her current situation as he did.

She'd wanted to come home—had allowed herself into being blackmailed into coming home, or the home she'd hoped to find. Why had she thought anything would be different? Because she'd been gone for eight years? Because her mother finally had a daughter as Magnolia Queen? Because her father was getting free publicity? Because Logan...because Logan had triggered memories of a time when she'd been happy?

Because, in spite of all evidence to the contrary, she'd felt a faint tug from the past and thought he'd felt it, too?

When would she learn that inner tugs were almost always hunger and nothing more?

She could end it all right here at the airport: announce the details of her flop of a life in front of the reporter, resign as queen and give back the roses while they were still fresh enough to be presented to another lucky queen.

Except, how would she get back to New York? She didn't have a ticket and no one here was likely to lend her the money, considering she'd be leaving them without a queen for the pilgrimage.

Yeah, she was stuck here for the next two weeks, until she could be sent back to New York in queenly splendor.

The photo session ended and Lily waylaid the reporter, handing him her official press releases for the pilgrimage.

"Oh, I made some notes, too." Gigi pulled bright pink paper from her tiny handbag.

"What is that?" Lily grabbed at the papers.

Gigi held them out of reach. "Information for the newspaper."

"That's Azalea Pilgrimage letterhead!"

"We've got tons of this pink paper—you don't want it to go to waste, do you?"

Conscious of the press, Lily said carefully, "It might be confusing to have information coming from more than one source."

"Oh, pooh." Gigi scribbled across the top of the papers. "There. Problem solved."

Wincing, Lily still managed a smile as Gigi added her hand-written papers in azalea pink to Lily's laser-printed pages in white vellum.

"So Mrs. Van Dell is the coordinator this year?" the reporter asked Lily and not Gigi.

"That is correct."

"And you are...?"

"I'm..." Lily's face went blank.

"She's the queen's mother, of course!" Gigi inter-jected.

"Yes, but what is her official capacity this year?"

Lily's mouth worked, but Gigi again answered. "Why, she's the mayor's wife and the queen's mother, and is on a whole bunch of committees—just how much do you expect the woman to do, anyway?" Gigi put her arm around Lily's waist. "This is her year to enjoy."

Forced to lean closer or stumble noticeably, Lily demonstrated her years of politicking by turning the situation to her own advantage. "Yes, I wouldn't want to miss one minute of my daughter's reign as queen. I remember when *I* was queen and my own mama..."

"Amazing," Amber murmured beneath her breath.

"It is," said a low voice beside her.

She hadn't been aware of Logan's approach. "I've heard this story before," Amber told him. "I'm going to get my luggage."

"The driver took care of that. It's in the limo."

"Thanks." Amber met his eyes, wondering why she wasn't angrier with him. It couldn't be just his looks, though he was admittedly good-looking in an appeal-ingly raw, polished way.

He reminded Amber of the rough beauty of some

precious stones in their natural state. There was a point in the cutting and polishing process when the precious stone still had some of the rock attached to it. Amber preferred the gems in this state rather than in their faceted yet sterile perfection.

That was Logan, she thought. He'd had all the polishing he needed. There was the smooth glitter revealing the value, along with enough roughness to keep it interesting. It was the roughness that made him genuine, as opposed to her parents who were all highly polished faux glitter.

"I imagine you're pretty pleased with yourself," she said.

"It was just luggage. That's his job."

"I'm talking about the pilgrimage deal you worked out, and you know it."

Logan continued watching the ongoing discussion with the reporter. "The key to my deals is finding out what people want most and making sure they get it, even if they lose something else in the process. That way everyone wins something."

"Even if it's the booby prize?"

He looked down at her. "If they want a booby prize, then that's what they'll get."

Her anger was growing a little now. "So you came to New York, checked out my apartment and decided I needed a booby prize? Gee, *thanks.*"

His eyes were dark. She'd known that, but she'd mostly been with him at night and, strangely, they'd been lighter then than they were now. She hadn't realized how black and unfathomable they could be.

"We weren't talking about you," he said.

"Weren't we?"

•

Logan shook his head. "You wanted to come home. You came home."

"I—" Ready to deny it, she broke off. As far as it went, he was correct. "I just didn't want to come home to *this* home."

"Is there another one?"

The reporter was headed her way. Behind him her mother gestured. Amber automatically smiled. "I guess not."

"LOGAN, LET ME RIDE HOME with you and not in the limo with that awful woman and her puppet of a husband."

"Don't let her get to you," Logan reassured his mother.

Gigi tossed her hair. "She doesn't *get* to me. She's never gotten to me. Your grandmother is another story. It's a good thing she isn't here or there'd be blood on the pavement by now."

"You're in charge of the pilgrimage, not Lily Madison. She'll take over if you let her."

"I don't know how to stop her! People just automatically look to her."

"Mama." Logan waited until he had his mother's attention. "The problem is that you're trying to run Lily Madison's pilgrimage instead of making your own. I do believe there are certain traditions that you ought to follow, but do what you want with the rest of it. Shuffle everything around. Break up the committees. Mix in the azalea folks. People are going to have to come to you if Lily doesn't know the drill."

"I can't do that this close to the beginning of the home tour!"

"Sure you can. You're in charge. You can do anything you want."

Gigi beamed at him. "How did you get so smart?"

"It's not so much about being smart as about having common sense." His mother was smart enough, but because of her striking looks and former profession, people discounted what she had to say and there were times when she encouraged it, to his irritation. His grandmother might be the guiltiest of all in that respect. Ever since Gigi and Logan had come to live with her, she'd ragged on her daughter-in-law.

Logan couldn't figure out why his mother had stayed all these years. His father must have left her *some* money. But maybe not, and now, since she and his grandmother had been running the bed-and-breakfast together, Logan figured she was there for good. It occurred to him that if Lily Madison accepted his mother, then his grandmother might soften toward her, as well. If that happened, then he'd have made the best deal of his career.

"Go on," he urged her. "Get in the limo."

"Okay." She gave him a look. "But only because I want the opportunity to get to know that cute Amber Madison. I like her style. Imagine wearing black on her first appearance as queen." Gigi smiled and shook her head. "That took guts. I think I'll reward her by distracting her parents."

"Mama," Logan warned.

"Don't worry." She actually reached up and pinched his cheek.

Logan gave her a reluctant smile. "Just don't be too distracting."

"I'll behave." His mother tossed her hair and walked

toward the limo. She was doing her showgirl strut. The mayor and his wife noticed—and the wife noticed the mayor noticing.

Logan gloomily watched the group get into the limo. Every instinct told him that this was a disaster in the making. Should he pretend that his car wasn't racking up a big parking bill in the short-term lot and ask for a ride? No, better follow the limo all the way into Belle Rive in case somebody got thrown out by the side of the road.

A leg appeared in the door. Great. They'd already started ditching passengers. Logan stopped at the entrance to the lot and watched as Amber got out, followed by Gigi. Then Amber got back in, then stormed out again, followed by her mother. Lily pointed and Amber snapped, "Are you sure?"

"Yes. I think that way we'll all be more comfortable," Lily said.

Amber climbed back in, followed by his mother, then Lily. The driver shut the door.

Logan took a deep breath. It was going to be a long two weeks.

5

"WE THOUGHT a pale pink would be the perfect color—
mixing the white of the magnolia with the hot pink of
the azalea. Rather symbolic, don't you agree?" Lily
Madison asked the room at large as she held up a color
swatch.

"It ought to be more of a blush," Amelia Jasper commented.

"This is the lightest shade, but Grishams said they
would be willing to formulate a special color for us."

"Oh, I like that!" Mrs. Jasper exclaimed to general
agreement.

"I do, too," Lily said. "We can call it Magnolia Blush
and it'll be exclusive to us."

They were talking about ribbons and napkins and
who knew what else. Amber had sat through the mind-
numbing "emergency" decorations committee meeting for the past hour and was ready to declare an all-
denim pilgrimage and see what happened.

"Grishams is being quite accommodating, considering that this will be a rush order," her mother said. "I
don't know what we would have done if they hadn't
called to inquire why we hadn't placed our order this
year. But after all, Mrs. Van Dell can't be expected to
think of every little detail."

"The ball decorations and pilgrimage wreaths can

hardly be called 'little'!" Mrs. Jasper made the comment Amber knew her mother had hoped for.

"I'm sure she's doing the best she can." Lily made it sound as though Logan's mother's "best" could only aspire to adequacy. "I'm just happy I could take care of this detail for her—even though the additional rush charges will affect the profits from the pilgrimage."

Oh, clever. If taxes had to be raised this year because the pilgrimage hadn't made enough money, Mayor Reginald Madison would just remind everyone that Gigi Van Dell had been in charge. Amber toyed with the idea of warning Logan, but then abandoned it. Had he warned her?

You didn't need warning, a little voice said.

"Oh, shut up."

"Amber?"

Everyone was looking her way.

"Did you say something?" her mother asked.

"Did I?" Maybe no one heard. "I'm going to have more lemonade. May I get some for anyone else?"

How wicked she was. The forced polite smiles as everyone desperately hoped enough lemonade had evaporated from their cups so they could take more and not offend Lily—it was great.

"I'd like some more." Mrs. Jasper smiled, her small eyes bright. Mrs. Jasper was still ever hopeful that Lily Madison would single her out for special attention. How many gallons of the horrible lemonade had she put away over the years?

Lots, since she had some each time she paid a call on Lily. Funny thing, after those visits, Lily always seemed to know Amber's and Stephanie's latest social transgressions. Amber was surprised Mrs. Jasper hadn't made her way up to New York.

Amber took the woman's cup and made her way to the punch table. Dipping the ladle and refilling the cup as full as she could, she gave it back. Everyone watched in fascinated sympathy as Amelia Jasper took a sip and swallowed.

Amber refilled her own cup with Bertha's lemonade, then snitched sugar from the coffee service.

It had been a very long and interesting day. The limo ride with Gigi Van Dell into Belle Rive had been the most interesting of all—even more than seeing her mother's blood pressure sky rocket when the Belle Rive High School Marching Rebel Band played "New York, New York" instead of "Dixie." That had been great. There had been an overly innocent expression on Gigi Van Dell's face that made Amber suspect that she'd had something to do with the musical selection.

Amber liked Logan's mother, mostly because it was obvious that she wasn't afraid of or impressed by Amber's parents. Her mother's arsenal of expressions of subtle disapproval washed right over Gigi Van Dell. One might think she was oblivious and one would be wrong. It was clear to Amber that her mother had met her match in the manipulation department. In any case, Gigi deflected her mother's attention and allowed Amber an hour of peace before arriving at the Belle Rive museum.

Logan was already there, holding a parasol over a tiny white-haired woman in a wooden folding chair whom Amber recognized as the charismatic Camille Van Dell, his grandmother. She was wearing an azalea-pink suit and wide-brimmed hat and looked more regal than Amber could ever hope to. Impulsively, Amber left the line of pilgrimage dignitaries and went over to Camille.

"Hi, Logan. Would you introduce me to your grandmother?"

His eyes warmed and fired an answering warmth in her. "Grandmama, I'd like you to meet Amber Madison, this year's Magnolia Queen."

"So you're Amber Madison." Blue eyes twinkled at her. "Well done, Logan."

Well done, *Logan*? "I hear you've become quite a success in New York," Camille said to her.

Oh, right. Well done, Logan. Amber flashed him a chagrined look. "New York has its moments."

Nodding to the group behind her, Camille reached for her hand. "We'll chat another time. I believe they're waiting for you."

Before she turned to go, Amber pulled a white rose from her bouquet and presented it to Camille. As she did so, there was a flash, followed by several more from the crowd and a smattering of applause as Amber returned to the gathered dignitaries.

"Amber," her mother said in a low voice.

"Where's *my* grandmother?" Amber cut her off in an equally low voice.

Her mother's face tightened as though it might crack. "With friends," she managed to say through gritted teeth.

"But—"

"Later."

The April sun was hot, especially if a person was wearing black wool, which Amber was. Nevertheless, she smiled her bright red smile, used the oversize silver scissors to cut the ribbon across the archway leading to the museum gardens and declared the pilgrimage under way.

During all of this, Logan worked the crowd like a pro. They flocked around Camille and whenever Amber glanced his way, he was talking and smiling with yet another group of people. Since when did he know so many people in Belle Rive?

Well, he was a Van Dell, she reminded herself. Everybody knew the Van Dells whether or not they'd admit to it. Since she'd left home, apparently a lot more people were admitting to it.

"Well, what does our queen have to say about it?" one of the committee women asked, jarring Amber back into the present.

All eyes in the room were trained on her. She smiled her best queenly smile, lips slightly puckered from the lemonade. "I'm sure whatever you decide will be lovely."

"Does it go with your gown?"

Amber actually saw part of her life flash before her eyes, then sparkly colors danced at the darkening edges of her vision. The queen was expected to wear a ball gown with an elaborately decorated train, embroidered and beaded in symbols important in her life. A coronation dress. Since there weren't many places to wear a coronation outfit, it was hard to buy one off the rack, not that Amber could afford to buy one anyway.

It wasn't as though she'd forgotten that she'd need a dress, but her plan was to drive into Louisiana where there was a shop that handled vintage Mardi Gras finery and rent a dress and train. She was hoping to find something that didn't have the telltale Mardi Gras col-

ors of purple, gold and green. She was hoping even
more to do it without her mother finding out.

"What color is your dress?"

"It's—" She'd started to say "a surprise" when her
mother broke in.

"It's antique white satin, of course. Her grandmother wore the dress when she was queen, I wore it
when I was queen, and Amber will wear it now that
she's queen. For her reign we'll add a border to the
stole and train, just as we did for me. I thought we'd
use an amber color because of her name and because it
echoes the brown on the underside of the magnolia
leaf. My color was forest-green, for that very reason."

"Oh, how lovely." There were other agreeable mur-
murers.

Amber gripped the edge of the punch table because
her knees were shaking. She felt light-headed with relief. "Mama, I'm going to refill the lemonade." She
picked up the heavy silver punch bowl and sloshed her
way into the kitchen, where she set the monstrosity on
the tiled counter next to the sink and then collapsed
onto a kitchen chair.

Saved. She was saved. It took three deep breaths for
her heart rate to slow.

Amber was still recovering when she heard the back
door creak open. Jerking around, she saw her grandmother sneaking into the kitchen.

"Memaw!"

"Shh!" Mary Alice Newhouse held a finger to her
lips and set down an overnight bag. Straightening, she
opened her arms.

Amber ran to give her grandmother a hug. "Trying
to avoid the decorating committee?" she whispered.

"Oh, Amber, child, it's so good to see you again."

For long minutes Amber hugged her grandmother and inhaled the familiar scent of her talcum powder. Memaw had lost weight and seemed frailer than the woman Amber remembered.

"Where have you been? You missed my big moment."

Memaw pulled back and eyed Amber shrewdly. "Didn't think you'd show. Last I heard, you'd rather eat a bug than be Magnolia Queen."

Amber gave her a wry smile. "So maybe I ate a few bugs and decided I didn't like the taste."

"Would I be a traitor if I admitted that I'm glad?"

Giving her grandmother's shoulders a quick squeeze, Amber laughed. "No. I can imagine what the talk is. 'That Amber Madison...putting it about that she'd never be queen, yet when the call came, she was just like any of us.' Is that about it?"

Memaw smiled. "That would be the polite version."

Amber made a face. "That bad?"

"Since when did you care about talk?"

If you only knew. "I guess I'm just like any of you."

Shaking her head, Memaw picked up her satchel. "Don't disappoint me, child."

"Memaw—"

Her grandmother held up a hand and headed for the kitchen stairs. "In the morning. I've got to get my sleep if I'm going to get up in time to fight Bertha for the privilege of making you your favorite biscuits for breakfast."

Amber gave a mock gasp. "Oh, then please go sleep! Bertha is a dear, but I hope you win."

Her grandmother chuckled. "It is good to have you

back. The house has been quiet with both you girls gone."

"I noticed Stephanie hasn't been by."

"Stephanie is doing penance in Natchez."

"Doesn't sound like much of a penance to me."

"Especially not when you meet her husband. He's almost too much of a man for one woman."

"Memaw!"

"Reminds me of Logan Van Dell."

At Amber's expression, her grandmother laughed softly and continued up the stairs.

Logan Van Dell. Why did her grandmother mention Logan? Did she know...? Of course not. No one knew. Amber had been too good at sneaking out.

In the background, sounds of the committee meeting rose and fell, indistinct, except for her mother's voice.

Amber couldn't bear to go back into the room. She glanced at the punch bowl and knew that no one would bother to draw attention to its absence.

Did she dare? She'd been very good all day. She deserved a reward.

Silently, Amber followed her grandmother up the back stairs into her old room. It had been converted into a guest room, but someone—her grandmother? Bertha?—had left a few of Amber's childhood possessions around, along with her debutante dresses encased in long plastic bags.

Amber opened her suitcase and hung up the clothes she'd brought. Black and beige. Her mother would have a fit. Underneath everything, Amber found the jeans she had been looking for and quickly pulled them on, along with battered tennis shoes and a T-shirt with a picture of a rock group that had long since broken up that had been left in her drawer.

She carefully stepped into the hallway, remembering to avoid the creaking board just in time, and gently pulled her door closed.

"Want to borrow the keys to my Cadillac?"

Amber started.

Framed in her doorway at the end of the hall, her grandmother dangled a set of car keys.

Amber grinned. "I love you, Memaw."

LOGAN SIPPED HIS BEER and stared at the moon's rippling reflection in the cold water spring. The more things changed, the more they stayed the same.

Amber Madison.

He'd been twenty. She'd been eighteen. Life took them in different directions and he'd neither tried to remember nor tried to forget her. She had been a part of his life and he recognized his role in hers for what it had been. Amber was rebelling and he'd been part of that rebellion. He was the forbidden. It had always puzzled him, though, why she'd been so careful when she met him. It seemed the object would be to get caught so her parents could forbid her to see him. Then she could keep doing it, anyway.

And what had she been to him?

Logan tipped his beer back. At first he'd been attracted to her because of who her family was. The way her mother treated his mother had angered him and being with Amber was a way of getting back at the Madisons.

He hadn't meant to fall for her, but what twenty-year-old male could be around a pretty girl and not fall for her?

However, now that eight years had passed what was his excuse? Nostalgia? He wasn't sentimental. Beauty? This older Amber was a little gaunt for his tastes and her expressions were sharper—edgier, with an underlying wariness that living in the city had given her. He liked his women soft and round and willing.

Amber had never been soft and round, but she had been willing—willing to get back at her parents. And Logan, to his surprise, found that he wanted Amber to want him for himself, not because she knew her parents would disapprove.

Had she ever considered him as something more than a way to annoy her parents?

And had he ever thought of her as anything more, either?

Yeah, he had. He knew, because he hadn't wanted to feel more. A man acted the fool when he started feeling more than he should. At that stage in their lives, he had nothing to offer her and she had nothing to give.

What about now?

Hell, he didn't know how he felt, then or now. Maybe if he'd gone ahead and slept with her, she would have become just another ex-girlfriend.

But he'd never know, would he?

Standing, Logan walked over to the tree house, set his beer on the floor above his head, and tested the boards he'd nailed to the trunk to use as a ladder. The bottom one broke off, but the rest held his weight. He climbed until he was waist-high with the floor.

He'd used treated lumber for the floor, and it had held up okay over the years. It had been years since he'd climbed up here to check it out, generally being content to sit on the rock. He jiggled the boards and noted with satisfaction that they were still tight and solid.

The property had once belonged to the old battery plant that was on the other side of a stand of trees. He'd come out here all the time before Amber, and then with her. He'd never brought anyone else here, male or female.

A couple of years after she'd left, some local kids had stumbled onto the place and had trashed the tree house pretty good, but Logan had rebuilt it, not even knowing why he'd done so. Since then, he didn't think anybody else had been here.

It was a place you had to want to find, since the battery plant, now the spiffed-up computer power supply plant, wasn't near anything else in Belle Rive. It was down by the river on a road that led only to it.

Logan wouldn't have found the place except that he'd gone for an unexpected long walk. It had been the time when the guys on the football team had been passing around an old publicity photo of his mother wearing nothing more than feathers and sequins. Logan had seen it before—his mother had it in her scrapbook after it had been published in the Belle Rive *Mirror* shortly after they'd moved to Belle Rive. When she'd seen it, his grandmother had gone to her room and hadn't come out for two days.

"I was wearing that costume when I met your daddy," his mother had told him. The young Logan had thought she was the most beautiful woman he'd ever seen. No wonder his father had fallen in love with her.

Hearing the sniggers of his friends had shamed him. He'd thrown his helmet at them and then, fists flying, had tried to take on the entire team. Coach had sent him to the principal's office, but Logan had walked right past the office and kept walking until he found this place.

He hoisted himself onto the platform and drained the rest of his beer. He was still taking on the entire team, only this time he wasn't using his fists.

No Trespassing.

Well, that was new. The headlights of Amber's grandmother's Cadillac illuminated not only a sign but a chain-link fence to go with it. There hadn't been any barriers when she'd come here with Logan.

Where there was a fence, there was usually a hole somebody had made to climb through. She could follow along the line until she found an opening, except the old Caddy wasn't exactly an off-road vehicle. Of course she was already off-road and hoping that the ground wasn't so damp that she'd get stuck in the mud. Right now she was okay, but any nearer to the river, and she wouldn't be. Amber drove the car into the shadows, climbed out and approached the fence.

She wasn't much of a climber, but there wasn't any barbed wire on the top, so she thought she'd give it a try. She stuck the toe of her tennis shoe in one of the holes as far as it would go and hoisted herself up. She got about two feet off the ground before her toe slipped out and she slithered down. Standing on the hood of the car would work, but then, how would she get back over from the other side?

She checked the fence a few feet in either direction

and discovered that there was a gate behind the sign. Just how strong was the lock, anyway? Amber braced herself, grabbed the horseshoe-shaped latch and jerked upward as hard as she could.

It shot up, smashing her thumb in the process.

She gasped in pain, then had to settle for fiercely whispered swearing.

Great. So the gate wasn't even locked. Figured. She pushed it open and headed toward the cold spring, hoping the clearing wasn't all overgrown. She was going to dunk her throbbing thumb in the icy water.

The path was still there, but not nearly as worn as when she and Logan had met here. A nearly full moon spilled silver patches between the shadows, but just in case, Amber had brought a flashlight. She flipped it on just as soon as she was far enough into the trees to avoid being seen by anyone passing by, not that that was likely. Still, Logan had said that the battery plant had changed hands. Maybe the new owners were more diligent about patrolling their property. They'd gone to all the trouble to post signs, after all.

Amber picked her way through the weeds, beginning to have second thoughts. She was alone in the middle of nowhere, having a nostalgia attack. For all she knew, others had discovered Logan's secret place, others who might be there even now.

Or the whole place could be a thicket of weeds. She and Logan had clipped the grass around the edge of the pool and had collected river stones to pave the edge and make a path to the tree house so they could walk without getting their feet muddy.

Amber stopped abruptly. She'd been walking too long. She shone the flashlight all around her and strained to find any familiar landmarks. Was she still on the path?

She was about to turn around and go back when her flashlight caught a reflection of something. At first she didn't recognize it for what it was—water. It must be the pool. Amber left the path, such as it was, and headed for the gleam.

A few hundred feet later she found the clearing. She'd never approached it from this direction before, but sure enough, there was the pool.

It didn't look too overgrown, and she was more relieved than she'd expected to be. She was on the far side of the clearing and headed toward the flat rock where she and Logan had sat and dangled their feet in the cold water.

Amber turned off her flashlight, finding that the moonlight was more than bright enough. She'd always liked the way the light filtered through the Spanish moss on the trees and made lacy patterns in the water.

Amber shivered and crouched on the rock, dipping her sore thumb into the cold water. It immediately felt better. Sighing, she stretched out on her stomach and dangled her hand in the water, listening to the gentle lapping and faint bubbling as the cold spring fed the pool. The rock still held a faint warmth from today's sun. That summer with Logan, she remembered that the rock was sometimes so hot they had to splash it with water from the pool.

The tension drained from her shoulders and the echoes of her mother's instructions faded from her ears.

She shouldn't let her mother bother her so much. She'd agreed to be queen and she'd known there were a lot of activities and appearances that went with the

MILLS & BOON®

An Important Message from The Editors of Mills & Boon®

Dear Reader,

Because you've chosen to read one of our romance novels, we'd like to say "thank you"!

And, as a **special way** to thank you, we've selected <u>two more</u> of the <u>books</u> you love so much **and** a welcome gift to send you absolutely <u>FREE!</u>

Please enjoy them with our compliments...

Tessa Shapcott

Editor, Mills & Boon

P.S. And because we value our customers we've attached something extra inside...

EDITOR'S "THANK YOU" SEAL

PEEL OFF AND PLACE INSIDE

How to validate your Editor's Free Gift "Thank You"

1. **Peel off the Free Gift Seal** from the front cover. Place it in the space provided to the right. This automatically entitles you to receive two free books and a beautiful gold-plated Austrian crystal necklace.

2. **Complete your details** on the card, detach along the dotted line, and post it back to us. No stamp needed. We'll then send you two free novels from the Sensual Romance™ series. These books have a retail value of £2.49, but are yours to keep absolutely free.

3. **Enjoy the read.** We hope that after receiving your free books you'll want to remain a subscriber. But the choice is yours - to continue or cancel, any time at all! So why not accept our no risk invitation? You'll be glad you did.

Your satisfaction is guaranteed

You're under no obligation to buy anything. We charge you nothing for your introductory parcel. And you don't have to make any minimum number of purchases – not even one! Thousands of readers have already discovered that the Reader Service™ is the most convenient way of enjoying the latest new romance novels before they are available in the shops. Of course, postage and packing to your home is completely FREE.

Tessa Shapcott
Editor, Mills & Boon

The Editor's "Thank You"

You'll love this exquisite gold-plated necklace with its 46cm (8") cobra linked chain and multi-faceted Austrian crystal which sparkles just like a diamond. It's the perfect accessory to dress up any outfit, casual or formal. RESPOND TODAY AND IT'S YOURS FREE.

Not actual size

◄ Detach along the dotted line and post this card today. No Stamp Needed ▶

Yes! Please send me my two FREE books and a welcome gift

PLACE EDITOR'S "THANK YOU" SEAL HERE

Yes! I have placed my free gift seal in the space provided above. Please send me my two free books along with my welcome gift. I understand I am under no obligation to purchase any books, as explained on the back and opposite page. I am over 18 years of age.

T1FI

BLOCK CAPITALS

Surname (Mrs/Ms/Miss/Mr) _____Initials_____

Address _____

_____

_____

_____Postcode _____

◄ Detach and keep your complimentary book mark. ▶

HOW THE READER SERVICE™ WORKS

Accepting the free books places you under no obligation to buy anything. You may keep the books and gift and return the despatch note marked "cancel". If we don't hear from you, about a month later we will send you 4 brand new books and invoice you for only £2.49* each. That's the complete price – there is no extra charge for postage and packing. You may cancel at any time, otherwise every month we'll send you 4 more books, which you may either purchase or return – the choice is yours.

*Terms and prices subject to change without notice.

The Reader Service™
FREEPOST CN81
CROYDON
CR9 3WZ

NO
STAMP
NEEDED

If this offer card is missing, please write to: The Reader Service, P.O. Box 236, Croydon, CR9 position. She should be able to handle being the center of Belle Rive society for two weeks. It was only for two weeks, not a lifetime.

It meant everything to her mother that one of her daughters was queen, so Amber resolved to do it up right. She'd smile and she'd schmooze and she'd be so gracious and friendly to tourists that Belle Rive would get a lot of repeat business.

Now that her thumb had stopped throbbing, Amber was enjoying the serenity of the place. The only times she'd ever been here alone had been the rare occasions when she'd beaten Logan here, and then it was only for a few minutes.

More often than not, Logan was waiting with chilled cola or, later on, beer or wine.

Just for fun, Amber scooted as far out on the rock as she could, rolled up her T-shirt sleeve and thrust her arm deep into the water under the rock. There were two bottles there!

Laughing in delighted surprise, Amber brought one out. "I wonder how long you've been there?" she asked out loud, turning the bottle so she could read the label in the moonlight.

There was a soft thud. "About an hour."

Amber started as a dark figure emerged from the shadows by the tree house. Every horror film she'd ever seen flashed through her mind. Out here alone and no one knew it—she was a poster girl for stupidity. She repositioned the beer bottle in her hand, ready to use it as a weapon.

The man stopped just at the edge of a patch of moonlight. "Hello, Amber. Welcome home."

6

ADRENALINE SPRITZED through her body before she recognized Logan. "You scared me!"

"I've been trying to figure out a way to let you know I was here without scaring you."

"Dropping out of the tree house *isn't* the way."

"Sorry." Logan reached for the bottle she held, twisted off the cap and handed it back to her.

Amber took a long swallow and noticed that her hand still trembled.

Well, maybe that wasn't entirely from being startled.

Like Amber, Logan had changed into jeans, but he still wore a white shirt with the collar open and the sleeves rolled up. It was a mix of the "then" Logan and the "now" Logan. An appealing mix.

He stretched out on the rock and retrieved another beer, just the way he'd done on countless nights long ago.

They sat on the rock in a surprisingly comfortable silence and watched clouds chase their way across the moon.

"This is nice," Logan said after a while.

"It was always nice."

"The silence, I mean. You used to talk a lot."

She had—constant whining and complaining and dreaming. "I'm kind of talked out after today."

She felt, rather than saw, his smile.

"I didn't expect you to come here," he said.

"Neither did I."

There was another silence. Then he asked, "Why did you come?"

"Why did you?" Amber countered.

"This has always been my thinking place, you know that."

"Yeah. I should have known a little thing like trespassing wouldn't stop you."

Logan sipped his beer. "Who's trespassing?"

Amber laughed. "We are."

"*You* are." He turned to her, his expression hidden in shadow. "I own this property."

"You *do?*"

"Yeah."

Amber was so surprised, she didn't know how she felt. "How? When?"

"It was my fee for negotiating the battery plant deal. Remember, in my deals, everybody gets what he wants."

"And you wanted this place? Why?"

Logan let several heartbeats go by before he answered. "I like it. I'm thinking about building a house out here someday."

She nodded toward the platform in the tree. "You already built a house out here."

Logan looked over his shoulder and smiled. "I'm talking about a real house. A big white one with columns and a circular drive and my name over a wrought-iron gate."

"In other words, Van Dell House Junior?"

"Maybe."

"Not to be morbid, or anything, but won't you inherit the real thing someday?"

He nodded. "But Van Dell House is a full-fledged B and B now, listed in the Historic Register and all that. I wouldn't want to go to all the trouble to turn it back into a private residence. Besides, my mother and grandmother are having a blast running the place. They'll never retire. To them, it's a continuous house party. I have a town house, but..." He looked around. "I'd rather live here."

"But there's nothing out here."

Logan gestured. "*This* is out here."

Amber exhaled. "It's so quiet. I'd forgotten how quiet the night could be."

"The night's not quiet. It's full of life going about its business. Listen."

Amber held her breath and heard the lapping of the water against the rock and the faint burbling of the spring. Water bugs plinked into the pool and scooted across the surface as a breeze combed through tendrils of Spanish moss. Amber didn't consider herself a "nature girl," but a sense of peace stole over her and she relaxed in a way that she hadn't for years.

"I haven't heard anything like this in a long while," she whispered. "From my apartment, I hear traffic. All the time, day and night."

"They say New York is the city that never sleeps."

"They're right."

Logan propped his beer in the earth by the rock and leaned back on his elbows. The moonlight made his shirt gleam blue-white as it stretched across his chest. It looked like a pose straight out of the macho-man-at-rest school.

He probably knew exactly how good he looked, too.

Amber drank her beer and ignored the good-looking man lounging next to her.

The good-looking man didn't want to be ignored. "Why *did* you come here tonight?" he asked.

She grinned. "To see if I could still sneak out." Her bottle was empty, so she set it aside and mimicked Logan's position. That hurt her elbows, so she lay down, sighing as the gentle curve of the rock fit perfectly in her back. Spas would pay a fortune for this rock.

"Obviously you've still got the touch."

"Nope. Memaw caught me."

"What did she say?"

"She lent me her car."

Deep laughter rumbled in his chest and he lazily shifted his position until he was propped on one elbow.

Amber could feel him watching her. Faint warning alarms went off and she immediately disconnected them. She and Logan were here in their old meeting place. This was where they'd spent hours kissing and nuzzling. He was obligated to make a pass. If he didn't, it would be insulting to her, and to the memory of this place. Besides she was curious to see if there might be any of the old magic left. Logan must be wondering, too.

So, Amber knew a pass was coming.

The only question was when.

HOW SOON could he kiss her? Logan wondered. Because he *was* going to kiss her, he'd known it ever since he'd decided to come down out of the tree house.

No. He'd known it ever since he'd held her when she cried in New York.

The only question was when.

That was the tricky part. Kissing Amber, especially here, sent a definite message. But until he was absolutely clear what the message was, he'd better keep his lips to himself.

He studied her face in the moonlight as she watched the night sky. Hollows shaded her cheekbones and her eyes were larger than he remembered. Yes, Amber had changed, and not just physically. She'd never been able to stay quiet for long and while he'd enjoyed listening to her talk, he'd also appreciated the silences, like tonight.

Back then, she'd talked endlessly about getting out of Belle Rive, telling him how wonderful her life was going to be when she did. He noticed she wasn't talking about how wonderful her life in New York was now. She hadn't said a word about her jewelry, or her job, or friends—male or female—or anything. It must be worse than he imagined.

But she wasn't talking about giving up and moving back here, either.

Logan thought about today: the stilted greeting with her parents, the endless photographs and her relentless red-lipped smiling. He wondered if she hated him for bringing her back. She'd done a good job with all the queen stuff, though. He remembered the rose she'd given his grandmother and how Camille had carefully put the white flower in her best crystal bud vase once she'd gone home. And he'd seen Lily's disapproving face when Amber rejoined the officials and knew that breaking away had been her own idea.

"Thank you for acknowledging my grandmother today," he said, wanting to explain how much it had meant to both of them, but not wanting to make a huge deal out of it.

"She's run the Azalea Pilgrimage for years. She deserved to be acknowledged. I would have done the same thing for *my* grandmother, if she'd been there."

Logan heard the hurt in Amber's voice and wondered if her grandmother was ill. But she didn't say, so maybe being queen meant more to her than she was letting on and her grandmother had just missed an important day in her life. "Are you enjoying any of this, or do you hate me for bringing you back?"

"I'm not *enjoying* it, but I don't hate it as much as I thought I would." She laughed softly. "Or as much as I *want* to."

"And me?"

She gave him a wry smile. "I don't hate you, Logan."

Something uncurled within him. "I'm glad."

Amber turned her head so that her cheek rested on the rock. "Why?"

Why, indeed. Logan didn't know the answer, much less want to think of it, so he hedged. "It would mean that you weren't happy with the deal and in my deals—"

"People get what they want. Yeah, so you've said." She turned her head back and stared at the sky.

Damn. He'd just missed the perfect opportunity to kiss her.

He wasn't usually romantically clumsy so maybe it hadn't been such a perfect time, after all. He rolled onto his back and joined Amber in stargazing.

Perhaps he'd better give kissing her more thought.

For instance, was it going to be just a kiss, or a prelude to more? They were adults now and his best kisses were prelude kisses, but he didn't want to presume too much. Besides, he wasn't prepared for a prelude to anything. Yet, he had enough pride to want to guarantee that any comparisons she made between his kisses now and his kisses then showed some progress on his part. If he gave her an old-time's-sake kiss, it wouldn't rate much on the hot scale.

If he gave her a prelude kiss and she only gave him a polite kiss back, that would be embarrassing.

Maybe the best way to go here was a quick, old-time's-sake kiss with a little taste of prelude at the end, just as he broke away. Leave her wanting more. Yeah. That could work. If all went well, he'd break away a few inches and she'd melt toward him and then he could segue right into a full-fledged prelude kiss.

If all went *really* well, it actually would be a prelude kiss. Unfortunately, not toni—

"When are you going to kiss me?"

Logan didn't move. He had to make very sure he'd actually heard what he thought he'd heard.

Amber propped herself up on an elbow. "And don't bother denying that you want to. I can practically *hear* you thinking about it."

Logan kept staring at stars. "Yeah, I'm thinking about it."

"Then why haven't you kissed me?"

"I wasn't sure you wanted to be kissed."

She laughed. "I can't believe Lover Lips Logan said that."

His eyes jerked toward hers. "*Lover Lips?*"

Amber nodded.

"Was that…was that your pet name for me or something?"

"Don't tell me you didn't know that's what all the girls called you. Well, most of the girls."

He *hadn't* heard. "What did the others call me?"

"Go-to-Hell Van Dell."

"What?"

"Those would be the former Logan's Ladies Club members."

"You're making this up, right?"

Amber grinned. "Some of it."

Logan didn't want to know which part.

"So?" She looked at him expectantly.

"So what?"

"So, are you going to kiss me or not?"

"Not now. I've lost the mood," he grumbled.

"Logan, you *are* a mood." Groaning, Amber sat up, stretched, and wrapped her arms around her knees.

Logan could see the bumps of her spine through her T-shirt. "It's really bad for you in New York, isn't it?"

She denied it, but he expected her to.

He didn't say anything more and after a while she starting talking. He figured she wouldn't be able to stay quiet for long.

"I think my problem was that I couldn't figure out what I wanted to do. All I ever thought about was getting to New York. I never actually thought about what I'd do when I got there. I mean, I suddenly had all this freedom and I wasn't used to it. Here, I always had something I was supposed to be *doing.* I had choir practice, cheerleading practice, I was on the teen board for Weiss's Department Store, I was the class vice president, I was on the student council, the drama club, the environment club, the—"

"I get the picture." She'd been a member of the "in" crowd. Logan had been on the football team and thought he'd finally been in, too. He hadn't.

"Well, what I'm saying is that everything was all planned out for me and all I could think about was getting away from it all." Her chin rested on her knees and the moonlight haloed her head.

He'd never seen it do that before, but he hadn't watched Amber from this angle before. "You used to say you wanted to be an actress," he said to prompt her reminiscences.

Amber sighed heavily. "So does everyone else in New York. I couldn't get an agent. I couldn't even get an *appointment* with an agent. And everyone told me to take voice lessons to lose the accent—"

"Guess what?"

She straightened and twisted to look down at him. "What?"

"The lessons didn't take."

Amber rolled her eyes. "It's just being back here," she said, and this time all the consonants sounded.

Logan smiled to himself.

"To pay for the lessons, I worked as a waitress in a twenty-four-hour deli. I lasted a week."

"A whole week?"

She turned back around. "I learned that people who order pastrami sandwiches at three-thirty in the morning don't tip. After two voice lessons, I was in the hole."

"So then what did you do?"

"I worked in a bar. Two, actually."

Logan tried to imagine Lily Madison's daughter working in a bar, and couldn't. "At the same time?"

She sighed. "No. At first, I worked at a sports bar and had to wear a cheerleader uniform. It was nothing like any cheerleader uniform *I* ever saw."

Logan laughed.

"You wouldn't be laughing if you saw the football uniforms the guys wore. Tight pants with interesting lacing and a cropped see-through shirt."

Logan's laugh changed to a cough. "So what happened?"

"The tips were better, but tips on happy hour beer and nachos don't add up to much and I also wanted to take acting lessons. So-oo, I took a job in a nightclub where I had to wear a short black skirt, fishnet stockings and these killer high heels."

She would have looked great in fishnet stockings and high heels.

"Men kept wanting to buy me drinks—"

"I'll bet they did," he muttered.

"—but I was under age. The manager decided we under-twenty-ones were costing the club money, so he made us into busgirls. I told him to forget it and quit."

Logan continued listening as Amber recounted her early years in New York where she bounced from one job to another and lived with a succession of roommates. She gazed out over the cold spring pool as she spoke and went from one episode to the next like an unending confession. He was surprised she'd stuck it out.

"I rented a couch," she said at one point.

"A lot of people rent furniture," he said carefully, not sure what she wanted him to say.

"No, you don't understand. I rented the couch in someone's apartment—I paid rent to sleep on their couch. I had to keep my clothes in a steamer trunk they used as a coffee table. Three other people lived there and we all shared the bathroom. I stayed there for two months. The apartment was in a great location and people treated me better when I gave it as my address, but if I wanted to use the fridge or the iron or the microwave, I had to pay extra."

Logan began to wonder if her situation ever got any better, then he realized that living in a one-room workshop *was* better.

Still, he kept waiting for her to get to the penthouse episode with the jewelry store owner, which was really what he was interested in. He could hardly blame her for jumping at the chance to live with him after all the moving around she'd done, but Logan didn't like thinking about her with another man.

Only Amber never mentioned the jewelry guy and Logan didn't want to ask. She kept talking, her voice a monotone, and finally he sat up and draped a hand across her shoulders. He only meant to let her know he was still listening, but her shoulders were so tense that he positioned himself behind her, one leg on either side of her, and used his thumbs to massage the kinks out.

"You don't have to tell me all this."

"Mmm." She tilted her head back, eyes closed. "I can't seem to stop. Hey, right there." She guided his hands farther apart.

Logan exhaled softly, feeling the tightness gradually ease. "I'm sorry, Amber."

"What for?"

"That...that you went through all that stuff, I guess."

She was silent, except for the little sounds she made when he found a spot that was more sensitive than the others. "I don't want you to apologize."

The tension had crept back. Logan increased the pressure in his thumbs and worked the muscles in her shoulders. "I'm not sure what else I can say."

"Nothing. It's not your fault."

"If I'd gone with you—"

"No—o-oh, on my neck." She pointed out the spot and sighed. "It's okay that you didn't go with me. I would have depended on you and then when things didn't go right in New York—and they wouldn't have—I would have blamed you and probably come running home, bitterly dooming myself to a life of good works and crustless chicken salad sandwiches."

Logan chuckled.

"This way, at least I know whatever I've done, or haven't done, I did on my own."

She spoke with complete sincerity and not a drop of self-pity. At that moment Amber Madison became more than just a Belle Rive social princess to Logan. He'd always thought there was more to her, sure, but it had just been potential. Now the potential had become reality. Amber had just become a very compelling woman. She, too, had been on the outside looking in. She'd understand.

He circled his arms around her. "Come here."

"Why?"

"If you don't, I'll break into a chorus of 'My Way.'"

"I might like to hear that. I always thought you'd make a good lounge lizard."

Laughing, Logan tugged her against him until she was leaning with her back against his chest.

"You gonna kiss me soon?"

"Thinking about it." He brushed her hair away from her neck.

"Is it going to be a pity kiss?"

"No, it's going to be a you've-grown-up-and-I-like-the-woman-you've-become kiss."

She turned in his arms until her mouth was inches away from his. "Really?"

"Either that or a tight-black-skirt-and-fishnet-stockings kiss."

She smiled. "That's the Logan I remember."

Logan was smiling, too, so they bumped lips more than kissed. They both laughed and pulled back. She felt good in his embrace. Real good. He ran his hands up and down her arms and his smile faded, as did hers.

Logan looked down at Amber's face in the moonlight, just as he had dozens of times in the past. And the moonlight shone in her eyes, just as it had done in the past. Then, it had made her look innocent and starry-eyed. Probably because she *had* been innocent and starry-eyed. Now, it reflected something deeper within her, something wiser and richer. Something more womanly.

Logan felt an instant's regret that he hadn't been the man to give her that womanliness before the lure of it made him forget about everything but kissing Amber Madison.

NOBODY COULD KISS like Logan Van Dell, probably because he got so much practice. It was worth a broken heart just to know what being really kissed was like.

Logan and broken hearts went together like picnics and deviled eggs. With Logan, it could never be just a kiss. By the time that man finished kissing a woman, he had her heart—and soul, too, if she weren't careful.

Amber hadn't been careful. Oh, she'd been warned. Repeatedly.

"You're thinking of going out with Logan?" her friends had asked about the fifth time she stopped to have her car checked at the fancy imported car garage where he worked.

"Maybe—maybe not," she answered, not wanting to admit to anything in case her parents heard about it.

"Be careful," they'd said, giving her serious looks and telling her about a sad-faced former Logan's Lady. "Men just aren't, well, *men* after Logan. And it never lasts with him."

Amber had given them a superior look. "Maybe he just hasn't met the right *woman*."

"Your mother's going to kill you if you go out with him. He's a *Van Dell*." They'd lowered their voices to a whisper as though they were swearing. "His two cousins got sent off to military school—and their girlfriends had to go to school up north where no one knew their background."

That would have been one way to get out of Belle Rive.

And Amber had liked the idea of going out with a Van Dell even more. So the next time she'd taken her car in for a funny noise, she made sure she was driving alone.

It never lasts with him.

Why hadn't she listened?

Probably because he was the best kisser in the known universe.

Amber thought her memory had exaggerated Logan's skill in the lip department. Nope.

The thing about Logan's kisses was that she never knew what to expect. Sometimes he was passionate and sometimes tender. Sometimes teasing and sometimes hungry.

Right now, he was sweet. Amber didn't remember sweet kisses. Sweet kisses were...sweet.

He'd stared deeply into her eyes and brought both hands up to hold her face, rubbing his thumbs lightly over her cheekbones. All the while, his gaze had traced the outlines of her face, then his lips had slowly descended to hers, barely making contact.

Sweet.

Amber leaned toward him, but his hands held her away as his tongue traced her upper lip, then took her lower one and gently pulled it into his mouth.

She could feel her pulse in her lips. They tingled and tickled at the same time.

Whoa. These weren't sweet kisses. These were seductive kisses. How sneaky. And how effective.

Amber made a tiny sound of frustration as she tried to get closer, tried to kiss Logan back, but he still held her away.

"Logan..."

He relented about a centimeter and Amber fastened her mouth fully over his.

He was familiar and new at the same time. His beard was rougher, his touch more assured. His jaw was more angular than she remembered, his hair shorter.

And he still kissed with his whole body.

Amber was shaking. She was actually shaking. She had to do something with her hands. One was caught between them, so she turned it and spread her fingers against his chest, working two in between the buttons of his shirt to stroke his skin.

That earned her another fraction of an inch and a series of nipping kisses that made her lips throb even more.

Amber brought her other hand around and quickly undid three shirt buttons, fanning her hands over his chest.

His skin was hot and his heart pounded against her fingers. The thought that she had the power—still—to affect him made her smile.

"Amber!" Burying his hand in her hair, he pulled her head away and stared down at her, his eyes dark.

She stared back and waited for the little warning voices to chime in, the ones that would point out that she was being unwise. The ones that would remind her that Logan was a heartbreaker.

For once, they showed the good sense to know when it was a lost cause.

An instant later Logan hauled her close and was kissing her as frantically as she was him. She couldn't get close enough to him.

She remembered the feeling all too well, remembered wanting to make love to him so badly and not understanding why he wouldn't.

But that was then and this was now.

She was a woman now and he was very much a man.

Amber lowered one hand to the juncture of his thighs and with the other popped the snap on his jeans.

And unbelievably his hands covered hers.

"Logan?"

Breathing heavily, he shook his head.

"No?"

"No," he whispered.

"I can't believe this!" She tried to pull away, but he held her fast.

"Amber," he said, his voice hoarse.

"What's wrong with me?" she pleaded. "Can you just tell me so I'll know?"

"Nothing's wrong with you. You're a beautiful, desirable woman—"

"That's just what you said before! Boy, isn't *this* like old times."

"Not exactly." He gave her a wry look. "Then I had condoms with me."

"Oh." She felt foolish until a thought occurred to her. "Well, then why didn't you ever want to use one?"

"I did, but...never mind."

"What? What do you mean, 'never mind'?"

He shook his head, then took her hands and placed a kiss in each palm before releasing them. "Let's just say the time wasn't right."

His face was partially shadowed in the moonlight and Amber wished she could see it fully. She sensed that she was missing something, but couldn't figure out what it was. "Will the time ever be right?" she asked.

"Come back here and find out." His voice was low, with a hint of grit in the syrupy drawl.

He moved his head slightly and Amber saw the half grin. The dimple she couldn't see, but she knew it was there.

He was just too full of himself for his own good. "I might not ever come back here."

He crooked his arm around her neck and dipped her down, then kissed her, movie-hero-style. "You will."

7

I WILL MAKE IT through the day. I will make it through the day. I will make it through the day. Amber took the last of several deep breaths, fought a wave of hyperventilated dizziness and determinedly strode into her mother's room for The Fitting of the Queen's Gown. Photographed for posterity, of course.

Or at least the Thursday society section of the Belle Rive *Mirror*.

Amber's mother, grandmother, and Bertha were waiting for her by Lily's triple-oval, full-length mirror. The photographer was cooling his heels downstairs until Amber could be decently clad.

I will make it through the day. I will make— "What the hell is that?"

Three female voices erupted simultaneously. "Amber Lynn Madison!"

"You watch your language, missy!"

"Why, it's a corset! Bertha's holding it upside down." Amber's grandmother took the aging white torture device from Bertha and inverted it.

Amber's mother gazed at her sternly. "During your years of life in the big city, you seem to have forgotten that you're a lady."

Even Bertha, who had been Amber's ally for years, looked at her admonishingly. Amber sent her a glance pleading for understanding, but Bertha didn't budge. She, too, was subscribing to this queen business.

I will make it through the day—by putting Mama's medicinal whiskey in the lemonade. The thought cheered Amber, even though she'd never craved whiskey before. "Is that what ladies wore back then?"

"Yes," her mother said, taking the thing and shaking it out.

"So *why* would anyone want to be a lady?"

There was a muffled snicker.

"You're only encouraging her, Mother." Lily sighed heavily. "But I've come to expect that. Here, Amber. Put this on."

Amber positioned the yellowing lace and cotton around her rib cage. "Don't I have to grab a bedpost or something?"

Her mother ignored her. "Turn around. Bertha and I will lace you."

A few seconds later Lily yanked the first of the laces. Bertha was gentler, but still Amber knew it would be a toss up whether she suffocated or died of heatstroke first. She had on pantaloons, or whatever they were called, and some flimsy undershirt-like thing on top. After this corset would come the hoops. "Do we have to do the whole Scarlett drill?" she complained. "I can hardly breathe in this thing."

"You're lucky that you're thinner than I was when I wore it."

Amber caught her grandmother's eyes in the mirror. "This was yours, Memaw?"

Mary Alice nodded, looking wistful.

Oh, hell. Amber supposed she could wear the thing if it had been her grandmother's.

At last, the corset was laced and Lily spun Amber back around.

The three women eyed her.

"It's..." Lily waved vaguely.

Bertha cut to the chase. "That girl doesn't have enough bosom."

Amber looked down at herself. The thing was actually comfortable up there. She knew there had to be a catch. The catch was about a two-inch gap between her breasts and the corset. She could see all the way to the bottom of her rib cage, where the tight boning was rearranging several internal organs.

"Well, we can't have that," Lily said, studying her daughter.

"But the dress is going to cover this, won't it?" Amber asked.

Silently, Bertha held up the white satin dress, which had a tiny little bodice and about a hundred yards in the full skirt.

"Whoa. Ladies must have suffered from chest colds back then."

"Those who had chests," Lily said with a disparaging glance toward Amber's neckline. "I blame your father's people for this."

"At least the women were healthy," Amber retorted.

"And single," Mary Alice added.

Fortunately the doorbell sounded before Amber's marital status became the subject of discussion.

"I'll get that." Bertha practically ran out of the room.

"Chicken," Amber muttered as Bertha passed by.

Bertha pretended that she didn't hear.

"I wonder if the boning bends," Amber said, trying it.

"No!" Both Mary Alice and Lily reached out to stop her. "That's an antique!"

"It's been on display in the Belle Rive museum," Memaw added proudly.

"You mean my underwear has been on display where everybody can see it?"

"Of course, don't be silly." Lily was rummaging through a drawer in her vanity.

"And it was *my* underwear," Memaw said. "There's a nice tasteful plaque explaining why it's temporarily out of the case."

"So everybody's going to know I'm wearing it?" Amber sighed, but couldn't get a really good breath going and ended up coughing.

Lily approached, carrying flowered chiffon scarves. "Here. Try to fill in the space with these."

Amber wanted to sigh again, but, remembering the trouble she'd had last time, simply took the limp material and tried to make a little ruffle with it, thinking her mother wanted to alter the neckline of the gown and was visualizing how it would look.

"Amber, for heaven's sake, inside."

"You want me to stuff this thing? Mama, I'm not twelve!"

"Which is why I'm allowing it."

"Mama—"

"Amber." Her mother closed her eyes, her mouth in a straight line.

From long experience, Amber knew that when her mother got that face, arguing was pointless.

In the distance, they could hear voices.

Lily's eyes flew open and her expression transformed into one of delight. "I'll bet the *Mirror* sent over the society columnist. I hope it's Rebecca Lee's daughter and not that other one. Hurry up, Amber!"

Amber jammed the scarves in the cavernous space left by the corset. The ends fountained out.

"Amber, please cooperate. We want a tasteful cleavage."

"I'm sorry, Mama, but there isn't that much to cleave!"

"Did I hear someone say 'cleavage'?"

Everyone's eyes widened as Gigi Van Dell's voice sounded just outside the door. Logan's mother, her arrival accompanied by the click of impossibly high heels on hundred-year-old wooden floors, swept inside Lily Madison's bedroom, followed by an ineffectually protesting Bertha.

"Well, here you all are!" Gigi beamed. She seemed incapable of smiling any other way. "It's okay, Logan, honey, she's decent."

Logan was here?

"It is *not* okay!" both Amber and her mother exclaimed, for once in agreement.

Bertha, wide-eyed, barred the door. "Mrs. Van Dell...*Mr.* Van Dell—"

Gigi pooh-poohed Bertha. "I swear, the way you were carrying on, you would've thought she was naked."

"Naked would probably look better," Amber said, trying to stuff the ends of the fluttering chiffon down before Logan appeared.

She almost made it.

"Is this command central?" he asked, peering in the doorway over Bertha's shoulder. "The photographer wanted me to remind you that he's got a twelve noon deadline.''

Amber vaguely heard her mother comment on the younger generation having no respect as Logan's gaze collided with hers.

She knew she was wearing more clothing than normal, but the fact that this was underwear—even ancient underwear—made her feel self-conscious. That, and the chiffon-filled gap.

Or maybe it was because kissing him at the cold spring last night had reawakened all the physical desires she'd once felt for him.

Still felt for him, if she was being honest. Amber wasn't sure she was ready for that much honesty right now.

He'd left her with a challenge last night, and was reminding her of it right now as his gaze skimmed over her. Rather than walking into the room, he remained in the doorway and leaned against the side, continuing to watch her and only her. His lips barely curved and his dimple was absent. And his eyes...his eyes were full of a passion so hot, Amber was surprised no one else felt the heat.

Or maybe someone did.

Lily moved to stand in front of Amber. ''Bertha, why don't you make us all some lemonade?''

Logan moved aside as lucky Bertha escaped. When he looked back at Amber, the fire in his eyes had been banked. But they both knew it could flame to life at any moment.

Amber's grandmother, who'd been watching Gigi with fascination, cleared her throat.

Probably coming down with a chest cold, Amber

thought grumpily as she introduced her grandmother to Logan's mother. "Memaw, this is Mrs. Van Dell."

Logan's mother responded with the perfect blend of politeness and respect. Even Lily couldn't fault her.

"And this handsome man is my son, Logan," she said.

Mary Alice dimpled. "Oh, I know this young scalawag."

Logan smiled. "How's the Caddy running, Miss Mary Alice?"

"Don't you know?" Amber's grandmother said with an arch look at Logan, and then Amber.

For just a second Logan's self-composure slipped.

Amber, herself, hadn't had any composure since he'd arrived in the doorway.

But his smile was quickly back in place. "Why don't you bring the old girl around to the garage before you take her out on the road again?"

Garage? Logan still worked at a garage?

"You boys are just too sweet to me."

If Amber didn't know better, she'd swear her grandmother was flirting.

"It's an honor to work on your car. She's a classic—just like you, Miss Mary Alice." Logan sketched a smooth bow.

"Oh, how you do go on!" Amber's grandmother revealed that she had a good set of dimples herself.

"Logan's car club is providing the cars for the queen and her court in the parade. Tell them what you got for Amber, honey."

Logan looked pleased. "Gerald Mahoney—"

"He's one of those computer gazillionaires from Atlanta," Gigi interjected.

"Gerald's lending us his 1956 Rolls Silver Cloud."
Logan looked like a little boy on Christmas morning.

Gigi clapped her hands. "Won't that just be gorgeous?"

Lily looked stunned. "Why...why, yes. Although traditionally we've used horses and buggies—"

"Oh, we're going to. We're offering a Moonlight Tour."

"'A Moonlight Tour'?" Lily repeated faintly.

"Yes, and people have just grabbed up the tickets, so we're running it all weekend."

"I didn't know anything about a Moonlight Tour."

"That's right." Gigi snapped her fingers. "You weren't able to make the committee heads meeting last night."

Last night her mother had been holding a rogue meeting of her own.

Amber could see her gearing up to talk about the decorations, but before she could, Gigi zipped open a silver leather executive organizer. "Here's the flyer we've mailed out to everyone who wrote for advance tickets for the pilgrimage. And here are the photo cards we're putting in all the B and B's. Aren't they cute?"

Amber peered over her dazed mother's shoulder to see a picture of Gigi, legs crossed, waving from an open buggy. The horse was wearing a pink hat and a wreath of magnolia blossoms. Van Dell House was in the background. At the bottom was reservation and ticket information.

"Very nice," Lily said unenthusiastically. She tried to hand the card back to Gigi, but Gigi waved it away and got out more to give Lily.

"Here are some in case anyone staying here for the pilgrimage needs the information."

"Thank you." Lily set the cards on her vanity.

"Well, Amber, look at you." With Lily out of the way, Gigi got a full view of Amber. "Now, what's going on up here?" Gigi pulled on the end of a scarf and tugged it out like a magician pulling tricks out of his sleeve.

Maybe Amber wouldn't make it through the day, after all. Logan must just be loving this.

"Got any more in there?" Gigi peered over the top of Amber's bodice, then reached her fingers inside.

"Mrs. Van Dell!" Amber squeaked.

"I think you better call me Gigi, honey." She pulled out the other scarf and peered over the top of the corset. "Hello down there! You hear an echo?"

Now would be an excellent time for an out-of-body experience, Amber thought.

"Just kidding." Gigi grinned. "Don't worry. I'll lend you my boobie buddies."

"'Boobie...buddies'?" Lily whispered, holding on to the edge of her vanity table.

"She means fakes, Lily. Do you think they'll work under the corset?" Amber's grandmother asked Gigi.

"Sure! I've worn plenty of corsets in my time."

"Well, bring them on, then."

"I don't suppose anyone has considered putting the corset *back* into the museum where it belongs and letting me wear modern underwear under the dress?" Amber asked.

"We have to be authentic," Mary Alice reproached her.

"And *boobie buddies* are authentic?"

"They would have worn them if they could have,

hon. Logan, sweetie, you know in my closet where I keep my old costumes?"

Amber risked glancing over at him. Yes, he was still there. A gentleman would have gone back downstairs, but not Logan. No, he was standing in the doorway, grinning from ear to ear.

"Yes, Mama," he answered on the verge of laughing out loud.

"There's a box where I keep my accessories. My boobie buddies are in there. Would you run home and bring them back here for Amber? Bring all of them."

"All? Don't we just need two?" Amber asked.

Gigi looked doubtful. "You're going to need more help than that."

Amber could hear Logan's laughter echoing in the hall and all the way down the stairs.

That would cost him. Let him go to the cold spring—alone—and soak his head.

"Mrs. Van *Dell!*" Lily had recovered her power of speech. "While I appreciate your help, we want to stay within the bounds of good taste."

"'Course we do, but you're an amateur at this. Padding has gone high-tech." She tossed the scarves at Lily. "That stuff doesn't jiggle. Ya gotta have a little jiggle." Gigi demonstrated, indicating her own breasts. "Now these are top of the line. Not like my first job—Logan's daddy paid for that one and he hadn't been having a huge run of luck at the tables, if you know what I mean. But he was a sweetie." She sighed, clearly remembering Logan's father.

For a minute Amber thought it was kind of nice, then Gigi looked up at her. "If you're ever interested, hon, let me give you the name of my second surgeon. Now he's the one you want to go to."

"I'll keep that in mind."

"Yes, well." Lily struggled to regain control of the situation. "Mother, while we're, er, waiting, we can get Amber into the hoops."

Mary Alice arranged them on the floor and Amber stepped into the concentric circles of lace and silk and bent to pull the center up to her waist. She couldn't. "Help?"

"Bend your knees," instructed Lily.

Amber squatted and felt around until she found the drawstring and pulled the whole cagelike contraption up to her waist.

"Look at that workmanship!" Gigi marveled, fingering the lace as Mary Alice tied the drawstring around Amber's waist.

"It belonged to my grandmother," Lily said, her voice thawing toward Gigi.

"Amber, you're so lucky to get to wear this," Gigi said with sincerity. "My folks are both long gone, and I don't have much of anything left to remind me of them. I was so young and didn't appreciate heirlooms for what they were...at least until I had Logan. That's why when Auden was sick, I insisted we come live with Camille. I wanted Logan to have a sense of his roots after his daddy . . . well."

"And you were quite right to do so," Mary Alice said, patting her arm.

Even Lily unbent enough to nod.

And Amber was struck with the sure knowledge that Gigi had loved her much-older husband. *Really* loved him, and loved him still years and years later.

Gigi blinked several times, then smiled. "Well, listen to me go on! I didn't mean to take up so much of your time, but I had a couple of things..." She looked at a list in her silver planner. "Oh! The crown—I'm told you have it here?"

"Yes," Lily told her. "It usually stays with the pilgrimage chairman."

A beat went by when she remembered she was no longer chairman.

"Could I see it?" Gigi prompted.

"Of course."

"No!"

Everyone looked at Amber's grandmother. "It's...there were loose stones. I took it to be repaired."

"Oh, Memaw. You should have waited for me," Amber said. "I would have fixed them for you. I brought my tools with me. I just haven't unpacked them yet."

Mary Alice swallowed. "I...forgot."

"Memaw?" Her grandmother looked horrible. "That's okay. I'm not offended or anything. You've never seen me work on jewelry, so you wouldn't know, but I'm really good."

Mary Alice tried to smile, but didn't quite make it.

"Mother, are you quite all right?"

"She probably needs some air." Gigi fanned her hands over Mary Alice's colorless cheeks.

"No...I—I'm a little tired. It's been an exciting morning. I'll go lie down for a bit."

Amber started forward to help her, but her hoops got in the way.

"Stay here. I'm fine." Mary Alice managed a trembling smile this time.

"Mother—"

"Lily, just leave me alone," she snapped. "If you all will excuse me." She slowly walked out the door.

She's getting old. Amber had never thought of her grandmother as old. She was just Memaw.

"You mentioned a couple of things?" Lily prompted into the uncomfortable silence.

"Yes. A courier from Memphis came by this morning." Gigi set her planner on Lily's vanity and withdrew an envelope. "He brought a huge invoice and wanted a fifty percent deposit." She took out three lengths of pale pink ribbon. "Something about special ribbon you ordered?"

"Those are the pinks!" Lily reached for them and walked over to the window to look at them in the sunlight. "You can always count on Grishams. When I realized you'd forgotten to order the ribbons for the wreaths and ball decorations, I knew Grishams would come through for us."

"But I ordered *plenty* of ribbon."

Lily shook her head. "Grishams didn't have a record of your order." She held up the center of what looked to Amber like three identical pieces of ribbon. "I like this middle one. What do you think?"

"I think you'll have to cancel the order with Grishams," Gigi stated calmly. "I ordered from a company that deals in Mardi Gras supplies out of Metairie, Louisiana."

"We always use Grishams," Lily stated, still examining the ribbons.

"But they're so expensive. I bought overruns from Bon Temps for considerably less than half this, I can tell you." Gigi tossed the invoice on Lily's now-cluttered vanity.

"Let me make sure I understand this," Lily said. "You propose to decorate the Magnolia Pilgrimage with Mardi Gras leftovers?"

Amber wanted to leave, but there was no way she could slip unnoticed through the doorway while wearing the hoops. After testing the knots at her waist, she knew she was stuck in here. At least if she stood between the two women, they'd be too far away to take a swing at each other.

And from the looks of things, it wasn't such a far-fetched idea.

"End pieces, not leftovers," Gigi corrected. "And they're plenty long enough for us. I wanted silver prism ribbon—"

"*What?*"

"It looks a like hologram, Mama. Like that little silver square on your charge card." Amber started moving and the hoops swayed.

Gigi and Lily stepped out of her way.

"Anything that tacky is completely unsuitable."

"And I suppose you think namby-pamby pink is better?" Gigi thrust her arm toward the ribbons Lily held. "I've got news for you. This show needs some razzle-dazzle if we hope to compete with Vicksburg and Natchez. That silver ribbon is going to flash and shine and keep the energy up, especially at the ball. If there's more energy, then there's more fun, and people will have a good time. Besides, the ribbon goes with everything. Black, white—even pink."

"This is not one of your Vegas shows," Lily said in a clipped voice.

"It's not a funeral, either."

"Mama," Amber said in warning. Where was Logan? The man was supposed to be mediating, wasn't he? Wasn't that the deal? Amber only had to be queen. Wasn't squashing herself into this thing enough? Did she have to do Logan's job, as well?

"But the pilgrimage is a memorial to a way of life!" Lily declared in ringing tones.

"I thought it was supposed to be a celebration of a way of life!" Gigi's voice was more clanking, but every bit as fervent.

"Gee, I wonder where Bertha is with that lemonade? Is anyone else thirsty?"

"You would, wouldn't you?"

"Just what do you mean by that?"

"*Mama.*" Amber wedged her way between the women. "You and Gigi can discuss decorations and pilgrimage philosophy later. Help me into my dress. The photographer is waiting."

"Just a minute. I want to know what your mother meant by her remark."

Lily set her head back. "I meant that you're a Van Dell. When Belle Rive faced her greatest threat, did your family fight? Did your family sacrifice? No, the Van Dells threw a party! I should have expected this from you."

Gigi's face turned luminous. "That's the nicest thing you could have said to me. Would you call me a Van Dell again in front of my mother-in-law?"

"I'll call you more than that!"

"Everyone's getting along as usual, I hear." Logan strode into the room. "And so can everyone else," he warned.

"Logan!" Amber sagged—as far as the hoops and corset would let her—in relief. "You're back!"

"Miss me?" He grinned.

"You have no idea."

Glancing over at his mother and Lily, who were still arguing, but in lowered voices, he said, "Oh, but I do.

The photographer is getting antsy downstairs." He handed a satin-covered box to Amber. "Here."

"What am I supposed to do with this?"

He held up his hands. "That's out of my area of expertise."

"You probably know more than you think." Amber opened the box and looked at the compartments of different-shaped, flesh-colored blobs. She poked one with her finger. "Ewww!" But they did feel lifelike, if cold. Curious, she picked one up and found that it both warmed and conformed to her hand. "Hey, these are kind of neat."

As she held it up, there was a flash of light followed by immediate silence and another flash.

The photographer knelt in the doorway and was preparing for another shot when Lily sprang forward, shrieking, "What are you doing?"

"Ma'am, I told you I had a noon deadline and it's eleven forty-five now." He took another photo as Lily, arms outstretched, charged him, before he raced out the door.

"Wait!" Lily started after him.

"Do you want me to catch him?" Logan asked.

"You and your mother have done enough!" Lily snapped. "I will handle this."

Which is how a photograph of Amber, wearing vintage underwear and holding a boobie buddie, ended up on the front page of the Belle Rive *Mirror* under the headline Borrowed And Blue.

8

"'CONTROVERSY ERUPTS in the queen's court...' Lily, would you explain this, please?" Reginald Madison pushed the front section of the evening edition of the *Mirror* across the dinner table.

"I told you." Lily's voice quivered and her eyes peered out of her blue plastic cooling mask. "The photographer forced himself into our bedroom like a..." She gestured for the word.

"Paparazzi, Mama."

"Yes. One of those horrible foreigners." She dragged her hand to her temple. "It's far too painful for me to discuss."

Amber had seen the picture—elevated from Thursday's society section to leading today's evening news—and it could have been worse. A lot worse.

The picture was a grainy black-and-white newspaper photo from a small-town paper. She looked as if she was wearing a strapless white evening gown. Logan was standing next to her as they looked at something Amber held. She was pretty certain no one would guess it was a boobie buddie. But behind them, Lily and Gigi were engaged in a finger-pointing argument. Their antagonistic expressions showed clearly, maybe they'd even been digitally enhanced, though Amber doubted Belle Rive had the technology.

Personally, Amber thought her mother ought to send the editor roses for not using the picture of her charging the photographer. But her mother was not taking it well. Besides wearing the soothing mask to ward off a potential migraine, she was having clear soup for dinner. She planned to retire to bed shortly thereafter.

Amber's grandmother had wisely remained in her room. When Amber had gone to check on her earlier, she'd been in bed with the covers pulled up to her chin, watching television.

"Don't bother about me, child, I've got three days' worth of my stories to catch up on."

"It's a good time to lie low. I don't suppose you want company?" After school, Amber used to climb into bed with her grandmother and watch her afternoon "stories" with her.

"Maybe some other time."

Amber nodded and closed the door, but truthfully, she felt just a little hurt. She acknowledged that she had no right to feel that way. She was the one who'd left.

And her decision to come back was looking more and more like a bad one. She tuned back into her parents' conversation.

"I'll be asked questions," her father stated. Her father stated everything. "Am I supposed to tell people that you find it too painful to discuss?"

"Daddy, just tell them that the photographer came up while I was still dressing and started taking pictures."

"Do you think it would be politically advantageous

for me to sue for invasion of privacy? After all, Amber is technically in her underwear."

"There's no 'technically' about it," Amber muttered.

"Sue and alienate the press in an election year? What a brilliant strategy, Reginald."

"Oh, right." He looked lost in thought. "What do you propose I do?"

"Why should you do anything? *I'm* the one on the front page of the paper in my underwear standing next to the most notorious ladies' man in Belle Rive."

"Those horrible Van Dells," Lily said with feeling.

"Mama, it wasn't their fault. You shouldn't have ordered the ribbon without checking with Gigi first."

Lily slowly pulled down the mask so she could see Amber better. Red imprints were on her forehead, cheeks and nose. "Thank you for reminding me of yet another humiliation. Can you imagine how I felt calling Grishams to cancel after they've supplied our ribbons for more than twenty years?"

Amber bit back her first response. "I imagine it was embarrassing."

"They supply my campaign ribbons," her father said. "I hope this won't affect their enthusiasm for my ribbon rosettes. Everyone is always impressed by those gray-and-gold rosettes. Very distinctive, they are."

Amber was suddenly very tired. She'd finished a huge portion of Bertha's meatloaf and mashed potatoes, which was her favorite comfort food, and now that she knew she had to get into the corset, she should probably skip dessert.

Excusing herself, she carried her dishes into the kitchen, rinsed them and put them into the dishwasher. Her parents were still talking, no doubt discussing every possible impact Amber's underwear photo would have on her father's political future.

That was the way it had always been. She and Stephanie were constantly reminded how their behavior not only affected them, but their father and the family, as well.

Amber crept up the back stairs, walking quietly down the hall. From under her grandmother's door, she could see the glow of the television and hear muted voices.

"Memaw?" She knocked softly on the door.

There was no answer. Amber slowly turned the knob and saw a lump in the bed. Her grandmother had fallen asleep. Amber silently turned off the TV and closed the door.

Once in her own room, she unpacked her equipment, setting up her polishing motor on her vanity table and her laptop on the desk where she'd done her homework as a student.

The queen was expected to give each member of her court a small remembrance. Amber had designed a free-form magnolia pin and planned to set a different semiprecious stone in the center of each. They were almost done, except that she didn't know how many duchesses were going to be in her court. Stephanie could be, even though she was married, but Amber figured she was still persona non grata since her mother never even mentioned her. Amber wondered when she was going to see her sister. If Stephanie didn't show by tomorrow, Amber was going to borrow her grandmother's Cadillac and drive to Natchez herself.

Amber spent a happy hour setting up a makeshift workshop. She then put on her goggles, screwed a pol-

ishing mop to the motor spindle, rubbed on tripoli polish, and polished a dozen silver pins, hoping that
would be enough. The brown tripoli was greasy and
messy, but using the motor was about ten times faster
than doing it all by hand. This was the first time she'd
made the same piece of jewelry in any quantity and
was hoping it might be the secret to actually making a
living at this.

She'd carried the pins into the bathroom to clean off
the compound and was drying each one when she
heard rain against her window. Or was it hail?

Whatever, it stopped. Amber went back to drying
her pins and then heard the noise again.

It sounded like rocks or...money.

Logan.

Surely he didn't think she would come to the cold
spring tonight. When he and his mother had finally
left, there had been no doubt that both he and Amber
were in for a long night of soothing their respective
mothers.

Besides, Amber didn't like him being so sure of her.
It was illogical, because he had every reason to be sure
of her.

Why, she didn't know. She wasn't sure she even
liked him. He'd manipulated her into coming back
here and having her insides squeezed and rearranged.
Then he'd witnessed the charming session where her
inadequate feminine attributes had been the topic of
discussion.

He'd brought her his mother's fake boobs.

There were some women who might like that in a
guy, but Amber had to draw the line somewhere.

The coins threatened to crack the glass in her window.

"All right!" Amber opened the curtains and unlocked her window, having to work to pull it open. Her room had been painted since she left.

With a screech, the paint seal broke and the window shot up. Sure enough, a familiar figure was out by the tree.

Amber leaned on the ledge. "What are you doing?"

"Picking up loose change. You need a ladder, or can you still climb down the tree?"

Did he have to be so darn sure of himself? "Logan, look, it's late and—"

"Hush." He positioned a shiny aluminum ladder against the tree, then climbed up.

"I figured you might be rusty," he said when his head was level with her window.

"Logan, we're adults. You can come to the front door." She might even change her mind and open it. He was looking mighty fine on that ladder.

"After today, are you kidding? Your parents would ride me out of town on a rail."

Amber sighed. "The picture wasn't your fault."

"I shouldn't have let your mother go after that guy. Threatening to get him fired wasn't the best strategy, under the circumstances."

"Did she?" Amber had been upstairs trapped in her hoops and had missed everything.

"Yes, among other things."

"Then she's *extremely* lucky they didn't publish that one picture of her."

Logan didn't look concerned. "Your dad's been the

mayor for, like, forever. You've gotta figure he's got some clout."

"Maybe." Amber thought her mother was the one with the clout.

"Hey." He ran a finger lightly across her arm. "Wanna come out and play?"

He'd said that to her the first time he'd come to her window and she'd been terribly thrilled and excited that the infamous Logan Van Dell had sought her out.

He'd been older. He'd had a reputation. Her parents would have had a cow if they'd found out. And he'd looked incredibly good standing under her tree.

He looked incredibly good right now. He wore jeans and a shirt and his hair was ruffled out of its styled cut. She might have been eighteen again and he might have been the dangerous Logan of old.

Come to think of it, he was still dangerous.

Slowly she shook her head. "I can't."

His dimple appeared. "Can't 'won't' or can't 'not tonight'—or can't 'not ever'?"

She didn't want to answer, but she did. "Not tonight." It was more than he deserved.

"Okay." He didn't sound disappointed in the least. "I can't tonight, either."

Amber gasped. "You jerk! I ought to push you down that ladder!"

Logan laughed, then quickly sobered. "No, really, I came here because I got a call from your grandmother."

"Memaw called you?" Was her grandmother matchmaking?

"Yeah. She's in Vicksburg and her car won't start. I

wondered if you wanted to ride to the rescue with me."

"Vicksburg? No way. She's asleep in her bed."

"She said she was in Vicksburg."

"Wait a minute."

Amber ran down the hall to her grandmother's room. She quietly opened the door a bit so she wouldn't wake her. The hall light behind Amber shone on the lump in the bed. She started to close the door, but, on impulse, went over and gently touched her grandmother's shoulder.

Her hand went all the way through to the mattress. Amber yelped before she could stifle the noise. Turning on the bedside lamp, she saw at once that pillows and blankets made the lump and that her grandmother was clearly not in her bed.

The sheets weren't even warm.

Amber didn't bother looking for her elsewhere. If Logan got a call from Vicksburg, then that's where she was.

She ran back to her room. Logan had climbed down the ladder and was waiting for her. "She's not there. Let me change my shoes and grab my purse."

"Sure."

Amber was glad of the ladder because either the tree had grown, or she was less limber. Maybe both. Eventually, she was on the ground and she and Logan were sneaking across the yard just like old times.

He'd parked a giant tow truck outside her gate.

"Where did you get that thing?"

"From the garage." He shoved the ladder in back, then opened the door and gave Amber a boost up. Amber tried not to notice that his hands were a little too low and lingered a little too long.

And felt a little too good.

She spent so much time trying to not react or remember anything about Logan that she ended up doing exactly the opposite. She saw hidden meanings in his smiles, felt the most casual of touches all the way to her toes and the not-so-casual touches...

Amber closed her eyes and swallowed as Logan jogged around the front of the truck. Focus. Her grandmother. They were on a midnight mission to rescue her grandmother.

Logan hopped into the truck and, gears creaking, turned it around and headed toward the highway.

Oh, the memories. Logan, his truck, rolling down the windows and letting the humid night air rush in, the quivering anticipation of spending stolen hours with him...it was all coming back to her when she wanted it all to go away. At least she knew why now.

She wasn't that girl anymore.

She knew better. Dreams just didn't happen. They were a lot of hard work and sometimes they even turned into nightmares. Being with Logan reminded her of how naive she'd been. No, not naive. Just inexperienced and wanting some experience so very much.

Amber swallowed the lump forming in her throat. How long could she keep chasing success? How long could she fool herself into thinking it was just around the next corner?

Shivering, she rubbed her arms and rolled up the window on her side. It was time to quit moping. They had at least an hour's drive ahead of them.

AMBER WAS A LOT QUIETER than she used to be. It was a change Logan had noticed right off. If it had been a happy quiet, he would have welcomed it, but he was convinced that Amber was deeply unhappy and it wasn't because she was missing New York.

Or if it was, he didn't want to know about it.

Logan started to turn on the radio, but returned his hand to the steering wheel. The radio in his old truck had been broken and, frankly, he was enjoying the feeling of nostalgia.

He wouldn't mind enjoying the feel of her. When they'd rode around together before, she'd sat pressed right up close to him and hadn't said anything if the arm he'd draped around her shoulder wandered the slightest bit.

Sometimes her hands wandered, too.

He hadn't expected to see her tonight. There was no way she'd come to the cold spring after a day like today. He hadn't even bothered checking and so, when Miss Mary Alice's call had come in, he'd been at the garage to take it.

Bringing Amber with him had been pure impulse, just like the impulse that had made him pursue her in the first place.

He'd known who she was from the first time she'd brought her car to the garage, way back when Mr. Fenton still owned it. Pretty as she was, Logan had decided that she came with too much baggage—her family, his family...there were a lot of pretty girls in Belle Rive who weren't such a hassle.

And then she'd looked at him. There had been something in her expression, not quite a dare, but damn close. It was a curiosity about the forbidden and it had resonated with him big-time.

In a play on the whole Romeo and Juliet bit, he'd come to her window one night. And she'd climbed out. He hadn't expected her to, at least not right away.

He smiled to himself, remembering how nervous he'd suddenly become. Now that she was out, what were they going to do? Where could they go and not be seen together?

So he'd taken her to the cold spring and it had been exactly right.

Only the thought of Miss Mary Alice waiting for him kept Logan from taking Amber to the cold spring right now.

THEY'D BEEN DRIVING for several minutes before Amber broke the silence. "I hope you've noticed that I haven't asked why my grandmother called you and not one of us."

They were stopped at the last light on Main Street before leaving the city limits. Logan glanced at her. "I'm the one with the tow truck."

Her eyes narrowed. "You told me you worked in a bank."

"I do. The garage is my hobby. You remember how I liked to tinker with cars."

"I didn't know you *liked* to. I just thought it was your job."

"It was for a while. When I came back from school—"

"School?" Logan had gone to school?

"Yeah. I'd been going to junior college and the fall after you left, I transferred to Ole Miss."

He'd gone to college. She'd had no idea. "What...what did you study?"

"Business. Anyway, I came back and worked for Mr. Fenton again while I was figuring out what I wanted to do." Logan smiled. "I helped him with the books, fine-tuned his business focus, that kind of thing, and he made me a partner. He didn't have any kids of his own, you know."

No, Amber hadn't. She hadn't known the garage owner's name. She'd only known Logan's name.

"I bought him out when he decided to retire a couple of years ago. Mr. Fenton always had a knack with cantankerous foreign imports and that's what he specialized in. Me, I like classics and that's mainly what we do there now. I belong to a vintage car club that meets on the weekends. It's all do-it-yourself. Everybody's got a key and last man out locks up."

She'd had no idea. None. Amber was struck with the lowering realization that she'd done a lot of talking about her life and hadn't listened, or asked, Logan much about his. "And you work on Memaw's car?"

"The guys love your grandmother's car. It's such a cream puff, or it was until she started taking these road trips. That's why I told her to bring it in for a check."

Road trips? A few stray comments made by her mother began to make sense.

"You'll notice that *I* didn't ask why you didn't know your grandmother wasn't at home."

"She snuck out," Amber said.

"I assume she learned from the master."

Amber laughed. "Well, she sure fooled me. Claimed she was tired and going to watch TV. I was using my polishing motor and didn't hear her leave. Did she say why she's in Vicksburg?"

Logan shook his head. "But the fact that her car is parked in the Isle of Capri Casino and RV Park kind of speaks for itself."

Amber bristled. "And what does it say—that my grandmother *gambles?*" What was her grandmother doing sneaking out in the middle of the night to gamble?

"Hey. I'm just the mechanic, here."

"But...but Memaw? At a casino?"

"Don't say it like it's a dirty word. A lot of the seniors go there. It's a social thing mostly."

"Then why didn't she just go? Why sneak out?"

"Why did you sneak out?"

"Oh. Good point." Amber looked over at him. "At least I was sneaking out to meet a good-looking hunk."

He grinned. "I was a hunk?"

Amber sighed. "You're still a hunk." She shouldn't tell him stuff like that.

"Yeah?" He sounded pleased.

"Yeah." As if he didn't know.

"Then what are you doing sitting way over there?"

"Because this is where my seat belt put me. Besides, that's one massive gear box." She indicated the large rectangle on the console between the bucket seats.

"That's nothing."

"Hmm. I think a girl would feel mighty safe with that thing between her and you."

"False security."

"Yeah?"

Logan's eyes met hers. "Yeah."

Glancing in the rearview, he slowed and pulled over to the side of the road.

"What's the matter? Why are we stopping?"

He grinned. "Security check."

No sooner had he ground the gears into park and released his seat belt than he'd closed the gap between them and fused his mouth to hers.

Amber hadn't been expecting him to move so fast—she didn't have time to erect any internal barriers. Logan's kiss cut clear through to her unprotected heart faster than a hot soldering iron.

And Amber didn't care. He didn't mean it to be anything more than a kiss for the moment, she knew. She was going to get hurt again. And still she didn't care.

It was so not fair.

When the pressure of his mouth lessened the slightest bit, she buried her hands in his hair and pulled him toward her.

It must have hurt, but Amber couldn't let go. She'd wasted a couple of days already. That was a lot of kissing to make up. And being in his arms felt so *good*.

"Ow," he mumbled against her mouth, gently pulling her hands from his hair.

"I'm sorry," she gasped. "It's your fault for being such a great kisser."

He rubbed his ribs, grinning and wincing at the same time. "You were right about the gear box."

Amber looked at the various knobs that must have been poking him. "What a time to be right."

Logan gave her an easy smile and refastened his seat belt. "You're a good sport, Amber. I know you're worried about your grandmother, so I was only planning on staying here about forty-five seconds." He looked at his watch. "A minute and a half. Wow."

Amber had forgotten all about Memaw. She'd forgotten everything except being in Logan's arms—or as close as she could get under the circumstances.

Tomorrow night, the circumstances would be different.

Tomorrow night, she was going to the cold spring.

And Logan had damn well better be there.

9

ONCE THEY WERE IN the Isle of Capri Casino parking lot, it was easy to spot her grandmother's car. For one thing, it was sticking halfway out of two parking spots. For another, there just weren't that many thirty-six-year-old, powder-blue Cadillacs in the lot.

Logan found a pink one of the same era, though, and a couple of really fine Buicks that he had to stop and peer inside.

Finding her grandmother, however, was another story. After Amber dragged Logan away from the parking lot, they went into the casino.

It was as bright as high noon—or brighter—and as crowded as Times Square on New Year's Eve. Flashing lights, buzzers, whistles, and sirens bombarded them, along with the chink of coins falling and electronic chiming that sounded as if it'd came straight from Amber's computer.

Row after row of slot machines were to their left and gaming tables were to their right.

"You think my grandmother is in here?" Amber asked, shouting above the noise.

"Where else?"

Amber could think of about a million other places.

Logan nudged her and pointed. "You take the slots, and I'll search the tables."

"No way." Amber took hold of his arm. "If one of us finds her, how will we let the other know?"

"Okay, then is your grandmother a slot machine queen, or a poker Patty?"

"She's my grandmother, that's who she is!" Amber glared at him and took off toward the slot machines, simply because they looked marginally less crowded.

After wandering up and down the aisles, they finally found her sitting in front of the nickel slots.

"Memaw?"

"Amber?" Her grandmother looked startled—and guilty. As well she might.

Amber caught the reproachful look she gave Logan before picking up a purple-and-pink cup half filled with nickels and sliding off the stool.

"Memaw, what are you doing here?"

"Well, you see I was waiting for Logan out by the Tradewinds and...and I found a ten-dollar chip that someone had left as a tip. I cashed it in for nickels so I wouldn't be bored while I waited."

"You—you *stole* a waiter's tip?"

"Don't be silly. I borrowed it. I was going to pay him back out of my winnings." She looked into her cup and shook the change.

Amber didn't have to count it to see that there wasn't ten dollars' worth of nickels.

"If I just had a couple more minutes, I know I'd hit the jackpot." Mary Alice edged toward the slot machine. "I need a jackpot." She sounded like a zombie.

Over her grandmother's head, Amber met Logan's eyes. He tilted his head toward the door.

Amber took her grandmother's arm. "Come on, Memaw. We're going to take you home."

"No!" Her grandmother jerked her arm away with a strength that surprised Amber. "You don't under-stand. I've been playing this machine for over an hour. It *owes* me a jackpot. If I leave now, someone else will win it. It's *my* jackpot."

"Memaw, you're tired. Let's go."

"No."

"*I'm* tired, then. It's going to be a long day—"

Her grandmother broke away and darted between the rows of slots and disappeared.

Amber stared after her, openmouthed. "She ran away!"

"Didn't know she had it in her." Logan was already on an intercept path.

Amber ran the other way in case her grandmother eluded him, keeping Logan's head in sight. When it stopped, she veered back into the rows of slots and spotted him with her grandmother, who was now shoving nickels as fast as she could into the quarter slot machines. Amber jogged up to her, but Logan held out his hand in warning.

Within a few minutes, Mary Alice had only fifteen cents left in the cup. "Logan, I need a dime."

"No."

"Amber!" She held out her hand without even look-ing at Amber.

Taking her cue from Logan, Amber shook her head. "No."

Her grandmother's face crumpled. "Please, you don't understand."

Tears stung Amber's eyes. "I do understand, Me-maw." She put her arms around the woman's shaking shoulders.

"No—it's the crown."

"What crown?"

"The Magnolia Queen's crown—your crown. I pawned it and I've got to win enough money to redeem it."

"You *pawned* the *crown?*" Amber was flabbergasted. "But why?"

"I needed a stake." Mary Alice made it sound perfectly logical.

Amber knew what was happening now. She was asleep and this was a dream. It had to be. "But the *crown?* There's a lot of other stuff you could pawn..." Amber trailed off at her grandmother's wary expression.

"You weren't supposed to come back and be queen," she said. "You always said you'd never be queen, and I thought we wouldn't need the crown this year."

"But somebody else would have been queen!"

"Lily said there wouldn't be a pilgrimage unless you were queen."

"But you must have known she didn't mean it!"

Logan broke in. "Have you got the pawn ticket with you, Miss Mary Alice?" he asked quietly.

His voice was the steadiest and sanest thing in the entire place. It cut through the bells and electronic music and gave Amber an anchor. She grabbed on.

Her grandmother sniffed and dug in her jeweled leather waist pouch, producing a crumpled receipt.

Logan smoothed it out. "Looks like the pawnshop is on Washington—just a couple of blocks from here."

"And how do *you* know?" Amber asked suspiciously.

Logan held up the receipt. "There's a map on the back."

She was being awful. This wasn't his mess. "I'm sorry, Logan. I—"

He touched her arm. "It's okay."

And as Amber felt the reassuring warmth of his touch, she believed it was.

He bent until his face was level with her grandmother's. "Miss Mary Alice, we're going to get the crown. You have to come with us now."

"Don't speak to me as though I'm a child!" she snapped.

"Then stop acting like one!" Amber snapped right back.

"Oo-ookay, you two. Time out." Logan stepped between them and draped an arm over each of them. "Now, what happened to the Caddy?"

Mary Alice sniffed again, making Amber feel guilty for losing her temper. "It won't start."

"There are a lot of reasons a car won't start." Logan kept up a steady stream of innocuous car talk until they were safely through the door. "Did you have any warning before she quit on you?"

Mary Alice shook her head, apparently not noticing that they'd left the casino. "It coughed, like cars sometimes do, you know."

Logan nodded.

"Then it chugged and then it just stopped right where it is now."

"Did you try to start it again?"

"Yes, but I told you it wouldn't."

"And you waited until midnight to call us?" Amber added, unable to help herself.

"I didn't want to miss happy hour at the roulette wheels. The chips are only a quarter then, you know."

"No, Memaw, I didn't know."

Logan squeezed her shoulder. Amber knew she should be quiet, but she was having a hard time assimilating all this. Did her mother know? Did her father? How was she going to tell them? Should she tell them? Knowing them, they'd be more concerned about how the mayor's mother-in-law's gambling habit affected the mayor's reelection chances than getting help for Memaw.

When they reached her grandmother's car, Logan popped open the hood and took a look, then got in behind the wheel and tried to start the car. It cranked several times before he got out and closed the hood.

"Is it serious?" Mary Alice asked, her voice quivering.

Logan nodded gravely. "'Fraid so. Stand back and I'll load her up."

Amber pulled her grandmother aside as Logan got into the tow truck and backed it to within a few feet of the Caddy. Jumping down, he lowered the loading platform and fastened a huge hook and chain to the underside of the car. Winching it forward until it was a little more than halfway, he raised the platform and then pulled the car the rest of the way onto the bed of the truck.

"All right, ladies, we're ready to go. Amber, why don't you get in first?"

Amber stepped forward and seconds later felt Logan's hands on her backside as he gave her a boost into the cab.

She couldn't believe he'd done that in front of her

grandmother. She glared at him and caught him smothering a smile as he turned to help her grandmother. For her, he laced his fingers together so she could use them as a step and Amber took her hands from the other side and steadied her.

It took several minutes and a trip around the block before they were able to pick out the Golden Ball from the other pawnshops.

Logan parked, and as they were approaching the fluorescent-lit doorway, Amber touched his sleeve. During the drive over, she realized she was in the humiliating position of not having the money to redeem the crown. And she knew her grandmother didn't, either. So that meant she was going to have to ask Logan for a loan.

"Logan," she whispered. "About redeeming the crown...I don't have enough money—"

"I'll take care of it," he offered, not making her actually say the words.

Amber was touched at his thoughtfulness. "Thanks." She closed her eyes. "I'll see that you're paid back."

Without warning, she felt the gentle touch of his mouth on hers, surprised to realize that it was exactly what she needed at that moment. Pleased that he'd known.

"It's okay," he breathed.

Amber opened her eyes and her heart lurched at the unLogan-like expression in his. There was tenderness mixed with nonjudgmental understanding.

There was friendship.

Amber needed a friend big-time right now. "It's not

okay, but you're a sweetie for saying so. Oh, and Logan?''

"Yeah?"

"I'm glad you're here."

He smiled down at her. "Glad I could help."

He spoke casually, but Amber could tell that her words had pleased him.

She liked pleasing Logan.

"Ma'am, you'll have to take a number," a bored voice told Mary Alice when they walked inside.

It was two in the morning and Amber was with her grandmother in a pawnshop in Vicksburg, Mississippi. There were seventeen people in line ahead of them. And New York was called the city that never slept?

Once they had their turn at the counter, it was bad news.

"Oh, the crown. Sorry, but it's been more than thirty days, ma'am. I sold it."

"But you can't! It was mine," Mary Alice wailed.

"Sure I could." He pointed to a sign behind him that said items would be sold after thirty days. "I had buyers lined up for it, too. We don't get too many crowns like that one. Most are just the white rhinestones, but that one had all those pastel sparklers in it."

"Who did you sell it to?" Logan asked.

"I'm not allowed to give out that information."

"Even if it's stolen property?" Amber interjected.

The man's face turned wary and his hand crept toward the telephone. "Are you telling me that crown wasn't yours to sell, ma'am? Because if you are, we can call the police and settle this right now."

"No!" Mary Alice clutched Logan's arm.

"Well?" The man's hand hovered over the phone.

They all looked at Amber. As if she had a choice. "Everything's fine. Thanks."

Why was she thanking him? Amber wondered. He'd probably put the thing on display the instant her grandmother had walked out the door.

Amber met the man's eyes and knew that he was the type who'd seen and heard it all, and wasn't interested in seeing or hearing more. Still, she swallowed and tried a last time. "Please tell us who bought it."

His expression didn't change as he leaned toward the microphone. "Number sixty-seven."

Amber turned away.

"Where are we going?" Mary Alice asked, clutching at Amber's arm.

"Home," Logan replied, opening the door for her.

"No." She backed away. "We can't leave without the crown."

"The crown is gone, Memaw," Amber said.

Mary Alice blinked twice, then her face went white a second before her knees sagged.

Logan caught her before she fell and swooped her up into his arms, carrying her back to the truck as though she weighed nothing.

And Amber's grandmother was no dainty pixie, either.

When she came to, she was in hysterics and refused to get into the truck. "The crown! We have to get the crown!"

"I'll make another crown," Amber rashly promised. "Just like that one. No one will ever know."

"Can you do that?" Mary Alice asked, at once calmer.

"Sure," Amber said, glancing at Logan. "Piece of cake."

YEAH, PIECE OF CAKE. Piece of rock-hard fruitcake.

First of all, Amber had to find pictures that would show her the crown from as many angles as possible. Second, she had to do it without her mother finding out.

Third, she had to find a way to pay for the vintage aurora borealis stones that would make up the crown.

And fourth? Fourth, there was Logan.

After last night, Amber was ready to melt into his arms at the very next opportunity. That is, until the next opportunity proved to be the luncheon honoring the owners of the homes on tour.

When had Logan turned into such a fuddy-duddy? Maybe because he didn't have to sit at the head table and smile until his cheeks cracked. Maybe because he didn't have to listen to small-town trivia until his teeth ached because he was gritting them so he could stay awake. Maybe because *his* mother wasn't draping bright colors all over him to perk up his black clothes.

No, Logan was reveling in all this "Magnolia" garbage. And reveling was the right word.

Honestly, she thought he'd burst into tears as they crossed the threshold of the Belle Rive Country Club for the luncheon. Well, not really, but he acted as though he was entering a temple or something.

"Never been here before," he said, looking all around. "Nice place." His words were casual, but his voice was awed.

"I haven't been here since I married," his grand-

mother stated. Amber remembered that the Van Dells
had never joined the country club.

Her mother reminded everyone of that fact by pretending to be helpful in conducting a tour and pointing
out everything in the restored plantation home until
Camille acidly reminded her that they *lived* in a plantation home.

Which naturally brought up all the old trouble and
Amber and Logan had to separate their families.

Only Gigi appeared oblivious to all, except that she
admitted being impressed by the ladies' powder room
and the "real lace-edged towels and perfumes! Why,
they had more in there than there were at the tester
counter at Weiss's Department Store!"

Both Camille and Lily gritted their teeth at that comment.

Amber also had to reap the rewards of the exagger-
ations—okay, the lies—that Logan had sown about her
success in New York. People wanted to hear all about
her life there and Amber got a headache from trying to
keep everything straight.

Also attending the luncheon was every young girl in
Belle Rive between the ages of fifteen and eighteen—
and several who were only related to people who lived
in Belle Rive.

These were the duchess hopefuls. The queen named
her court at a luncheon on the Friday before the balls
began, but it was tacitly acknowledged that she ap-
proved names from a list proposed by the pilgrimage
committee. Naturally each and every young girl there
wanted to be Amber's new best friend.

And Logan was in the thick of everything, introduc-
ing them all to Amber and her mother and his mother,

and generally acting as a lightning rod for any incipient storms between the two factions. By the time the luncheon was over, Amber never wanted to see him again.

But of course, she did.

She'd fled to the powder room Gigi had so admired and when she came out, Logan was sprawled on one of the velvet brocade love seats that lined the quiet hallway.

"What are you doing out here?"

"I'm not allowed in there."

"Logan—"

"Were you alone?"

"Yes, blessed silence." She sighed.

"You might try thanking your blessed guard out here."

"You?"

He nodded. "I directed traffic to another powder room."

He slid over and Amber collapsed onto the tightly padded seat, resting her head against the carved wooden panel behind her, which wasn't exactly comfortable, but she was too tired to move her head.

"I'd say I owed you, but won't, considering you got me into this mess in the first place."

"Isn't it great?"

Amber groaned. "It's like swimming with a bunch of lip-gloss-wearing piranhas."

"Hey, this is important to them. And you really are like royalty."

Amber rolled her head toward him. "Earth to Logan. This is make-believe."

"Not to them."

"That's my point! Don't you understand that to some of them, being Magnolia Queen is the pinnacle of achievement? The ultimate success? They start out taking charm with Miss Nancy and dancing in the pageant. Then they're junior pages. Then senior pages. Then they're ladies-in-waiting. Some of them wait a long time. After that, they become duchess and from the former duchesses, except in rare circumstances, come the queens."

"And you're a queen. Think of it, Amber."

"I am thinking of it and I'm thinking it's a bunch of nonsense." Amber didn't like the admiring way he was looking at her. In fact, Logan's whole attitude made her uncomfortable. "After queen, then what? I'll tell you. You become a member of every committee in town and spend the next hundred years reminding everybody that you've been queen. Oh, if you get married, and you'd better, you try real hard to have a girl so you can start the whole process all over again. It's so stupid!"

"Why? Because Amber Madison isn't interested, and therefore it's got to be stupid?"

Most men would think it was stupid by default. It was just like Logan to be contrary. "Logan, it's just all so unimportant in the grand scheme of things."

"Let me tell you something. It's real easy to say it's stupid and unimportant from the inside, but try living and working on the outside. Try making business deals in this town when you can't invite prospects to have lunch in one of the private rooms in this club, or play eighteen holes of golf. There are people who won't do business with me because I'm not a member here."

"Then they're not worth doing business with."

"Your father is one of them."

She should have seen that coming. "I'm sorry, Logan."

His face hardened. "Don't feel sorry for me. Van Dell House serves better food than this place, anyway."

"Okay, I'll concede that you've had a rough time, and that's my point." She made a broad gesture with her arms. "This whole society thing is stupid. Think what could happen if those women put their energies into trying to solve world hunger or entering politics, or—"

"Designing jewelry?"

He made it sound petty. He clearly felt that she was just as frivolous as these women were. For a minute Amber couldn't breathe. She just stared at Logan, who looked back at her without a hint of apology.

Amber called on all the long-buried lessons from Miss Nancy's Charm School and rose in a perfectly graceful, and yes, queenly movement. "A gentleman doesn't hit below the belt."

"When have I ever claimed to be a gentleman?" he asked harshly.

Amber slung her purse over her shoulder. "Perhaps that's why you aren't a member of this club," she said, and walked off.

THAT WOMAN was always getting to him one way or another. Logan watched her walk away and considered whether he ought to apologize.

He wasn't sorry. Amber was being so hypocritical he hadn't been able to restrain himself.

He'd been working toward this day for ages. A long

time ago he'd promised himself, and his grandmother, that she would lunch at the club again. Her family had been members, but once she'd married a Van Dell, she'd been barred.

Camille had pretended it had meant nothing to her, but he'd noticed the care with which she'd dressed today and her proud posture as he'd escorted her into the club.

It had made all the garbage he'd put up with in trying to gain acceptance in Belle Rive worth it. He'd wanted to share the moment with Amber, and realized she was incapable of understanding, after all.

So she wasn't perfect. Neither was he.

Logan jogged until he caught up with her.

"Have you come to apologize?" she asked, staring straight ahead.

"No."

"Good."

He stopped her. "Good?"

She nodded. "Because if you apologize, then I'd have to apologize, and I'm not sorry."

Logan grinned. "I'm not sorry, either."

"Okay."

"Okay."

She walked on.

"So we're okay?" Logan asked.

"We're okay."

And that worked for him.

They walked out onto the front verandah. At the end of the flowered path, Amber's mother chatted with a group of women.

"What's next on the schedule?" Logan asked.

"The meeting to decide the duchesses. I got out of it because I don't know any of the girls."

"So what are you going to do now?" Should he push his luck and suggest an afternoon trip to the cold spring? They'd never been there in the daylight. And if they were truly okay... An image of Amber diving into the cold spring formed in his mind. He'd be with her in the water, of course. The clear, cool, transparent water...

"I'm going to drive to Natchez and visit Stephanie." Amber looked hopefully at him. "I don't suppose there's any chance of Memaw's car being fixed?"

Logan squinted off into the distance, losing the image of Amber skinny-dipping in the sunlit pool. "There could be."

"What was wrong with it?"

"In layman's terms, she ran out of gas."

"Well, why didn't you say so?"

"Are you sure you want your grandmother driving?"

"Ah. Good point." She gave him a thumbs-up.

"I thought I'd tell her that we needed to order a part. In the meantime, maybe her gambling fever will cool."

"Sounds great. Except..."

"Except you need wheels."

She sighed. "I can ask Mama."

"But you'd rather she didn't know you were visiting your sister."

"You are getting very good at this." She gave him an approving look out of the corner of her eye.

Logan reached into his pocket. "You can borrow one of my cars. C'mon. I'll drive you over to the garage."

10

ON HER WAY OUT OF TOWN, Amber stopped at a drug-store to buy queen supplies. If she had to make her mouth red, then it was going to be a flattering red, if such a thing were possible. After she found a color she could live with, she stocked up on mascara and bought a hair spray that wouldn't contribute to the deteriora-tion of the ozone layer every time she used it. For good measure, she bought a new blush.

There. That ought to make everyone happy.

Logan had lent her his BMW, which she thought was very decent of him. The garage he owned was a sur-prise—very clean and surprisingly large. Not like a typical garage at all. She saw her grandmother's Caddy, which Logan had covered with a protective cloth.

Logan proudly gave her the grand tour. He'd re-stored a car with huge fins, which he kept telling her had the original this and the original that, and his old truck gleamed as though it were showroom new. Am-ber didn't have the heart to drive those vehicles, in case, heaven forbid, she should scratch one.

Then he'd removed a fabric cover to show her his pride and joy—a '61 'Vette. It didn't run—yet. But it would.

Amber stared at the dinged white Fiberglas shell

and the ripped red leather upholstery and tried to vi-
sualize it as an actual working car. Then she looked at
Logan's face.

And had a revelation. Logan was seeing the car the
same way Amber looked at raw stones and hunks of
metal, seeing their potential instead of what they were
now.

Amber felt a bond form between them. She didn't
want any bonds with Logan. Not that she was mad at
him. But any bonds forged with Logan were "one way
only" and would have to be cut in a couple of weeks.
From prior experience, Amber knew that one-way
bond-cutting hurt.

And so, feeling mean and petty, she feigned disinter-
est until his happy expression closed and he gave her
the keys to his BMW.

And now, Amber was on her way to see her sister for
the first time in eight years knowing that before she
left, she was going to have to hit her up for a loan.

Some role model she was, Amber thought, remembering the tributes to her at lunch.

An hour later Amber reached the city limits of
Natchez, a pretty river city filled with pre-Civil War
buildings. Following the directions that Stephanie had
given her when Amber had called, Amber soon found
the apartment complex.

The area wasn't bad, especially, just not a really
great one. Amber tried to keep an open mind, but she
still locked Logan's car.

And then she was straightening her shoulders and
knocking on Stephanie's door.

Stephanie answered it and the sisters stared at each
other before hugging fiercely.

"You're all grown up!" Amber couldn't help saying the cliché. "You were just a kid when I left."

"I was afraid I wouldn't recognize you," Stephanie admitted, and led the way to a sofa, which, other than a couple of folding chairs and a definite flea market stuffed chair, was the only furniture in the room.

Amber was telling Stephanie all about the doings in Belle Rive when the sliding door on the patio opened. "Hey, Steph, why didn't you call me and tell me your sister was here?"

An extremely tall man with kind eyes and sandy-brown hair held grease-covered hands out of the way and closed the patio door with his elbow. "I want to meet her, but let me wash up first."

"That's Doug." Stephanie glowed. "He starts med school in the fall, so we're both working and saving money now."

"He's going to be a doctor?" What could her mother possibly object to? Amber decided to ask.

"Well, at first, it was because he still has all his schooling ahead of him." She leaned forward and whispered as the water in the kitchen shut off. "But I think it's because he's a scholarship student."

"That means he's smart, doesn't it?" And that was bad?

Stephanie nodded, with that goofy look people get when they're in love. "I wanted to tell you all about him, but I was afraid Mama might overhear and find a way to stop us from eloping."

Doug came into the room, hand outstretched. "Hello, Amber. You caught me changing the oil in my car."

He was moderately good-looking, with a genuine

smile and a manner that made all the difference in the world on the attractiveness scale. Amber knew within seconds that he was perfect for her sister—and that Stephanie had been very wise to snap him up before somebody else did.

What on earth was the matter with their mother? Most mothers would gladly take on extra crow's feet in exchange for nabbing a son-in-law like Doug.

He reminds me of Logan, her grandmother had said. How? And then Amber intercepted a look Doug gave her sister. It was exactly the same look Logan had given her the day she'd been fitted for the queen's gown. Remembered passion with a promise for later.

Was there ever going to be a later with Logan?

After several minutes of easy conversation, Doug stood. "I know you two have a lot of catching up to do, so I'll just go back to fiddling with the car. I'll see you at supper, Amber."

"Isn't he cute?" Stephanie sighed, watching until he was out of sight.

"Yes, he's cute. Good call on the eloping."

Stephanie laughed, but seemed uncomfortable.

Amber poked her arm. "Hey, I have no problems with your decision."

"It's not that."

"Okay, then what's up?" Amber asked. "You sounded funny on the phone when I called earlier."

Stephanie looked down at her hands, then met Amber's eyes. "Did you come here to ask me to be one of your duchesses?"

Amber had thought it was a done deal. "Well—"

"Oh, Amber!" Stephanie wailed. "You know I'd do it if you really want me to, but...I've been so *happy* away from all that. *Please* don't ask me. I'll do almost anything to get out of it."

"Yeah, I notice that you very cleverly timed your elopement so I'*d* have to be queen."

Stephanie looked sheepish. "I know. Are you mad?"

"No."

"I know I owe you."

"Not really, but if you insist, there's a way you can pay me back." Amber explained all about Memaw and the crown and that she needed money to buy the stones to make another one.

"I thought you were rich," Stephanie said.

"That's because I wanted everybody to think I'm rich."

"You sure fooled Mama. So how's it really going?"

Amber decided to come clean. "My whole apartment is the size of this room, and I'm getting minimum wage and commissions working as a salesclerk in a jewelry store. I also sometimes wait tables at the Chinese restaurant down the street in exchange for tips and leftovers. But the good part is, I'm designing jewelry. Someday I'll make it big."

"I believe you."

Amber almost burst into tears.

"But in the meantime, I'm getting my checkbook."

Guilt struck Amber as she looked once again at the shabby furniture and the tiny apartment. "Stephanie," she called. "Forget it. You can't afford this."

Her muffled voice sounded from the bedroom. "It'll be cheaper than a dress."

"Yes, but we probably shouldn't bail out Memaw. That would make us enablers."

Stephanie came back into the room and proceeded to

write a check. "And how many times did she bail us out?"

Amber groaned and held her head in her hands. "Hundreds. Probably thousands."

"This is Memaw's money, anyway. She gave it to me when I got married and told me to keep it for an emergency." Stephanie tore out the check. "Sounds like this is what she was talking about."

AMBER HAD NEVER FELT like such a failure as when she had to take the check from her financially struggling, newlywed, husband-almost-in-medical-school sister.

She hated doing that. *Hated* it.

It was long after dark when she drove back to Belle Rive, feeling sorry for herself.

Having dinner with Stephanie and Doug had only made it worse. Stephanie had rebelled and was deliriously happy.

Amber had rebelled and wasn't. It was her own fault, too. Why had she allowed herself to be blackmailed into coming back here? Why did she care what anyone thought? Why hadn't she just called home and said, "I want to come for a visit and can't afford the ticket"?

Memaw would have sent her the money, or at least she would have—before she'd gambled it all away.

The lights of the old battery plant glowed on the horizon reminding Amber that the turnoff to the cold spring was coming up over the next rise. What she didn't know was what she was going to do when she got to it.

Amber crested the hill and saw the plant. She should keep going, just keep going.

Logan probably wasn't even there.

But when the turnoff was in sight, Amber slowed the car and pulled off onto the side of the road.

Logan. It was easier to ignore him when she didn't like him, when it was only rebellion and lust. It was girl-boy lust then, anyway.

Now it was man-woman lust and Amber discovered that the lust was affected by the liking thing. In fact, she was understanding the subtle differences between lust and desire. With lust, she didn't have to think. With desire, she thought. A lot. Such as right now, with her head resting on the padded steering wheel.

Just when she thought he was a heartless jerk, he turned into a nice guy. Then, when she thought he was a nice guy, he acted like a jerk.

What an irresistible combo.

She didn't want to know that Logan had hopes and dreams and had fulfilled a bunch of them. She didn't want to know that he was nice to his grandmother—and to hers. She didn't want to know that he was manipulative, or that he was a love-'em-and-leave-'em type, even though she was technically the one who left.

He was Logan, he was Belle Rive.

She was Amber, she was now New York.

And that was going to have to be that.

Sighing, she pulled back onto the road and drove home.

"WHERE HAVE YOU BEEN?" Amber's mother demanded the minute she walked in the door. She was clearing away the coffee cups from whatever meeting she'd held this evening. "Who's car is that?"

"Logan's."

"You've been with *him?*"

Amber just looked at her mother and felt something break loose. Wistfully, she realized it was the hope that once, just once, her mother might put Amber's happiness before the Madison family reputation.

"How could you after the day I've had?" Lily pressed her fingers to her temple. "That I should have not only lived to see the Van Dells in the country club, but that I should have had something to do with it...Amber, you could have shown a little more consideration for my feelings."

There was a time, she realized, when she would have felt guilty and would have vowed to try harder to be a good mayor's daughter. Now she didn't. With all her hope gone, what was the point? Her mother—and her father, too—would never see her as anything other than a political tool or liability.

"Logan lent me his car so I could drive over to see Stephanie." Amber bent and picked up a crumpled napkin. Paper? There was a time when her mother only used cloth. In fact, if Amber remembered correctly, her mother had pronounced people who used paper napkins as tacky.

"Oh, Amber! Why didn't you say something? I would have driven you. I need to see Stephanie, anyway. Your sister is being very vague about her dress. It's obvious that husband of hers can't afford an appropriate one, and it would be just like her to make an issue of it to embarrass me and her father." Lily sighed. "We'll have to pay for one, even though I'd rather she bore the consequences of the choice she made. She needs to understand what a mistake it was to marry beneath her."

"I like Doug," Amber said mildly.

"Of course you do. The man has to have charm, since he doesn't have money."

"Logan's family has money *and* charm."

"But they do not have breeding."

"They use cloth napkins."

Lily sniffed. "They've turned their home into a business."

As Amber tried to follow the intricacies of her mother's logic, Bertha entered the room and Lily handed her a tray loaded with lipstick-stained cups and plates sprinkled with powdered sugar from the lemon bars.

Smiling, Bertha brought the tray over to Amber. There were a couple of lemon bars left and Bertha knew she liked them.

Amber took one, remembering all the others she'd sneaked before and after her mother's meetings. Except for the paper napkins, nothing had changed.

If she didn't go back to New York, this would be her life—unless she aligned herself with the disreputable Van Dells and ended up a social outcast.

How very appealing.

Lily bustled around the room straightening pillows and putting chairs back into their proper places. "I don't suppose Stephanie showed you a dress, did she?"

Damn. Confrontation time and a mouthful of lemon bar was no excuse. Amber swallowed. "If you're talking about a duchess dress, then, no. Stephanie doesn't want to be a duchess."

"And you said you didn't want to be a queen, but you are. And Stephanie will be a duchess. Why is it my daughters must have honor forced upon them?" Lily swatted a pillow.

"Stephanie isn't going to be a duchess."

"She certainly is. Her name is on the list, along with Amelia Jasper's younger daughter who is *only* fifteen." Lily carried the silver tea service back to its place on the buffet and wiped her fingerprints off the handles of the tray. "It's plain to see she expects her to be queen one day."

"The queen approves the duchess list, doesn't she?"

"Yes, but it's just a formality."

"Formality or not, if Stephanie's name is on the list, I won't approve it."

Her mother straightened and froze. "You will *not* blackball your own sister! Think of the...well, you just won't."

Amber found it surprisingly easy to stand firm. It was almost as though she was watching the confrontation with her mother instead of participating in it. "I promised Stephanie she didn't have to be a duchess. If you don't want a fuss, or a scandal, then take her name off the list."

"I will not!"

"It's your decision." Amber knew there would be more arguing, along with lip-tightening and vein-bulging, so she pivoted on her heel and pushed open the front screen door.

"Amber Lynn Madison, where do you think you're going?"

Amber smiled and looked over her shoulder at her mother. Yes, there was the vein in the forehead. "Skinny-dipping."

AMBER FELT A THOUSAND percent lighter as she drove toward the cold spring. At last, she'd been successful. She'd saved Stephanie. And soon she'd save her grandmother.

Right now, Amber knew she ought to be in her room figuring out how many stones of which color she needed to order tomorrow, but she wanted to go to the cold spring. For the first time, she'd left by the front door *and* told her mother what she intended to do.

But not who she intended to do it with.

But Amber didn't even care if Logan was there or not.

Well, she did. But she wouldn't mind the time alone to think, either.

She pulled Logan's car right up to the fence, noticing that there wasn't another car around. His car hadn't been visible the other night, either, she remembered.

Amber pushed open the gate and followed the path, much more sure-footed this time, even though she didn't have a flashlight with her.

The moon was nearly full, the sky was clear, and it was a warm, humid spring night.

Perfect.

She entered the clearing, immediately searching for Logan in spite of her resolve. He wasn't there, but she saw evidence that he had been.

The place had been weeded, almost manicured. The paving stones that led from the spring to the tree house were smooth and clear of mud and debris with only soft moss left to grow between them. All the tall weeds and grasses had been mowed around the edge of the spring.

The tree house sported a canvas half-roof, leaving

the rest of the platform open to the stars. It appeared that several boards in the siding had been replaced, as well.

Amber approached the gently curved flat rock and saw a plastic storage bin next to it. Curious, she pried off the lid and laughed out loud. The box was filled with towels.

What was she waiting for?

She slipped out of her shoes and pulled her black sweater over her head at the same time. Seconds later, her black pants pooled at her feet. Amber kicked them away, not caring if they got wrinkled or not.

She felt free. Or she would as soon as she took off her underwear.

There. Amber kicked the filmy lace toward her pants. Then thinking about ants and assorted bugs that lived in the grass, she retrieved her clothes, folding them and leaving them on top of the bin lid.

Okay, *now* she was free. Spreading her arms wide she spun in a circle, enjoying the gentle breeze on her body.

She was a woodland nymph, queen of the—no, no queen stuff. A nymph was enough. Nymphs were cool.

She'd never been naked outside before.

Naked was cool, too.

But dancing while naked was even cooler. Amber caught sight of her shadow in the moonlight. Her legs looked miles and miles long. She stuck one out, then kicked Rockette-style.

She was not Rockette-limber, so she contented herself with whirling and skipping and giving a leap or two.

Dancing naked in the moonlight was great therapy.

Her mother had no control over her here—or anywhere else now. The judging eyes of Belle Rive society were far away and New York was even further.

Amber was out of breath when she stopped at the edge of the pool and raised her arms to the moon.

"I wonder if you can get moonburn?" she murmured out loud, running her hands over her skin.

WHAT THE HELL was he supposed to do?

After hanging around the cold spring for hours, Logan had left for thirty minutes to grab a hamburger and had come back to this.

When he'd noticed his car parked by the fence, he'd almost rammed it with his truck, so certain had he been that it was just a mirage.

She was there. He'd closed his eyes for a moment. Quite a few of the female population of Belle Rive would be astounded to learn that Logan hadn't been sure that Amber would return. And he himself was surprised how much he'd wanted her to.

He wished he knew what it was about her that appealed to him so much. He'd long since moved past any nostalgic attraction for the girl she'd been. He wanted the woman she was now.

Once he knew Amber was at the spring, he'd tramped through the underbrush like a wild boar and emerged at the clearing to find a naked woman prancing around.

At first, he hadn't recognized Amber. This wasn't Amber-like behavior.

And then...and then he'd realized it *was* Amber.

Totally nude, she stood, reflected in the pool and the moonlight, and held out her arms and legs at strange angles. When she laughed, he saw that she was making shadow pictures, and he smiled, too.

She threw back her head and stretched her arms high, then brought them down, sinuously outlining her body.

Logan's mouth went dry and his skin chilled at the same time his insides got hot.

Amber must have heard him crashing through the brush and was doing this to turn him on. Of course, just showing up naked had pretty much taken care of that.

As he watched her hands move over her skin, he could feel the corresponding parts of his body—those that corresponded—warming. The part that didn't correspond was plenty warm enough.

Logan yanked his shirt over his head. By his count, he figured they'd already had about eight years of foreplay and time was a 'wastin'.

But something about the uninhibited way Amber held herself in her shadow dance stopped him from interrupting her.

She didn't know he was there. She was dancing for herself.

So what was he supposed to do? he asked himself as Amber took off leaping and skipping around the pool.

Was this some precoitus ritual the elite of Belle Rive practiced?

An image of Amber's parents started to form and he quickly shut it down before he short-circuited his brain. Looking at Amber was cause enough for short-circuiting.

The full moonlight caught her right then and Logan could see her body as clearly as if a spotlight shone on her. Her skin was gleaming white without any distracting tan lines. Logan had always appreciated a good tan, but after watching Amber tonight, he never would again.

He wanted to go out there and be with her—not to dance, but to scoop her up and carry her to the nest he'd made in the tree house.

But he didn't know what she expected of him. It was the first time in his life he'd felt uncertain about anything to do with a woman.

Trust Amber to figure out how to befuddle him.

She skipped to the rock and stopped, breathing heavily.

Logan caught himself breathing right along with her, his gaze hypnotically watching the rise and fall of her breasts.

He made a mental note to tell her at some point tonight that she didn't need boobie buddies. She looked perfect without them.

Amber lay on the rock on her back, her hair and arms splayed behind her, her breasts and belly defenseless and exposed.

She looked like a painting, like Victorian erotica.

Logan wished he could freeze this moment forever. Though the anticipation of making love to Amber was driving him insane, looking at her and wondering how she'd feel inside—before he knew for certain—had a unique appeal. And now was the only time he'd feel that particular form of sweet anticipation.

And so he watched her in the moonlight until he started sweating and knew it was time for action.

He didn't know what he was going to do yet, but he knew he was going to do it without clothes.

11

SHE WAS FREE...free, free, free.

Amber closed her eyes and stretched on the warm rock, wondering if it were possible to dig it up and transport it to New York, when she heard a measured step.

"Amber?" a familiar voice whispered before she had time to become alarmed. Logan.

"No. I'm a lizard sunning herself in the moonlight. Or should that be mooning herself?"

"A lizard?"

"Yes." She languidly raised an arm and pointed in the general direction of her clothes. "See? I've shed my skin. Shed my old life. I've emerged from the cocoon and am drying my new wings."

There was a silence. "I thought you said you were a lizard."

"I'm whatever I want to be."

More silence. "Amber?"

"Yes, Logan?"

"Are you drunk?"

She smiled and sighed. "Yes—drunk on the moonlight."

"Don't you mean moonshine?"

"A joke. Logan, you made a joke. A funny, funny

joke." She giggled, which made her back bounce against the rock. "Ow."

"Is there room on the rock for company?" he asked, and she could hear the uncertainty in his voice.

"No." Amber liked Logan being uncertain. Eyes still closed, she stretched again, making sure she took up all the room.

"You look beautiful in the moonlight." His voice was husky with a longing that made her shiver.

"Only in the moonlight?"

"I've only seen you naked in the moonlight."

"And you like what you see?"

"Oh, yeah."

Amber smiled, feeling very womanly and in control. "So what are you going to do about it?"

"Whatever you want me to do."

Amber liked the sound of that. "I want you to seduce me."

She sat up to get into a more seduceable position and opened her eyes.

A naked Logan stood in front of her—a naked aroused Logan. Amber swallowed. "Good job."

The moonlight sculpted his muscles and a hint of uncertainty shadowed his eyes. "Amber, I...I don't want to mess up here. I've waited too long."

An endearing touch of humility. Damn, he was good. "Seduction accomplished." Amber gingerly scooted off the rock and walked up to Logan.

They stood inches apart, but he didn't kiss her the way she expected. He didn't even touch her, so Amber decided to touch him in all the places she'd longed to but never had.

She spread her hands across his chest, something

she'd done before, but Logan's chest was always worth touching at any opportunity. He had enough muscle to look solid without looking beefy. Moving her hands around to his back, she lowered them down the satiny skin, not encountering the waistband of his pants this time, but pure Logan.

She cupped his buttocks and sighed. "No wonder you look so good in jeans."

A smile touched the corner of his mouth. He was watching her face intently, but hadn't moved since she approached.

"You can touch me, too, you know." Amber took his hand and brought it to her breast. "Right here, in case you couldn't find it," she added.

"I can find it." Logan brought his other hand up all on his own. "But I enjoyed watching your face. You have a very expressive face."

His fingers warmed her and she hadn't even known she was cold.

"It's like you're a dream." He barely breathed the words as he slowly dragged his hands over her skin the same way she'd touched him.

And it was perfect, the slow sensual exploration of each other inspired by being outdoors in the moonlight.

Amber loved the way the muscles in his legs bunched and the way his stomach quivered when she lightly scraped her fingernails across his skin. She also liked the way he bent close and inhaled the scent of her.

She sighed. In all the times they'd been together, she'd never noticed the different textures of his skin, the rhythm of his breathing, or even the way he liked to nuzzle the side of her neck and inhale deeply.

Logan's touch changed and became more urgent, demanding a response from her.

It didn't have to demand too hard. By that point Amber pretty much hung on to Logan's shoulders and gave in to the sensation of his hands moving over her.

"Will it break the mood if I tell you that you don't need boobie buddies?"

She made a sound low in her throat. "Yes."

"Will it break the mood if I kiss you?"

"No."

Logan swept her off her feet and brought her lips to his.

Amber sighed into the kiss, locking her arms around his neck.

A smart move on her part. Logan had abandoned slow and sensual and was kissing her with a definite purpose. His kisses took her breath away, and she was pretty sure she wouldn't have been able to stand, either, so it was a good thing Logan was holding her.

And then her world began to spin. Amber opened her eyes and realized that Logan was twirling them around in his own version of a moonlight dance.

Laughing, she flung her arms out and her head back and enjoyed the sensation, until a grinning Logan staggered and had to set her on her feet.

"Quick, turn around in the other direction and you won't be dizzy anymore!" Laughing, Amber watched their shadows as they spun around.

"Okay, enough of that," Logan said.

She laced her fingers with his. "You want to dance with me?"

"Sure." He gestured to the tree house. "Up there—and horizontally."

Wait a minute—what happened to her seduction? A little fondling and one kiss—admittedly a great kiss—and she was supposed to fall into...into tree with him?

He'd made her wait eight years and a few days. Let him wait for a change. "If you're not going to dance, then I want to go for a swim."

Amber tugged at his arm, but he shook his head. "Think of it, Logan...a midnight swim in the moonlight—how romantic is that?"

"You remember how cold that water is?"

Amber ran toward the pool. "Then you'll just have to keep me warm!"

The water was inky black with a silvered sheen. Her toes sank into the soft earth at the edge of the pool. The cold soft earth.

Maybe Logan was right. As the mud oozed through her toes, she was pretty sure he was right. Well, she couldn't chicken out now. Amber held her breath and jumped in.

As the frigid water enveloped her body, all the air came whooshing from her lungs and she had to force herself to not gasp until she reached the surface.

During the oppressively hot days of August, this would feel refreshing. Now, it just felt cold. Very cold. And dark.

Amber broke the surface and treaded water, moving closer to the edge until her feet touched the slimy, gritty bottom. Ick.

Arms crossed, Logan stood at the edge and watched her. "How is it?"

"Great," she lied. "I feel very romantic." She tried

floating on her back, but her teeth were chattering, which made it hard to float, so she took a few lazy strokes—at least she hoped they looked lazy and that Logan didn't notice her quivering arms.

After about thirty seconds, Amber decided she'd made her point and could climb out—always assuming her feet were still there. They'd gone numb, so she wasn't sure.

She had taken two strokes toward the bank when a shadow blocked the moon and an instant later, there was a huge splash as Logan joined her.

"Wow!" He broke the surface breathing heavily. "I see what you mean. This is great! Really gets the blood moving."

Hers was no longer moving—it was frozen. She grabbed a tree root with one hand and a board someone had put in the side of the bank with the other, then felt cold arms encircle her waist and pull her back into the pool.

"Come here, you." Logan kissed her. His lips were cold. Or maybe hers were cold. Who could tell? Everything was numb.

"L-Logan, I've had enough romance. Time for me to get out."

"But I just got in." He held her close as they bobbed in the water. "I'll keep you warm."

His body was rubbing against hers. It had to be, but she couldn't feel it.

What she could feel, vaguely, was the yucky slime and assorted plant life at the bottom of the pool.

"Logan! This is horrible. I've had enough nature. I'm freezing!"

Logan kissed her but her teeth chattered. Laughing, he pushed her to the bank and helped her climb out.

Crossing her arms around herself, Amber ran for the towels. She dumped her clothes on the ground, but her fingers were so numb, she couldn't work the lid off the plastic bin. "Hurry up!" she urged Logan, who was taking his own sweet time about getting over there.

He popped the lid off, grabbed a towel and wrapped her in it. Then he got another one and draped it over her head.

Amber couldn't stop shivering.

"I—I really blew this, didn't I?" she said as Logan finally got a towel for himself.

"Nah." He rubbed down his torso and legs, then wrapped the towel around his waist and finger-combed his hair back from his face. "I'll remember your moonlight dance for a long time."

Smiling, he pulled out another towel and rubbed her arms and shoulders.

"If you knew the water was so cold, then why did you bring all these towels?" she grumbled.

"It's warmer in the daytime."

He must have been waiting here for hours. Amber's heart gave a little blip. Good. It was still working.

Logan sat her on the rock and knelt at her feet, vigorously rubbing them until they regained feeling. He did the same for her legs and arms.

Amber simply sat there and tried to keep her teeth from chattering, convinced she would never be warm again. Convinced that Logan must be seriously ticked at her right now.

At some point the nature of his touch changed. Amber wasn't sure when, but briskly impersonal rubbing became slow, personal stroking.

Amber's teeth stopped chattering.

He had lovely strong arms and equally lovely strong hands. Rivulets of water from his hair glistened in the moonlight as they trickled down the center of his back and over his shoulders. Lovely, strong, shoulders.

Logan massaged her calves, working his way ever higher.

The tiniest flame ignited in Amber's middle. The warmth grew and spread as Logan's strong hands reached under the towel to caress her thighs in a slow, strong and steady rhythm.

There was feeling in all parts of Amber's body now. Warm feeling. And getting warmer.

Logan looked up at her as he inched his way ever higher, his thumbs nearly reaching the juncture of her thighs.

She bit her lip.

And then they did reach the juncture of her thighs, rubbing and caressing until Amber was like molten silver through and through.

"Better?" he whispered.

"My lips are still cold," she whispered back.

"We can't have that." He slowly leaned forward, then stopped.

Their eyes met. She heard their breathing in the silence. She could hear her *heart* beating. Or was that his?

"Amber—"

Logan barely voiced her name before they tumbled into each other's arms and his lips were on hers in a fierce kiss that she matched wholeheartedly.

There was a different quality to this kiss, she sensed.

It was deeper and richer, not just physically, but including their recent shared experiences. She knew more about him, more about the man he'd become. She was connecting with him on a broader emotional scale than ever before.

She liked him. Liking hadn't been a part of the equation before. She hadn't known him well enough to like him, and now she did.

In fact, Amber was afraid she'd gone and done something extremely stupid. Such as falling in love with him.

What she'd thought was love before was shallow and wouldn't have lasted. Even back then, once she'd gotten over her initial anger, she'd sensed that it wouldn't have stood up to the hardships in New York. But this was a love that would take root in her heart and grow if she'd let it. It would weather any storms.

If she'd let it.

Logan wrenched his mouth from hers, gulping in deep breaths. "It's time."

"No kidding."

They stood, but couldn't stop kissing each other, taking a step, then stopping and pressing frantic kisses on each other wherever they could.

"Let's try this again." Logan swept her into his arms and crossed the clearing, setting her down by the tree house.

Amber had climbed the boards nailed to the tree dozens of times before, but never so quickly.

Once on the tree house platform, she sat back on her heels as she saw the pillow-covered bed Logan had arranged. "Logan!"

He swung himself beside her and dropped a kiss on the back of her neck. "You like?"

"I like." Amber crawled into the satiny softness. "It sure beats the old sleeping bag."

"I have fond memories of that sleeping bag," he said, and then added as he lay beside her, "I have fond memories of you."

"And now?"

"And now I want to make new memories."

Coolness caressed her heated skin as Logan loosened her towels and tossed them away.

Moonlight filtered through the Spanish moss and made lacy shadows on the wooden platform, just the way it always had. But Amber spent only a moment admiring the effect before she and Logan were hungrily kissing and she forgot everything else.

HE WANTED IT to be perfect. Absolutely, soul-meltingly perfect.

So perfect that Amber would choose to stay with him in Belle Rive.

She was the woman for him. The only woman. Maybe she always had been. They both had had to accomplish a few things on their own before they were ready to make a life together. They'd had to grow apart before they could grow together. Logan was proud of his twenty-year-old self for recognizing it.

Amber must have recognized it, too. Why else would she have come back to this spot tonight?

He'd given her time to think. Logan didn't want her swept away by passion, he wanted her to make a conscious decision whether or not she wanted to take their relationship to the next level.

And she had.

Amber hadn't made a tentative decision, either. She'd come here and reveled in the place, embracing it completely. He hadn't understood at first, not until he'd spun around with her in the moonlight. This place had always called to something inside him and now it called to Amber, too.

If he were the sort of person who needed signs, then this was a blinking, full-color neon one spelling out Amber.

Logan had always come here to think. It seemed fitting that now he came here to love.

And the loving was going to be perfect. All for her.

Gazing down at her, all white against the silvery-gray satin sheets he'd bought just for the tree house, his heart was gripped by an emotion so strong, he knew he couldn't speak, at least not with words. Tenderly pushing the damp waves of hair away from her face, he kissed her gently, prepared to take it slow, to draw out the lovemaking until she was flushed and sated.

Amber had other ideas and she wasn't shy about making them known. No sooner had their lips met than she'd gripped the back of his head and pulled him close, opening her mouth under his, meeting his tongue with hers.

When he tried to pull back, she wrapped her legs around his waist.

Okay. He would concentrate on kissing her mouth and ignore the fact that parts of him were pressing against parts of her in a way they'd wanted to press for a very long time.

Amber pulled his head away. "Logan?"

"Yes?" he whispered.

"Are you trying to be a generous lover?"

"Yes," he answered more cautiously.

She nodded to herself. "What if I told you I didn't want a generous lover? That I want a selfish lover? One who has lost all conscious thought because he desires me completely and is incapable of doing anything else until he's lost himself within me during several bouts of lustful, sweaty sex?"

Logan stared at her. "If you were to tell me that, I would make a slight mental adjustment, and then do my best to comply."

She smiled. "Adjust away."

Which he didn't find difficult to do at all.

LOGAN TOOK DIRECTIONS extremely well.

He unleashed the passion Amber had known he was keeping in check and, within moments, her own matched it.

His mouth and hands were everywhere, as were hers, until she was literally trembling with desire.

At the exact moment she reached her limit and thrust her hips upward, Logan entered her.

They both stilled, breathing in great gulps of air.

For a moment Amber felt relief at finally being joined with him, and then she was rocked with feelings so powerful they threatened to overwhelm her.

"Oh, Logan..."

"I know. Me, too." He dropped a light kiss on her forehead and then began to move.

Waves of pleasure quickly rolled through her until one crested and she gasped, feeling a thunderous rush and then countless bubbling ripples.

She had barely drawn a breath before Logan gripped her, shuddered, and was still.

Amber tightened her arms around him and enjoyed the echoes of their passion as they faded.

Finally. At last.

"Oh, Logan," she said on a sigh. "That was perfect."

He raised his head and smoothed a piece of hair off her cheek. "That," he said, "was just the warm-up."

"AMBER?" Logan was about to break all the rules here.

She stirred in his arms. "Mmm."

"Tell me about that guy."

"Mmm?"

"You know, the Barclay guy. The one whose penthouse you were living in."

She was silent for so long, Logan thought she'd fallen asleep.

"He has cats."

Now it was Logan's turn to be silent. What did she mean by that? He didn't care about some dude's cats, he wanted to know if she'd loved him.

"When he travels, which is all the time, the staff at the store takes turns going to the penthouse and feeding them and playing with them. Well, my turn came and one of them was sick. Everywhere. It was awful. The place reeked. Since I'd found her, I had to take her to the vet. Well, the vet gives me all these medicines. One, I have to give every four hours, another every six, plus I had to make this mush and feed it to her every two hours for a day. How was I supposed to sleep? Anyway, I didn't want a sick cat at my place, so I just stayed in the penthouse. That way, I could be there when the cleaners came, and all that."

"And that's when your mother came, wasn't it?"

She sighed. "It was so easy. Like it was meant to be."

Logan rolled onto his back. "I've been jealous of a man who keeps cats."

"You've been jealous?"

"Big-time," he admitted.

"You realize the penalty for that, don't you?"

"No."

Amber rolled on top of him and pinned his arms down. "You become my love slave for the next hour."

IN ALL THE TIMES she'd climbed out to see Logan, Amber had never had to sneak back at dawn. Of course, she'd never felt so incredibly relaxed, she'd never fallen asleep before, either.

This morning, in the gray dawn, she'd awakened, full of energy. Logan was less energetic, but infinitely more serene. He followed her to an all-night convenience store where they bought huge refillable mugs of coffee. Amber was in such a good mood, she didn't even mind the powdered creamer.

By the time they got to the garage and dropped off Logan's truck, the sun had started to brighten the sky.

Logan drove her home. Amber tried to convince him to bring her right up to the front door, then remembered that she didn't have a key, so he gave her a boost up her tree. Amber scooted along the branch until she reached her window, which had been left open about two inches. Wondering if that had been her grandmother's handiwork, Amber opened the window, blew Logan a kiss, and climbed inside.

She was too wound up from the coffee to go back to sleep, so instead, she sat at her desk and wired a guide frame for the queen's crown, using copper wire she'd salvaged from old electrical cords.

The crown's center floral piece was really quite lovely, she thought, looking at one of the pictures. Impulsively she sketched out a tiara incorporating the same floral piece. That triggered another idea and by the time she thought she could take a shower without awakening the household, Amber had a dozen sketches of crowns, tiaras and hair ornaments.

It had been so easy. So fast. She stood under the shower and marveled at how the ideas had flowed out of her. Designing wasn't usually this painless. And she had even more ideas.

Obviously being with Logan had great side effects.

Smiling to herself, she went back into her room and called one of her jewelry suppliers, one she'd only been a little late paying last time, and rashly put in an order for jumbo bags of pastel aurora borealis stones and the luxury of ready-made collets for the stone settings, since there wouldn't be time to make her own.

Even the fact that she had to assure him she had cash this time didn't detract from her good mood. By tomorrow, the stones would be here and Amber wanted to be ready to solder them into place. The stones would be individually prong-set, which would take hours of tedious work. To finish in time for the coronation, Amber would have to shirk some of her queenly duties in the coming days, because she sure wasn't giving up her nights with Logan.

She sighed. Working like this gave her time to think and, naturally, she thought about him. She wanted him to come to New York with her. They wouldn't have to live in the city. In fact now that she knew about his car restoration hobby, city living wouldn't be practical.

As she worked, she kept hearing his voice as he told her how there were people in Belle Rive who actually wouldn't do business with him because he wasn't a member of the country club. How stupid. How small-minded.

In New York, he wouldn't have that problem. Sure, there were power circles there, too, but if Logan could put together the deals such as the ones she'd been hearing about while operating under the Belle Rive handicap, think what he could do in New York.

It would be a relief for him to leave Belle Rive.

As it would be for her.

When Amber finished calculating the size and materials needed for the queen's crown, she quickly fashioned forms for a couple of tiaras, then simpler headbands and barrettes. She was only aware of the passing of time because her stomach growled about the same time as there was a tentative knock on her door.

"Amber?" came a whisper.

"I'm here, Memaw."

Mary Alice quickly came into the room and closed the door behind her. "You're back." She sighed and leaned against the door. "You were with Logan." It wasn't a question.

Amber nodded.

"He's a fine boy."

"I think so."

"Don't pay any attention to your mother."

Amber gave a short laugh. "I didn't."

Mary Alice came into the room. "I think the crown

was set in silver," she said, doubtfully eyeing the copper.

"This is just a guide," Amber told her. "Hey, I ordered the stones. They're overnighting them."

Looking guilty, her grandmother sat on the bed. "I feel awful."

"Good."

"Amber," she said reproachfully.

"I want you to feel awful. You've got a serious gambling problem and you need help."

She bowed her head. "With Stephanie gone, I just felt so unneeded. There was nothing to do! I always seemed to be in the way. So I went on one of those senior's bus trips to the casino and I won a little money. And then I won a little more. And then I lost a lot and tried to win it back."

"That's pretty much how it goes."

"Amber, it became the only reason I got up in the morning." She covered her face with her hands.

"Oh, Memaw." Amber sat on the bed with her grandmother and put her arms around her shoulders.

"And now look what you have to do!"

"But I'm having a great time."

Mary Alice raised her head. "You are?"

"Oh, yes. I've got so many ideas . . . but they'll be for later. The crown is going to take hours."

"I'd help you if I could."

Amber smiled. "Oh, you can. And you will." Standing, she opened her tackle box of supplies. Taking a stone, a collet, a pair of tweezers, and a brash pusher, she brought them over to her grandmother. "Each stone in that crown is going to have to be put in one of these." Using tweezers, she picked up the stone and

dropped it into the collet. "And then the prongs are going to have to be bent to hold it in place." She used the
brash pusher for that.

Mary Alice looked eager. "May I try?"

Amber gave her another stone and collet. It took her
grandmother several tries, but she did a credible job.

"This is fun!"

"But will it be fun the thousandth time you do it?"

"Won't it?"

Her grandmother looked so eager. And the thought
occurred to Amber that if her grandmother was up
here setting stones, she wouldn't be finding a way to
get to Vicksburg and gamble. She smiled and nodded.
"Yeah."

"I wish...I wish there was something I could do right
now. Gigi Van Dell called this morning and I don't
want to go downstairs. She's probably on her way
over."

"Why hasn't Mama been up here to wake me up?"

"We heard you in the shower."

"That was at eight o'clock."

"Perhaps she thinks you're putting on your
makeup."

"For an hour and a half?" Only her mother. Amber
went to her closet and pulled out a simple black cotton
sleeveless sheath. She had a heavy silver and chunky
raw stone necklace, bracelet and earrings set that was
quite an attention getter, and the dress would be the
perfect background. She felt powerful with all that
metal around her neck and today she had a feeling
she'd need all the power she could get.

She caught her grandmother looking longingly at
her worktable. "Here, Memaw. See this color picture of

the crown? You can catalog all the stones in it, so we'll know how many of each color and shape to set."

Mary Alice brightened and when Amber left, she was happily counting stones, which was actually going to be a huge help.

She stopped off at the bathroom to put on her new red lipstick, wanting to give her mother as little as possible to complain about.

It was remarkably silent as Amber crept downstairs. Shouldn't there be yelling?

She found her mother and Bertha polishing silver in the kitchen.

"Good morning, Amber." Her mother gave an energetic rubbing to a teaspoon. "I trust you slept well."

"Uh, yes. Memaw tells me we're expecting Gigi Van Dell?" Too late, she caught Bertha's warning look.

"No." Lily picked up another spoon.

"Oh." Amber waited, but when her mother said nothing more, she asked, "Then what is my schedule for today?"

"Your schedule is to announce the duchesses."

"I know they'll be presented at the ball, but isn't there some sort of event connected with this announcement?"

"I believe I'll just pour myself another cup of coffee. Would you like one, Amber?" Her hands on the table, Bertha pushed herself to her feet.

Amber shook her head as her mother spoke. "Bertha, that will be your third cup and you know how caffeine gives you heart palpitations."

Bertha scowled. "I'll put plenty of milk in it."

"Suit yourself," Lily said, attacking another spoon. "Everyone else around here does."

Oh, great. Lily Madison, martyr. Amber groaned in-wardly. "Mama, I'm still working on the gifts to the duchesses, so if there's nothing scheduled for me to-day, then I'll go back upstairs."

"You're to name the duchesses at lunch today," Ber-tha told her. "It's gonna be held at Van Dell House."

Lily shot her a poisonous look.

"Fine. When do we leave?"

"We don't." Lily had moved on to the dessert forks. "I am not going to set foot in Van Dell House and nei-ther is my daughter."

"Mama." Amber spoke as firmly as she could with-out crossing the line into sassiness. "You're being dif-ficult. You agreed that Gigi Van Dell was in charge this year. It's entirely appropriate for her to hold a lun-cheon in her own house. It's a B and B, for pity's sake! People hold weddings and receptions there!"

"The duchess luncheon has always been held at the club."

"Well, now, the Van Dells aren't members, are they?"

"With good reason. And as long as your father is on the board, they never will be."

Amber stared down at her mother, who was system-atically working her way through the forks.

She could not wait to leave this place. "I am the queen, so if the luncheon is at Van Dell House, then that's where I'll make the announcement."

"That's my girl."

"Bertha!"

"Miz Madison, now you know she's right."

Lily's mother pressed her mouth into a straight line. "What time is the luncheon, Bertha?"

"Eleven-thirty."

"Mama, you've got a little over an hour to get dressed. If you aren't ready when it's time to leave, then I'll go without you."

12

VAN DELL HOUSE was lovely. Best of all, Logan was there, sitting with his grandmother. Amber caught his eye and nearly melted all over again. She couldn't wait to get him alone and ask him to come back to New York with her.

Her mother was never going to change. At the last minute, she'd appeared at the top of the stairs dressed in her very best luncheon suit. Amber smothered a smile when she saw that it was mostly black with white trimming on the lapels.

Lily wore her heirloom pearl necklace, bracelet, earrings, brooch and ring. Amber had never seen her wear all the pieces at once before.

She looked very haughty and regal all through the luncheon. And it was a wonderfully feminine lunch with hand-painted flower-themed china and matching nosegays of flowers on each table. Everyone seemed in a really good mood, especially the large table of women by the window. Gigi sat with them and several times the entire group broke into raucous laughter that drew the looks of some of the other women.

Lily barely touched her food.

Right after lunch, Amber excused herself to reapply her lipstick—honestly, she was getting addicted to the stuff—her lips looked naked without it. She wasn't at all surprised to meet Logan in the back hallway.

"I've missed you," he whispered, pulling her close for a kiss.

"I wish I could leave with you right now." With a regretful moan, she pulled away. "Tonight? Same time, same place?"

He grinned. "Music to my ears."

Amber put on her lipstick and returned to her place. Under cover of the tablecloth, Lily passed her a piece of paper. "The duchesses," she whispered.

Amber unfolded it and immediately saw Stephanie's name. Well, she wasn't going to announce it and that was that. Let her mother argue about it when it was too late for anything to be changed.

"Amber, honey." Gigi pulled up a chair next to her. "I'm glad you're feeling better," she said. "When I called this morning, your mama told me you had a headache."

Amber glanced at her mother's rigid countenance. "I feel fine now."

"Well, I didn't get a chance to go over the duchesses with you ahead of time. Were there any special friends you wanted to ask?"

Amber shook her head. Her mother had never even asked. But most of Amber's close friends had already been duchesses.

"I gave Amber the list of duchesses," Lily said.

Gigi blinked at her. "But how could you?"

"We met yesterday and decided on the girls." Lily sounded as though she were speaking to a child.

"Excuse me, but you're not on that committee."

"Of, course I am! I've always been on the duchess selection committee."

Gigi shook her head. "Not this year." She handed
Amber a piece of paper.

Amber looked at Gigi's list hoping against hope that
it would duplicate some of the names on the list her
mother gave her.

Nope.

"I don't recognize any of these names," she told
Gigi.

"I don't suppose you do, hon. These are friends from
my showgirl days. I thought the pilgrimage needed a
little flash, you know? And they've got their own
Southern costumes from a show we used to do. They'll
make great duchesses."

Her mother wore a look of utter horror. "Do I understand that you have asked showgirls to be our duchesses?"

"Oh, their showgirl days are long past."

Oh, this was too, too much. Amber swallowed, trying to hide her quivering lips. "Are they the ladies who
were sitting with you at lunch?"

Gigi nodded enthusiastically. "It's great. We haven't
seen each other in years and everyone's having such
fun." She waggled her fingers at them. "Well, give me
a knife to rap the ole water glass and you can make
your announcement." She picked up Amber's knife.

"No!" Lily grabbed her wrist. "I won't let you do
this."

Gigi's always-present sunny smile faded. "You
don't have anything to say about it."

"What about these girls? Being named duchess
means the world to them."

Amber showed Gigi the other list.

"Well, make them duchesses, too. There isn't a rule about how many you can have, is there?" She laughed. "And if there is, we don't have to pay any attention to it, anyway!"

"It is completely inappropriate. I cannot allow those young girls to associate with...with..." Unable to finish, Lily waved in the general direction of Gigi's friends. "Their mothers would never forgive me."

Unfortunately, as their discussion had gone on, conversation in the rest of the room had ceased and Lily's words carried clearly.

Amber's eyes met Logan's in mute appeal. His chair scraped across the wooden floor as he stood, patted his grandmother's hand and approached them. "Have we run into a problem?"

"A problem has run into us," Gigi said. Unsmiling, she stood, looking as formidable as Lily could. "You are a guest in my mother-in-law's home," she said to Amber's mother. "As are my friends. I will not have anyone insulted here."

"Just a minute." Camille Van Dell's voice rang out. Everyone waited as the tiny woman made her stately way to the group. "Gigi, you are wrong."

"That's what I was trying to tell her," Lily said.

Camille took her daughter-in-law's hand. "This house is every bit as much your home as it is mine." Still holding a visibly moved Gigi's hand, Camille turned to Lily. "Her friends have been staying here since Wednesday, and I find them utterly delightful."

The two women stared at each other. Without taking her eyes from Camille's, Lily said, "Amber, make the announcement."

"Both lists?"

"Yes," said Camille.

"No!" Lily said at the same time. Then she added, "I would rather cancel the pilgrimage than have that lot be connected with it in any way." She stood, as well.

"Mama!" Amber felt her face flush.

"Let's take this discussion outside," Logan murmured, and ushered his mother and grandmother forward.

Camille smiled. "I'll remain here and see to our guests."

Amber's mother didn't want to be ushered. Amber leaned close to her and whispered, "Right now, you look like the bad guy, Mama."

Without acknowledging that she'd heard, Lily stiffly left the room leaving a trailing Amber to follow in her wake.

It was easy to find Logan and his mother—all they had to do was follow the sound of raised voices. Logan had led Gigi to the conservatory in the back of the house.

"I have tried and tried to get along with that woman," Gigi was saying as Amber and Lily entered the room. "But has she made even the slightest effort? No."

"I'm here in your house, aren't I? That was quite enough effort."

"Mama!"

Amber faced Logan, expecting sympathy, and was shocked to see his face tight with anger, anger that apparently extended to all Madisons, including her.

"Let me tell you something," Lily said to Logan's

mother. "Being a duchess is an honor, not a part in some tasteless costume extravaganza."

"Oh, please! This whole thing is just a show for tourists!"

"I wouldn't expect you to understand."

"If everybody would take a couple of deep breaths and calm down for a minute, we can work out a compromise," Logan said.

"There is nothing to work out," Lily stated. "Amber, please announce the duchesses and then we'll leave. I have developed a headache."

"That's fine, as long as she announces my duchesses," Gigi insisted.

Lily turned to her. "If she does, then I'll cancel the pilgrimage."

"You can't do that!"

Lily smiled coldly. "My husband is the mayor and grants the permits. I can't imagine him approving an event that involves women of questionable character. Amber, if you wish to be Magnolia Queen, then I suggest you make the correct announcement."

Amber looked at them and couldn't believe it. Even Logan. There were so many more important things in the world to argue about. Amber inhaled deeply. "Then the correct announcement is that we won't be holding a pilgrimage this year."

AMBER COULD HARDLY WAIT to get to the cold spring. She was free, free of the whole Magnolia Queen mess. She and Logan could leave as soon as he could pack. After today, Amber couldn't imagine that he would want to wait.

She found him sitting on the flat rock, staring into the water. He was fully clothed, but she could fix that.

Amber crept up behind him and covered his eyes with her hands. "Guess who!"

"Hello, Amber." His voice was colder than the water in the pool.

He was sitting right in the middle of the rock. Amber didn't have enough room to sit next to him, but she decided to, anyway, bumping him with her hips until he reluctantly moved to one side.

"Tell me you aren't holding my mother's arrogant close-mindedness against me."

"Would it have killed you to have just gone ahead and named the damned duchesses?"

"Did you miss the entire argument? I had two lists, one of which consisted of your mother's showgirl friends. Now, my mother was out of line to assume she'd choose the duchesses, but even I know having your mother's friends wouldn't be right."

He turned his head to look at her. "Why not?"

"Logan!" She couldn't believe he didn't think the whole thing was as hilarious as she did. "Well...they don't even live in Belle Rive."

"Neither do you."

"But I was born here. My family lives here. Come on, Logan. You know the duchesses are mostly in high school, or a couple of years out."

"It doesn't matter now, does it? There isn't a pilgrimage."

"I know!" Amber laughed. "I can't believe I lucked out! I don't have to be a stupid queen in the stupid pilgrimage. Listen...come back to New York with me."

He just stared at her. "You don't get it, do you?"

"Of course I do. You and your family are being snubbed by a bunch of close-minded people here. So leave. It's not worth it."

"It's worth it to me. It's worth it to my mother and grandmother. We live in a home that's been in the Van Dell family for more than a hundred and sixty years. I have spent a long time carefully building connections and laying the foundation so that one day no door in town will be closed to me or my family. And then finally, *finally* I got a break. With my mother in charge of the pilgrimage, no one would dare snub her. And now you've ruined it."

Amber's jaw dropped. "You've confused me with my mother."

Logan shook his head. "If you'd truly wanted to be queen, she wouldn't have made that threat. It was her dream to see one of her daughters as Magnolia Queen. You blew that, too."

How did everything suddenly become her fault? "I take it this means you won't be coming to New York with me this time, either?"

"No—but you could stay here in Belle Rive with me."

He was obviously still mad at her. "Oh, no."

"Why not? What have you got to go back to? I've seen the life you lead in New York. You'd rather go back to that than stay with me?"

He was serious! "Logan, I—"

"You're just like your mother. I'm not good enough for you, am I? Not to be seen with in public in Belle Rive, anyway. Isn't that why you only meet me here at night?"

"You're being ridiculous."

"Am I? Then why hadn't you asked me to be your escort for the ball?"

This stuff actually mattered to him. A lot. And he couldn't believe that his social standing or lack of it didn't matter to her. "I...I hadn't got around to it. Frankly, I forgot about needing an escort. Get real, Logan. Remember last night? Who else would I ask?"

"Someone your mother picked for you. I'm sure she's called a committee meeting to discuss it."

That would be so typical of her mother that Amber laughed.

Logan didn't. "Look, Amber, it's late and I'd like to be alone."

She couldn't believe it. Well, he didn't have to tell her twice. "Sure." She got off the rock and began walking quickly, hoping to make it back to her mother's car before she started crying so hard she couldn't see the path.

"Amber."

She turned back, hoping he'd come to his senses.

"Have a nice flight back to New York."

AMBER STOPPED feeling heartbroken—again—the minute she got out onto the open highway. Now she was mad. At Logan. At her mother. At Logan some more, and then at Gigi. And mostly at herself for not realizing that all Logan had ever wanted was social acceptance in Belle Rive.

In fact, that was probably the reason he'd hooked up with her in the first place. He didn't love her, he loved her social standing. She'd had a close call and was due for a few weepy Saturday nights, but she'd come through this okay.

Apparently she was due for a weepy Friday night, too, because she spent more time than he was worth crying into her pillow after she got back. She overslept and was awakened by the doorbell the next morning. Dragging herself into the bathroom, she stared at herself in the mirror. Great. Puffy eyes. She'd have to borrow her mother's stupid mask.

Her grandmother was waiting in her room when Amber got back from her shower.

"They're here!" Mary Alice had opened the box from the jewelry supplier. "I didn't take anything out," she said anxiously. "I just wanted to see them."

The damn crown. Amber had wanted to go to the airport and camp out until a standby seat to New York became available, but how could she abandon her grandmother? "That's good, Memaw. We need to make sure everything on the packing slip is in there."

It looked as if she was going to make a crown, after all.

Actually, after a couple of hours spent with her excited grandmother, Amber reluctantly admitted that it had been the best thing for them both. Mary Alice quickly became such a pro at setting the different-shaped stones and bending the prongs to hold them, that Amber started soldering the completed ones into the outline of the central flower design.

They managed to keep their work a secret for three days. During that time, Amber didn't visit the cold spring and Logan didn't come to her window.

Her mother went to bed and stayed there, and Amber's father, without his advisor to guide him, made several political gaffes.

Amber also made an appointment with her grandmother's doctor, who recommended a therapist in Vicksburg. Mary Alice had agreed to see him, but as she happily told Amber, "Who has time for gambling when there's work to be done?"

Amber finished a tiara as practice and, on a whim, listed it at an Internet auction site. She and her grandmother were having a great time, becoming as close as they'd been before Amber had left.

And then one morning, there was a knock on the door.

Amber and her grandmother froze and before either could say anything, the knob turned and Lily entered.

She stared at the nearly covered copper wire form and the pictures of the crown that Amber had taped to the wall above her desk. "What's that?"

"It's going to be the magnolia crown."

"What happened to the real crown?"

Mary Alice looked at Amber pleadingly.

"The shop where Memaw took it sold it. Apparently someone offered the guy enough money so that he wouldn't tell us who bought it."

Lily looked horrified. "That's...that's outrageous!"

"But I'm making another one. When I'm—I mean, when we're finished, no one is going to know the difference." Amber looked fondly at her grandmother.

Lily came forward and studied all the glittering stones. "Yes, they will. After fifty years of hair spray, the thing was looking pretty dingy. This looks like new."

Amber and her grandmother glanced at each other.

"You're not mad?" Amber asked.

Lily shook her head and her lip quivered. "I just want to see you wear it!" And she burst into tears.

Amber had never seen her mother cry before.

What a mess. Amber looked at the crown. She actually was kind of disappointed that she wouldn't get to wear her creation. Unless...

She could fix this. She could fix everything. It would be so easy. She could even fix things with Logan. Who knew why it was important for him to see his mother in charge of the pilgrimage, but it was.

And... Amber picked up the partly finished crown and put it on her head. Since she'd been using herself as a model, it was a perfect fit. But it felt right, too.

Oh, good Lord, she was happy. Working with her grandmother was a riot and she'd never had so many ideas when she was in New York. Life was so hard there and these past few days had been... Amber exhaled softly. She wanted to stay. Preferably with Logan, but yes, here in Belle Rive.

Life sure threw some curveballs sometimes.

Well. Amber took off the crown. If she was going to stay here, then she'd better set about getting things in order.

"I'VE INVITED YOU ALL here to see what we can do about getting the pilgrimage back on."

"It was too late to cancel the home tours. It was only the parade and coronation ball that got canceled," Gigi said with a look at Lily.

Lily glared at Reginald, who blurted, "But, Lily! Be reasonable."

"That was the problem," Gigi said.

Camille shushed her.

Logan said nothing.

"Bertha, Mr. Van Dell would like some more lemonade," Amber said. Was it her imagination, or did the edges of his mouth turn up just the slightest bit?

In any case, he held up his newly filled glass in a silent toast to her and drained it in a single gulp.

"Did I get the sweetening right for you, Mr. Logan?" Bertha asked to everyone's astonishment.

"Perfect, Bertha."

"Miss Mary Alice told me you like it mighty sweet." Smiling, she returned to the kitchen.

Logan raised his empty glass to Amber's grandmother.

Bertha had added sugar to her famous lemonade. If she could compromise, then, Amber wasn't letting anybody leave the room until the pilgrimage was back on.

"Okay. Here's what we're going to do and there will be no discussion. Agreed?"

"But—" sounded many voices.

Amber held up her hands. "No discussion. Now, Gigi, there's just too much tradition attached to the position of duchess. They're usually young girls from Belle Rive families. Mama, Gigi's friends have come to help our pilgrimage and I want them to participate. Therefore, they will be given the new position of Ladies of the Court and act as hostesses at the ball and on the home tours. The ball and parade will proceed as scheduled. Everyone understand?"

There were stiff nods all around.

"Daddy, you get down to the courthouse and issue those permits."

"Yes, ma'am." He smiled broadly and winked at her.

"Logan?"

He looked up at her. "Yes?"

"You are hereby appointed official queen consort."

His smile grew until she saw the dimple again. It had been a long time since she'd seen that dimple. "Yes, ma'am," he said, echoing her father.

"That ought to take care of everything. Any questions?"

There weren't any, which was good since Amber had planned to answer them all "Because I say so" anyway.

"Oh, and Logan?" she said as the group was breaking up. "We've got a date for later. You know the time and the place."

SOLVING THE Dueling Duchesses Scandal, as the paper had called it, had been so easy. So ridiculously easy. Amber shook her head and headed back to her room. The crown had to be done in forty-eight hours.

Her grandmother was already at work, but she gave Amber a worried look when she entered.

"I think there's something wrong with your computer. It keeps dinging."

Amber went over to check out her laptop. "That's the sound for incoming e-mail messages." Seventeen? What was going on?

Amber opened them and read query after query about her tiara. Curious, she checked on the auction and stared at the total bidding. "Memaw! The bidding is up over two hundred dollars and there's still three days left on the auction!"

"Is that good?" her grandmother asked.

"It's fabulous!" Amber stared at the screen. It figured that it would take something like a glittery crown to finally click with the public. She could pay Stephanie back in no time.

"I wonder what they'd bid on this one," Mary Alice mused, looking at the queen's crown.

"Don't even think about it!"

Later, when she brazenly borrowed the mayor's car and drove to the cold spring, Amber discovered that she was nervous.

Would it be as easy to patch things up with Logan?

LOGAN SAT ON THE ROCK and waited for Amber. He'd spent two days in purgatory thinking that she'd gone back to New York, thinking that maybe he'd have to follow her, after all, when the message about the meeting had come.

She'd stood up there and told everybody what they were going to do in the best imitation of her mother he'd ever seen. He knew better than to say that to her, though.

Still, when he realized what she'd done, even though it meant she had to act as queen—and he knew how much she hated that—Logan realized that he loved her and that he was going to have to be with her no matter where she wanted to live.

He'd been doing a lot of thinking. He always gave people, including himself, what they wanted in deals. In this one, he'd wanted his mother to be in charge of the pilgrimage because he'd wanted Belle Rive society to accept her. And why? Not for himself, but because he thought it would make his grandmother stop resenting her. Seeing his grandmother tell Gigi that Van Dell House was her home, too, well, wasn't that what he'd truly wanted?

"Logan?"

He'd been listening, but hadn't heard her approach. "Hey," he said.

Amber climbed onto the rock. They sat in silence and Logan knew he'd have to be the one to break it.

"You were great today."

"Just like my mother, huh?"

He gave her a wary look.

She laughed. "It's okay. I've watched her in action so often, I absorbed it. So.... The pilgrimage is back on and you get to be right in the thick of it."

"Thanks. I know how much you hate it."

"It won't be so bad. By the way, if you want to join the country club, you can. I made Daddy promise."

"Maybe I don't want to join anymore."

She swatted him on the arm.

"Kidding."

"You better be!"

He let a beat go by. "Are you going back to New York after the ball?"

"I suppose."

He swallowed. "Would you like some company?"

Amber turned to look at him. "What are you saying?"

"That I'd like to come to New York with you."

"You'd give up this place?"

Logan touched the side of her face and tilted her chin toward him. "I'd rather give up this place than give up you."

She searched his face. "You're telling me you love me, aren't you?"

"Yeah."

"It would be nice to hear the words."

"I love you, Amber."

Her face broke into a huge smile.

And as long as he was on a roll, he added, "I want you to be my wife."

She gasped softly. "Those were more words than I was expecting."

"If you need time to think—"

Amber covered his mouth with her fingers. "I've been thinking for years. I've been in love with you for years—except it wasn't really a forever love."

"And now?"

"And now it is."

"I'm hoping that's a yes."

She melted into his arms. "Of course it's a yes, and, I can't believe I'm going to say this, but I want to stay here in Belle Rive."

He gave a crack of laughter. "I can't believe you said that, either."

"Well, you know, my grandmother and I have been working on the queen's crown and, you'll never believe it, but I have all these designs in my head. I'm selling one of them at an online auction and the bidding is already over two hundred dollars! Anyway, I think the rush of ideas has something to do with being here, in this place, with you. So, I'm going to propose a deal. I'll stay here and marry you, if you'll build that house you were talking about."

Logan closed his eyes. How could he love her more now than he had five minutes ago? "So that's the deal?"

Amber smiled. "Yeah. Everybody wins."

He pulled her close. "Then let's seal it with a kiss."

Epilogue

"I STILL CAN'T BELIEVE you let them make our wedding part of the Christmas Pilgrimage. I thought for sure we'd just elope," Logan grumbled.

Amber and Logan sat on the cold spring rock and drank hot chocolate as they looked at the skeleton of their new house. It wouldn't be finished until next spring, but when it was, it would be perfect.

"Sure you can. You know that by letting our mothers plan the biggest blowout Belle Rive has ever seen, they'll leave us alone afterwards. They'll owe us."

"Okay, I understand the strategy behind the giant wedding, but during the pilgrimage?"

"The last one made so much money that Mama wanted your mother to try a winter one."

"So whose mother's idea was it to make us the main attraction?" Logan asked.

Amber set her mug down and burrowed her arms in Logan's jacket, then kissed him. "Do you really want to know, or do you want to go play in the tree house?"

Logan gave her a slow smile. "Why, Amber Madison, are you offering me a deal?"

She stood and pulled him up with her. "As long as I get what I want."

MILLS & BOON®

Makes any time special™

Mills & Boon publish 29 new titles every month. Select from...

Modern Romance™   Tender Romance™

Sensual Romance™

Medical Romance™ Historical Romance™

MAT2

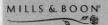

2 BOOKS
AND A SURPRISE GIFT!

We would like to take this opportunity to thank you for reading this Mills & Boon® book by offering you the chance to take TWO more specially selected titles from the Sensual Romance™ series absolutely FREE! We're also making this offer to introduce you to the benefits of the Reader Service™—

* ★ FREE home delivery
* ★ FREE monthly Newsletter
* ★ FREE gifts and competitions
* ★ Exclusive Reader Service discounts
* ★ Books available before they're in the shops

Accepting these FREE books and gift places you under no obligation to buy; you may cancel at any time, even after receiving your free shipment. Simply complete your details below and return the entire page to the address below. *You don't even need a stamp!*

YES! Please send me 2 free Sensual Romance™ books and a surprise gift. I understand that unless you hear from me, I will receive 4 superb new titles every month for just £2.49 each, postage and packing free. I am under no obligation to purchase any books and may cancel my subscription at any time. The free books and gift will be mine to keep in any case.

T1ZEC

Ms/Mrs/Miss/Mr ....Initials ....
BLOCK CAPITALS PLEASE

Surname ....

Address ....

....

....Postcode ....

Send this whole page to:
UK: FREEPOST CN81, Croydon, CR9 3WZ
EIRE: PO Box 4546, Kilcock, County Kildare (stamp required)